Table of Contents

Introduction

This is the second supplement to *Alcohol On Campus*. The original book included statutes and judicial decisions regarding the use, possession and distribution of alcoholic beverages in each of the fifty states through July 1, 1988. However, as Justice Cardoza once said, "The law never is, but is always about to be." Thus, it has been necessary to update *Alcohol on Campus*.

The *1990 Update* to *Alcohol On Campus*, included statutes and judicial decisions from July 11, 1988 to January 1, 1.990. The supplement included the same topics addressed in the original book, organized in the same fashion, but was not a cumulative supplement. Thus the *1990 Update* must be read along with the original book for a comprehensive review of a state's alcoholic beverage laws.

This *1999 Update* serves as a supplement to *Alcohol On Campus* and the *1990 Update* and includes cases decided and statutes enacted between January 1, 1990 and January 1, 1999. As with the previous supplement it must be read with the original book and the 1990 Update for a comprehensive review of each state's alcoholic beverage laws.

The 1999 Update was researched in the same manner as the *1990 Update;* however, electronic research methods were employed for this supplement. The reader is cautioned that each state legislature meets on a different schedule and the codification and publication of a particular state's laws will vary from each of the others. Thus, there may be laws that have been enacted, but not yet published when this research was completed. **Where there is a concern about a specific law, counsel in that jurisdiction should be contacted for the most upto-date information.**

Not all cases or laws dealing with alcoholic beverages are included. The authors selected cases and statutes that would be of interest and applicable to college and university administrators. The cases included have direct application to institutions of higher education although often not involving a college or a student or faculty member. Each state is followed by a listing of the most recent state supplement consulted.

The tables showing dramshop and social host states are cumulative and up-to-date at the time of this writing. These tables provide a quick reference and cite the statute or judicial decision creating the law.

1999 Update to
ALCOHOL
ON CAMPUS:

*A compendium
of the law
and a guide to
campus policy*

Terry W. McCarthy
Donald D. Gehring

1999
UPDATE

COLLEGE ADMINISTRATION PUBLICATIONS, INC.

Library of Congress Cataloging-in-Publication Data
McCarthy, Terry W. and Gehring, Donald D.
   '99 Update to Alcohol on Campus: a compendium of the law
and a guide to campus policy   /   Donald D. Gehring.
       p.   cm.—(Higher education administration series)
     ISBN 0-912557-11-7
     1. College students—Legal status, laws, etc.—United States
2. Tort liability of universities and colleges— United States.
3. College students—United States—Alcohol use.
   I. Title.   II. Series.
KF4243.G44   1999
344.73'075—dc20
[347,30475]   8915904
                                                          CIP

Brief quotation may be used in critical articles or reviews. For any other reproduction of the book, however, including electronic, mechanical, photocopying, recording or other means, written permission must be obtained from the publisher.

The views expressed in this book are those of the individual authors and are not necessarily those of College Administration Publications, Inc.

This publication is designed to provide accurate and authoritative information in regard to the subject matter covered. It is sold with the understanding that the publisher is not engaged in rendering legal, accounting or other professional service. If legal advice or other expert assistance is required, the services of a competent professional person should be sought.

—from a Declaration of Principles jointly adopted by a committee of the American Bar Association and a committee of publishers.

248

1991-99 Highlights

In the eight years since the *1990 Update,* the federal and state legislatures have given considerable attention to alcohol on campus. The federal government enacted the Drug Free Schools and Communities Act Amendments of 1989 (20 U. S. C. 1145) with implementing regulations at 34 C.F.R. 86. This law requires that institutions provide every student and employee with a written statement of the following information:

• standards of conduct prohibiting, at a minimum, the unlawful use, possession or distribution of illicit drugs and alcohol by students and employees;

• a description of applicable laws related to unlawful possession or distribution of illicit drugs and alcohol;

• a description of counseling and treatment programs available;

• a clear statement that the institution will impose sanctions for violations of its standards and a description of those standards;

• a description of health risks associated with the use of illicit drugs and alcohol; and

• a description of the applicable legal sanctions under local, state and federal laws for the unlawful use, possession and distribution of illicit drugs and alcohol.

The Drug Free Schools and Communities Act Amendments also mandate a biennial review to determine the effectiveness of the institution's programs to reduce the use, possession and distribution of alcohol and illicit drugs on campus and the implementation of changes suggested by the review. *A Handbook for Complying with the Program and Review Requirements of the 1989 Amendments to the Drug Free Schools and Communities Act* was published in 1992 by College Administration Publications Inc. to assist institutions in understanding their obligations under the act and to assist with the biennial review.

The federal governnment continues to be concerned with issues of alcohol on campus. In 1998, included in legislation primarily designed to combat campus crime, there was a section entitled "Collegiate Initiative to Reduce Binge Drinking and Illegal Alcohol Consumption." While this section only set forth the "Sense of Congress" and was not a legal mandate, it is very intrusive and suggests that presidents establish and support task forces to examine academic life and recommend changes to reduce alcohol and drug problems, Congress also suggests alcohol free housing and other alcohol free environments as well as a zero tolerance policy for illegal consumption and the vigorous enforcement of campus policies. While this "Sense of Congress" is not law at the present time, it seems only inevitable that it will be soon.

Finally, Congress also amended the Family Educational Rights and Privacy Act (FERPA) in 1998 to allow institutions to disclose to the parents of students information regarding the violation of any federal, state or local law or policy of the institution, governing the use or possession of alcohol or a controlled substance if the student is less than 21 years-of-age, and has been found responsible for violating the institutions rules.

State legislatures have also been busy making changes to their alcoholic beverage laws during the past eight years. Several states including **Colorado, Illinois, Montana New Mexico, South Carolina** and **Virginia** have recodified their alcoholic beverage laws. Several others have increased penalties for minors who possess or consume alcohol (**Kansas** and **New Jersey**) while **Oregon** doubled the fine from $500 to $1000 for mi-

251

nors who misrepresent their age. Still other states have amended their statutes to revoke the driver's license of a minor who attempts to purchase (**Massachusetts,** possesses or consumes alcohol (**Texas** and **Washington**), misrepresents his or her age in an attempt to purchase alcohol (**Virginia** and **D.C.**) or who possesses or consumes while driving (**Indiana**). **Georgia** made it unlawful for minors to "attempt to purchase" while **Iowa** repealed a law permitting underage persons to possess alcohol in a private home with the knowledge and consent of the minor's parents. It is now a class D felony in **Arkansas** to sell alcohol to a minor. **Maine** enacted a statute requiring permits for BYOB parties. Sponsors of the parties may not permit minors on the premises nor allow minors or intoxicated persons to possess or consume alcohol on the premises.

In 1997 **Iowa** amended its dramshop law to include service to minors. Vendors who serve or sell to those they know or should have known are minors may now be liable to those injured as a result of that service.

Dramshop liability was also litigated extensively during the past eight years. While **Delaware, Maryland** and **Nevada** courts reaffirmed their reluctance to impose dramshop liability, the **Arkansas** supreme court overruled a 1965 case holding if the law was to be changed the legislature would need to do it. In a 1997 decision **Arkansas** joined the majority of states when its supreme court held a vendor can be liable for injuries resulting from the unlawful sale of alcohol to a minor.

The courts in several states interpreted their dramshop laws to provide a remedy only for innocent third persons injured by an intoxicated tavern patron. The consumer of the alcohol who suffers an injury has no remedy against the vendor. This interpretation was rendered by courts in **Hawaii, Iowa, New York, Oklahoma, Oregon** and **Washington.** However, in both **New Jersey** and **Texas** the courts reaffirmed the liability of vendors for injuries suffered by patrons but applied the doctrine of comparative negligence. Thus, if the consumer of the alcohol was fifty percent or more at fault recovery would be barred.

Alaska amended its dramshop law by making the vendor liable to the state for the prosecution costs and eliminating the defense of voluntary consumption.

The **South Carolina** supreme court has held that a licensed vendor who sells alcohol to a minor is negligent *per se*. The state's appellate court also decided that the statute prohibiting the sale of alcohol to an intoxicated person is designed to protect the public at large as well as the individual served.

The liability of a social host for injuries caused by an intoxicated guest seems to have been litigated more during this eight year period than in the past. In 1980 only one state recognized the liability of a social host. In 1990 there were 19 states that held a host liable for the injuries caused by intoxicated minor guests while an additional 9 states would possibly impose liability on the host. Eight states had not faced the question while the courts in 15 states held fast to the old common law rule of the liability resulting from the consumption rather than the furnishing of alcohol or stated that if the law was to be changed the legislature must do it. Today 25 states recognize social host liability where a minor is served and five more would possibly impose liability. Only 14 states specifically refuse to impose liability on hosts who serve minors. 5

In the past eight years nine states reaffirmed their position of not recognizing social host liability **Florida, Hawaii, Illinois, Kansas, Louisian , Missouri, Oklahoma, Rhode Island** and **West Virginia**). However, two of those, states have left the door open for future litigation. The **Illinois** supreme court imposed social host liability but limited it to situations where:

1. a social host knowingly served alcohol and permits the liquor to be served to youths under eighteen years of age at the social hosts   residence;

2. the social host permits the minor's consumption to continue to the point of intoxication; and

3. the social host allows the inebriated minors to depart from the residence in a motor vehicle.

In **Missouri,** an appellate court noted that while the state does not hold social hosts liable, a cause of action was available to the estate of a student who died after consuming a large portion of alcohol as part of an organization's initiation ceremony. The alcohol was provided by the organization and the student was a minor.

Two states previously listed as possible social host states (**Arizona** and **New HMpshire**) imposed liability on social hosts for the first time. The Idaho supreme court also reconfirmed the liability of social hosts. **North Dakota** will probably also join the growing number of social host 6 states. In 1994 the state's supreme court held that the dramshop statue was not limited to those who professionally sell alcohol and could be used to impose liability on a host who served an intoxicated adult who subsequently injured a third person.

Still other state courts which have imposed social host liability have, during the past eight years, limited the factual basis for imposing that liability. **Alaska** courts have determined that social hosts can only be liable for injuries on their premises while **New Jersey** only holds the host liable if the guest is driving. The New Jersey Superior Court said:

> A social host may only be directly liable to minors, and to third persons injured in automobile accidents. A social host is not liable to anyone else injured as a result of the social host's serving of intoxicating beverages to a guest.

In **Georgia** a state appellate court held that a social host has a duty to take "... some action to prevent the guest from driving once he or she is discovered to be intoxicated." **Washington** applies a traditional negligence analysis to determine the liability of a host using the statute prohibiting furnishing alcohol to a minor as the duty.

The liability of a social host in **Colorado** and **Iowa** is limited to serving minors. In **Colorado** the host must "willfully and knowingly" serve a minor while in **Iowa** the host must "know" a minor is being served. Colorado also recognized the theory of negligent entrustment. In 1992 the state supreme court said, "entrustment of an automobile to one who is likely to operate it under the influence of intoxicating liquors soon after obtaining possession of the vehicle presents an unreasonable risk of physical harm to the entrusted or others." In **Pennsylvania** the state's supreme court said a minor could not be liable as a social host since "one minor does not owe a duty to another minor regarding the furnishing or consumption of alcohol." The opposite result was arrived at in **New York** where an appellate court held that minors could be liable as social hosts for serving other minors.

Utah is unique in its social host liability. In 1997 the state supreme court held that the Dramshop Act could be applied to social hosts since it imposes liability on anyone who provides "liquor" to minors or those '4apparently under the influence." The alcoholic beverage must however, be liquor as opposed to beer or other alcoholic beverages. The court even pointed out that Utah is the only state that differentiates on the basis of the type of alcohol in its imposition of liability.

Finally, **Massachusetts** imposes liability on social hosts only where an innocent third person is injured. Much like the dramshop legislation in most stakes, the guest who consumes does not have a remedy for injuries suffered because of intoxication.

There were also some very interesting cases reported involving suits against parents whose minor children hosted parties in their parents' homes—sometimes the parents knew a party was to be held while other times they did not. In **Georgia** a mother purchased the alcohol for her teenage son who made it available at a party he hosted, The parents of a girl who was killed in an accident after the party sued the mother of the host under a state statute which allows parents to sue anyone who provides alcohol to their child without their permission. The host's father, who was out of town, but knew his wife regularly provided alcohol for the teenage friends of his son could also be liable.

Three other cases also involved the liability of parents who were not at home when a party took place. A **New Jersey** court held a parent liable for injuries sustained by a guest of her son. Although the mother was out of town the court said:

> [p]arents have a duty to provide for reasonable supervision of their minor child if it is reasonably foreseeable that, in their absence, the child will invite friends to a beer party at which one of their minor guests injure himself.

The highest court in **New York** also had to address the issues of the liability of a social host for injuries sustained at a party hosted by a minor whose parents were out of town. The court found that the teenage daughter, but not her parents could be liable; however, in a different case an appellate court held that parents could be liable as landowners who have a duty to act responsibly. The **Ohio** supreme court also said that parents, even though out of town, can be liable for injuries resulting from intoxication of minor guests attending a party hosted by their child if they gave permission for the party, knew or should have known that alcohol would be present and did not provide supervision.

The **Oklahoma** supreme court, however, disagreed with the decision above when it held that parents who are out of town could not liable since "in order to be a social host some degree of control is necessary."

Several decisions were issued during the past eight years that more directly involved colleges and universities. During this time period at least eleven different states reported cases involving the death, rapes, or serious injury to fourteen college students. However, colleges and universities continue to enjoy deference from the courts. In **California** where a student was raped after being served alcohol at a party in her residence hall a state appellate court said "universities are generally not liable for the sometimes disastrous consequences which result from combining young students, alcohol and dangerous or violent impulses."

A **Pennsylvania** court also found in favor of a university where a female student was injured on her way home after attending several fraternity parties at which she was served alcohol. The fraternities had not followed the university rules related to student organization social functions. The student argued that the university having established rules failed in its duty. The court, however, found the rules only to be guidelines which place responsibility for compliance on the fraternities.

An opinion of the Attorney General in **Louisiana** also involved fraternities. The state statute prohibiting public possession of alcohol by a minor provides an exemption for possession in a private residence, The Attorney General has issued an opinion that off-campus fraternities are not within the definition of "private residence" for purposes of the exception to the law.

In both **New York** and **Missouri** the courts have held that if a student is injured as a result of consuming alcohol during an initiation ceremony a jury might decide if the consumption was in fact coerced. The **New York** court said the fraternity would be liable if:

> the evidence shows that the drinking was imposed upon the pledges, and that their obedience was extracted as an express or implied condition of membership.

Campus judicial administrators may also be interested in decisions by courts in **Virginia** and **Washington.** In both sates the courts have indicated that if one has used a substance then there was possession. The **Virginia** court said "use of a substance necessarily implies [its] possession." The **Washington** court observed that "evidence of assimilation is circumstantial evidence of prior possession" and convicted the individual of possession based on his slurred speech, alcohol breath and blood shot eyes.

Finally, three states have gone on record stating that minors are not competent to assess or deal with the risks associated with alcohol. The supreme court of **Alaska** stated that society has decided ". . . children are not competent to assess in any meaningful way the risk involved in the use of alcohol." While the supreme court of Connecticut said ". . . minors are presumed not to have the capacity to understand fully the risks associated with intoxication" and the **Oklahoma** supreme court observed that "Minors are incompetent . . . to deal responsibly with the effects of alcohol." Yet in the face of this expression the **Michigan** supreme court has held that "criminal or violent acts are not foreseeable results of the serving of alcohol to minors, and therefore, cannot serve as a basis for social host liability."

These are simply the highlights of the statutory and case law for the past eight years. Many more interesting issues can be found in the various state annotations.

About the Author

Dr. Terry W. McCarthy is an honors graduate of the University of Alabama School of Law and is employed with the Birmingham law firm of Lightfoot, Franklin, and White. Before beginning his law career, Dr. McCarthy served as Director of Student Affairs at Jacksonville State University.

In addition to his law degree he holds a Bachelor of Science degree in Finance from Auburn University, a Masters of Education degree in Counseling and Guidance from the University of Montevallo, and a Doctorate of Education degree in Higher Education Administration from the University of Alabama.

Dr. McCarthy publishes and lectures regularly in the area of education law. He may be reached at tmccarthy@collegepubs.com.

The author would like to express his appreciation to Edward Peterson for his assistance in preparing this manuscript.

1999 Updating
STATE
ANNOTATIONS

This section updates, for the period of January 1, 1990 through January 1, 1999, the State Annotation information contained in the 1989 edition of Alcohol on Campus and its 1990 updating supplement.

Alabama

1998 Cumulative Supplement

Definition of a Minor

In **Kelly v. Ryals Services, Inc.**, 585 So. 2d 1371 (Ala. 1991), the Alabama Supreme Court held that for the purposes of Code 1975 §6-5-70, a minor is a person under the age of 21.

Sale to a Minor

In **Funari v. City of Decatur,** 563 So. 2d 54 (Ala. Crim. App. 1990), the court held that anyone who sells alcohol to a minor is responsible for the sale even if they did not know the purchaser was a minor.

In **Mcleod v. Cannon Oil Corp.**, 603 So. 2d 889 (Ala. 1992), the Alabama Supreme Court gave a sound analysis of how to interpret Code 1975 §6-5-70. First, the court ruled that under Code 1975 §6-5-70, "a plaintiff must prove that the defendant (1) sold spirituous liquor to a person who was a minor, and (2) was chargeable with notice or knowledge of the minority" (p. 891). Once the plaintiff meets these two elements, the defendant must show that he complied with all the appropriate regulations. In this case, a store was liable for the death of a passenger in a car accident because they sold alcohol to a minor and did not ask for the minor's identification. The court used strong language to analyze the statute and stated that:

> [j]ust as the Dram Shop Act creates strict liability in cases of its violation, the Civil Damages Act creates strict liability in cases of its violation . . . . The Act provides that a seller of spirituous liquors sells them at his peril. . . . It places the burden on sellers of such beverages to determine that the purchasers are not minors. (p. 893)

Misrepresentation of Age

A 1995 amendment states that it is unlawful for a minor "to knowingly use or attempt to use a false, forged, deceptive, or otherwise non-genuine driver's license to obtain or attempt to obtain alcoholic beverages in this state" [Code 1975 §28-3A-25(22)].

Dramshop Liability

There have been several cases of interest that have further interpreted the Alabama Dramshop Act. **McIssaac v. Monte Carlo Club, Inc.**, 587 So. 2d 320 (Ala. 1991), addressed an issue of Dramshop liability that was of first impression in the Alabama courts. The court addressed "whether a person who allegedly participated in drinking that led to the intoxication of another can recover damages under the provisions of the Act for injuries incurred in an accident allegedly caused by the intoxication of the other person" (p. 321).

This case involved a plaintiff who was drinking alcohol with a friend at a bar and was injured in an accident that resulted from the friend's intoxication. The trial court held that the plaintiff could not recover because of the doctrine of complicity. Complicity precludes recovery under Dramshop for a plaintiff who willfully participates in the intoxication of the inebriate.

However, the decision of the trial court was reversed on appeal and the Alabama Supreme Court held that Code 1975 §6-5-71 "creates strict liability in favor of those persons covered under the provisions and authorizes those persons to maintain an action without regard to complicity or contributory negligence" (p. 324). The court did rule that the defendant could raise the defense of assumption of risk, which could immunize the defendant from liability if the plaintiff knew and understood the risks involved and voluntarily assumed those risks.

In **Duckett v. Wilson Hotel Management Company, Inc.,** 669 So. 2d 977 (Ala. Civ. App. 1995), the court held that a Dramshop action can still proceed even for the *intentional* criminal behavior of the intoxicated patron. In this case, an establishment allegedly served alcohol to an intoxicated patron who later shot and killed the plaintiff's father. The court allowed this case against the establishment to be decided by the jury because the purpose of the Dramshop Act is to punish establishments that continue to serve intoxicated customers. It is irrelevant in Alabama whether the actions of the patron are intentional or unintentional if the establishment violated the statute.

In **Attalla Golf & Country Club v. Harris,** 601 So. 2d 965 (Ala. 1992), the Alabama Supreme Court specifically articulated the three elements a plaintiff must prove to be successful in a Dramshop action. "The sale must have (1) been contrary to the provisions of law; (2) been the cause of the intoxication; and (3) resulted in the plaintiff's injury" (p. 967). The court reiterated that selling alcohol to a visibly intoxicated person was illegal, but they also held that "it is illegal for a private club to sell liquor or alcohol to a nonmember or a nonguest" (p. 968).

It appears that the Alabama Supreme Court will not hold an establishment liable for selling liquor to an adult who subsequently provides the liquor to a minor. **Epsey v. Convenience Marketers,** 578 So. 2d 1221 (Ala. 1991), put to rest a question concerning the interpretation of Code 1975 §6-5-70. The Supreme Court interpreted Code 1975 §6-5-71 and gave an example of how the statute would apply to this common situation:

> A clerk sells beer to an adult, who can legally buy the beer, and that adult later gives the beer to a minor. The clerk in the example has no right to refuse to sell the beer to the person legally entitled to buy it. [To hold the retailer liable for the minor's injuries] would for all practical purposes impose strict liability on retailers of alcohol; we expressly reject such a holding. (p. 1232-1233)

Jones v. BP Oil Co., Inc., 632 So. 2d 435 (Ala. 1993), reaffirmed the decision from **Epsey** that "a direct, rather than an indirect, sale of alcoholic beverages to the person causing the injury is required in order to create a claim under Code 1975 §6-5-71" (p. 438).

This type of situation was present in **Parker v. Miller Brewing Co.,** 560 So. 2d 1030 (Ala. 1990), when the mother of a minor daughter who was killed as a result of driving while intoxicated sued the beer retailer and distributor who sold the beer to the sponsors of the party where the beer was consumed. The court did not impose liability under Dramshop because the beer was not purchased directly by the minor daughter.

Similarly, in **Moreland v. Jitney Jungle, Inc.,** 621 So. 2d 285 (Ala. 1993), the court did not impose liability on the establishment when the minor was present when the purchase was made. In this case, a grocery store that sold beer to a 21-year-old who gave the beer to a minor was not liable under Dramshop even though the minor was present at the check-out line when the beer was purchased. The plaintiff argued that the court should look at the "totality of the circumstances" and see that it was obvious that the minor would also consume the beer. The court held that the "totality of the circumstances" test only applies to Code 1975 §6-5-70.

Weeks v. Princeton's, 570 So. 2d 1232 (Ala. 1990), and **James v. Brewton Motel Management, Inc.,** 570 So. 2d 1225 (Ala. 1990), both held that "an intoxicated person's minor children can bring an action ..." (p. 1232) under Code 1975 §6-5-71. *See also,* **James v. Najor,** 575 So. 2d 1105 (Ala. 1991). However, **Weeks**

continued to uphold the rule in Alabama that the intoxicated person is not a protected party under the Dramshop Act.

In **The Booth, Inc. v. Miles,** 567 So. 2d 1206 (Ala. 1990), a man who was struck by an intoxicated driver sued the driver and the tavern who served him the alcohol which caused him to become intoxicated. The driver settled the case before trial for $15,000 and the court upheld a jury verdict against the tavern for $50,000 in punitive damages. The facts indicated that the driver had consumed six beers and two shots of liquor. He was served while visibly intoxicated and his blood alcohol content was .32.

In **Adkison v. Thompson,** 650 So. 2d 859 (Ala. 1994), the Alabama Supreme Court continued its policy of refusing to recognize a claim based on negligence in the distribution of alcohol. This was reaffirmed in **Williams v. Reasoner,** 668 So. 2d 541 (Ala. 1995), which noted that the only civil liability in Alabama for the unlawful dispensing of alcohol is under the Civil Damages Act and Dramshop Act.

Social Host Liability   The Alabama courts still refuse to hold a social host liable under the Dramshop Act unless the social host serves alcohol to a minor. In **Gamble v. Neonatal Associates, P.A.,** 688 So. 2d 878 (Ala. Civ. App. 1997), a guest of a company party at the home of one of its shareholders was served alcohol to the point of intoxication. He left the party in his car and he was in an accident with the plaintiff. The plaintiff sued, but the court refused to hold the social host liable because the guest was an adult—not a minor.

Alaska

1998 Replacement Volume

Definition of a Minor   In **Loeb v. Rasmussen,** 822 P.2d 914 (Alaska 1991), the Alaska Supreme Court held that a licensee cannot reduce its liability with the defense of comparative negligence when the licensee illegally serves alcohol to a minor and the minor is subsequently injured. In this case, the parents of a minor brought this action against a tavern that served their daughter alcohol to the point of intoxication which later caused her to be in a car accident. One year later she committed suicide. The jury returned a verdict against the tavern in the amount of $144,593.09 and the trial court reduced the amount in accordance with the principles of comparative negligence. On appeal, the court held that comparative negligence does not apply to a licensee who serves alcohol to a minor. The court stressed:

> society's belief that children are not competent to assess in any meaningful way the risk involved in the use of alcohol. [The tavern] was able to exploit this lack of competence when it sold liquor unlawfully to [the minor]. However, we can think of no legitimate reason to allow [tavern] to exploit it further, by having its liability to the plaintiff reduced. (p. 919)

Possession or Consumption by a Minor   A 1995 amendment to Section 04.16.050 added a new section which fines a person who violates this section not less than $100.

Sale or Gift to Minor   A 1994 amendment to Section 04.16.051 makes it a class C felony if, within five years preceding the violation, the person was previously convicted under this section or any other section substantially similar to this section.

Miscellaneous   According to Section 4.16.080, "a person may not sell or consume alcoholic beverages during a school event at the site of the event."

In 1995, the legislature adopted A.S. §04.16.055 which makes it unlawful for anyone to rent a room in a motel or other similar place for the purpose of providing alcohol to minors.

Dramshop Liability

The legislature amended Section 04.21.020 by adding some additional sections which became effective July 1, 1997. The new sections state that a person who sells alcohol in violation of Section 04.11.010 (this is the section which forbids the sale of alcohol without a license) is strictly liable to the recipient or to other third persons for civil damages if the recipient's alcohol consumption substantially contributes to the harm. Further, the seller is liable to the state for all the prosecution costs of the recipient. The new section also specifies that the seller cannot assert as a defense that the person voluntarily consumed the alcohol.

As the amendment states, the seller is only liable if the alcohol is served in violation of Section 04.11.010, which says a person may not sell alcohol without a license. However, Section 04.11.020 exempts from this section private gatherings of co-workers or private gatherings of fraternal organizations "if equal contributions are made by all in attendance and only the amount required to purchase the alcoholic beverages is contributed."

In **Williford v. L.J. Carr Invs., Inc.**, 783 P.2d 235 (Alaska 1989), the court held that the Dramshop statute is only designed to protect vendors who serve alcohol in a legally permissible way. Thus, if a vendor sells alcohol to an intoxicated person in violation of Section 04.16.030, the statute does not immunize the vendor from liability.

Gonzales v. Krueger, 799 P.2d 1318 (Alaska 1990), involved a situation where a store sold alcohol to an intoxicated passenger of a car after a store employee was convinced that the driver of the car was sober. The passenger shared the alcohol with the driver and they subsequently were in an accident. The court held that the store was not immune from liability and sent the case to the jury to determine if the sale by the store was the proximate cause of the accident. The basis of this lawsuit is that a licensed provider of alcohol is only immune from liability if the licensee does not sell to an intoxicated person or a minor.

On remand, in **Gonzales v. Safeway Stores, Inc.**, 882 P.2d 389 (Alaska 1994), the jury returned a verdict that the store was not negligent. The decision was affirmed on appeal because there was enough evidence to support the jury's finding that the store did not sell alcohol to an intoxicated person with criminal negligence.

It was held in **Lord v. Fogcutter Bar**, 813 P.2d 660 (Alaska 1991), that the purpose of the Dramshop Law in Alaska is not to protect people from the consequences of their own intentional criminal conduct. Therefore in this case, even if the tavern violated the dramshop law by selling alcohol to an intoxicated person, the tavern was not liable for crimes that that person subsequently committed against a third party.

Social Host Liability

The issue of social host liability appeared to be unsettled in Alaska for some time. Two cases seem to indicate that the courts would not impose liability on a host for the injury of an innocent third party. However, liability would be imposed for injuries that occur on the premises of the event.

Gordon v. Alaska Pacific Bancorporation, 753 P.2d 721 (Alaska 1988), involved a company that provided alcohol at a party it sponsored for its customers. At the party an altercation broke out. The court held that the company would be liable for injuries that occurred because they had a duty to provide protection since they knew that intoxicated people would be on the premises. Even though they did not have a liquor license the court determined they were not immune from liability.

Mulvihill v. Union Oil Co., 859 P.2d 1310 (Alaska 1993), involved a Christmas party of UNOCAL. An employee became intoxicated at the party and after having a couple of beers at a tavern afterwards, he was driven home by another employee who had been at the party. Later, the intoxicated employee tried driving and fell asleep at the wheel, killing himself and two others and seriously injuring a passenger in the other car. That passenger and the estates of the victims sued UNOCAL and the employee who drove the intoxicated employee home.

The court held that "UNOCAL, as a social host, owed no duty to [the victims]" (p. 1312). The court ruled this way because the company had no liquor license. Further, the employee who drove LeMay home was a volunteer who had no liability because he exercised reasonable care. The court stated that if he were liable,

> then every designated driver who agreed to drive a friend home after a night of drinking would risk liability if that friend chose to drive after the designated driver left. Such a result would undermine society's well-founded desire to encourage sober people to volunteer to drive their intoxicated friends home. (p. 1314)

The court quoted a similar federal case which said, "persons who otherwise have no liability should not be discouraged from making reasonable efforts to remove an obviously intoxicated driver from behind the wheel" (p. 1314). *See,* **Prelvitz v. Milsop,** 831 F.2d 806, 810 (8th Cir. 1987).

The issue of social host liability in Alaska was given some clarity in **Chokwak v. Worley**, 912 P.2d 1248 (Alaska 1996), a case where a minor who was injured in a car accident after he was provided alcohol at a party brought this action against the hosts of the party. The court performed a thorough analysis of the legislative history of Section 04.21.020, the Dramshop statute, and concluded that it "grants civil immunity to social hosts who unlawfully provide liquor to minors and that this grant of immunity is not unconstitutional" (p. 1255). The plaintiff unsuccessfully argued that the statute granted immunity only to licensees. Therefore, in Alaska, a plaintiff cannot "borrow" the Dramshop statute to create social host liability.

Arizona

1998 Cumulative Pocket Part

Definition of a Minor The section that lists the legal drinking age at 21 is now A.R.S. §4-101(18).

Sale or Gift to an Intoxicated person A 1994 amendment to A.R.S. §4-244(14) inserted "obviously." So the statute now provides that no licensed vendors nor other persons may "serve, sell or furnish spirituous liquor to a disorderly or *obviously* intoxicated person" (emphasis added).

Definition of Intoxicated Persons A 1994 amendment to A.R.S. §4-244(14) defines obviously intoxicated as "inebriated to the extent that a person's physical faculties are substantially impaired and the impairment is shown by significantly uncoordinated physical action or significant dysfunction that would have been obvious to a reasonable person."

While there is still no statutory Dramshop Act in Arizona, the courts have continued to apply common-law Dramshop liability. In **Carillo v. El Mirage Roadhouse, Inc.**, 793 P.2d 121 (Ariz. App. 1990), the court held that a liquor licensee has a duty not to provide alcohol to anyone, regardless of their condition, if the licensee is aware that an intoxicated person will consume the alcohol.

In **Petolicchio v. Santa Cruz County Fair and Rodeo Association, Inc.**, 866 P.2d 1342 (Ariz. 1994), the court held that a liquor licensee who stores alcohol has a duty to use reasonable care to guard against those who would foreseeably endanger the public through its use.

In **Riddle v. Arizona Oncology Services, Inc.**, 924 P.2d 468 (Ariz. App. 1996), an employer ordered an employee to leave the work premises because of her intoxicated condition. The employee subsequently drove her vehicle and caused an accident, injuring the plaintiff. The court refused to impose liability because the employer had no duty to control the actions of the employee.

Dramshop Liability

A recent Arizona Supreme Court case implies that social host liability will apply when a social host serves alcohol to minors. **Estate of Hernandez v. Arizona Board of Regents**, 866 P.2d 1330 (Ariz. 1994) involved a fraternity that purchased alcohol with money obtained from members who contributed to a social fund. The majority of the members of the fraternity were minors. John Raynor, a contributing fraternity member, consumed alcohol purchased from the fund at a party one night. Later, he crashed his car into another, killing the driver. The estate sued the following parties: (1) fraternity (2) each fraternity member who contributed to the fund (3) Arizona Board of Regents (4) national fraternity (5) lessor of the fraternity house property (6) the student assigned through the university to educate the fraternity about alcohol.

Social Host Liability

The court sent this case to the jury to decide liability because the defendants had a duty to avoid furnishing alcohol to *underage* drinkers. Because minors were involved, there was no protection under A.R.S. §4-301, (the statute which exempts social hosts from liability for injuries caused by social guests of the legal drinking age). In the subsequent history of the case, **Estate of Hernandez v. Flavis**, 930 P.2d 1309 (Ariz. en banc, 1997), the pledges who were named as defendants were released from the suit because of their relatively limited role in the incident.

The Arizona courts have continued to not apply social host liability where the alcohol is sold to those of legal drinking age. In **Bruce v. Chas Roberts Air Conditioning**, 801 P.2d 456 (Ariz. App. 1990), the court held that an employer was not liable for the actions of an employee who was drinking on the employer's premises. The court stated that the "Legislature has foreclosed liability for anyone, other than a licensee and his or her employees from the serving of alcohol" (p. 459).

In **Knoell v. Clerkvenik–Anderson Travel, Inc.**, 917 P.2d 689 (Ariz. 1996), the parents of an eighteen-year-old brought this wrongful death action against a travel agency which supervised a trip which lead to the son's alcohol related death. The travel agency argued that they were immune from liability as a social host under A.R.S. §4-301. However, the court disagreed because a social host only receives immunity in Arizona when the person served is of the legal drinking age. Although the death occurred in Mexico, where the legal drinking age is eighteen, the court held that §4-301 refers to the state's legal drinking age of twenty-one, rather than the drinking age of where the alcohol was consumed.

An Arizona appellate court addressed the issue of the potential liability of a person who takes the car keys of an intoxicated per-

Other Cases of Interest

son but returns them while the person is still intoxicated. In **Ocotillo West v. Superior Court,** 844 P.2d 653 (Ariz. App. Div. 1 1992), some golf course employees took possession of the car keys of a person who had become intoxicated from alcohol he purchased while playing a round of golf. The employees then turned over the keys to the inebriant's friend, who assured them he would be responsible. Subsequently, the friend returned the keys to the inebriant, who drove from the golf course and was killed in an accident.

Although the common law does not instill a duty on a person to gratuitously help another, if a person does choose to help, he must use reasonable care. The court held that a "reasonable fact finder could conclude that [the friend's] actions contributed to" the death of the inebriant. Therefore, because the friend did not use reasonable care in handling the keys, he assumed liability that he would not have had if he had never taken the keys in the first place.

Arkansas

1998 Replacement Volume

Definition of a Minor	The statute providing that the age of majority is eighteen and the minimum age to consume alcohol is twenty-one in Arkansas is codified at Arkansas Code §9-25-101(b), rather than §9-25-10(b).
Possession or Consumption by a Minor	According to **Kastl v. State,** 796 S.W.2d 848 (Ark. 1990), a defendant must be in actual possession of the alcohol to be convicted.
Sale or Gift to a Minor	A 1993 amendment to Arkansas Code §3-3-202 makes it unlawful for "any person to sell alcoholic beverages to a minor." A person who violates this section will be charged with a class D felony. A 1995 amendment requires that a warning notice with the provisions of this section be posted in any place where alcohol is sold.
Sale or Gift to an Intoxicated Person	A 1993 amendment changed the fines under Arkansas Code §3-3-201 to not less than $200 nor more than $500 for the first offense. For subsequent offenses, the fine is not less than $500 nor more than $1000 and/or jail for not less than one year.
	According to Arkansas Code §3-3-209, any person who provides alcohol to an intoxicated person or habitual drunkard is guilty of a misdemeanor. This was incorrectly listed as Arkansas Code §3-3-201 in *Alcohol on Campus.*
Dramshop Liability	In **Shannon v. Wilson,** 947 S.W.2d 349 (Ark. 1997), the Arkansas Supreme Court held that a vendor of alcohol can be held liable for injuries that occur as a result of the unlawful sale of alcohol to a minor. It is important to note that **Shannon** overruled the old common-law rule of **Carr v. Turner** which was that vendors are not civilly liable for the sale of alcohol. Under the new rule of **Shannon,** a party may have a cause of action in negligence against an establishment if the party is injured by an intoxicated minor.

California

West's Annotated Business and Professional Code (1998 Replacement Volume)

Sale or Gift to a Minor	In **Provigo Corporation v. ABC Appeals Board**, 28 Cal. Rptr. 2d 638, 869 P.2d 1163 (Cal. 1994), the court stated that the law against the sale of alcohol to minors can be violated even though

the seller does not even know the buyer is a minor and they routinely check IDs.

Section 25658(b) makes it unlawful to sell, furnish, or "cause to be sold" alcohol to a minor. Under §25602.1 it is also unlawful when the alcohol is provided to an intoxicated person. According to **Hernandez v. Modesto Portuguese Pentecost Association**, 48 Cal. Rptr. 2d 229, (App. 3 Dist. 1995), the term to "cause to be sold" alcohol to an obviously intoxicated minor requires an affirmative act—not just acquiescence or inaction. In this case, a ballroom owner rented his ballroom for a one day social event. At the event, alcohol was sold to an obviously intoxicated minor who drove and struck a utility pole, killing himself, two others, and injuring a third passenger.

The court refused to hold the owner of the ballroom liable because it was not he who "caused to be sold" the alcohol as required in §25658(b) and §25602.1. There was no evidence to indicate that he was in a position to know that the minor was obviously intoxicated and the owner did not affirmatively act. Also, the court concluded that his failure to adopt affirmative policies did not rise to the level of being an affirmative act.

Sale or Gift to an Intoxicated Person

According to **Schaffield v. Abboud,** 19 Cal. Rptr. 205 (15 C.A. 4 Dist. 1993), the standard to determine "obviously intoxicated" is that of a reasonable person.

Miscellaneous

A 1993 amendment added §25659.5, which requires licensees who sell kegs of beer to tag all kegs sold for identification purposes.

In 1992, West's Ann.Cal.Bus. & Prof. Code §2566.5 was added. According to this section, if a person violates §25658(b), §25658.5, or §25662, and is put on probation, the court may order, with defendant's consent, that the defendant participate in a program described in Art. 1.7 (starting with section 23145) of Chapter 12 of Div. II of Vehicle Code.

Section 25608 states the general rule that alcohol cannot be present on school grounds. However, there are several exceptions, such as football games, religious purposes, and courses when alcohol use is approved by the school's administrative head or governing board.

Dramshop Liability

In **Cantwell v. Peppermill, Inc.**, 31 Cal. Rptr. 2d 246 (Cal. App. 1 Dist. 1994), a patron who was stabbed in a bar fight sued the bar owner. The court held that "although a proprietor of a place where intoxicating liquors are dispensed is not an insurer of its patrons' safety, he has a duty of care to protect patrons from reasonably foreseeable criminal or tortious conduct of third persons" (p. 248). Even though §25602 insulates an innkeeper from liability for selling to a drunk person, the seller still has to take reasonable steps to protect guests from aggressive conduct of other guests.

One interesting decision is important for all campuses that allow "tailgating" before and after athletic events. In **Leong v. San Francisco Parking, Inc.**, 1 Cal. Rptr. 2d 41 (Cal. App. 1 Dist. 1991), the parents of a child who was killed by a drunk driver brought this action against the San Francisco baseball team and others, alleging that since the baseball park served alcohol, and since alcohol was consumed on the premises via "tailgating," that they should be liable. The court refused to impose liability because §25602 precludes it. The court held that the defendants could not be liable "for simply permitting [the driver] to consume alcoholic beverages on [their] premises" (p. 44).

The immunity of §25602 even applies when a tavern serves alcohol to a person who is mentally incompetent. [**Cardinal v. Sante Pita, Inc.**, 286 Cal. Rptr. 275 (Cal. App. 4 Dist. 1991].

Other Cases of Interest   One California case should make those party hosts who collect keys be extremely cautious. In **Williams v. Saga Enterprises,** 274 Cal. Rptr. 901 (Cal. App. 2 Dist. 1992), the passenger in an automobile who was injured in a car accident brought this action based on the claim that the bartender was negligent in holding the driver's keys as a precautionary measure and returning the keys to the driver after he became intoxicated. The court held that there was enough evidence to send this case to the jury to decide if liability should be imposed. The court stated that if the bar and patron had an arrangement where the bar was to withhold the patron's keys if he were to become intoxicated, that the bar could be liable. Because fraternities and sororities often collect keys at parties, this case is one they should know.

In **Tanja H. V. Regents of the University of California,** 278 Cal. Rptr. 918 (Cal. App. 1991), a minor female student was served alcohol at a party in her residence hall and was subsequently raped by four members of the football team. The court refused to hold the university liable and cited the current rule in California that "universities are not generally liable for the sometimes disastrous consequences which result from combining young students, alcohol, and dangerous or violent impulses." (p. 920).

Colorado

1998 Cumulative Pocket Part

Possession or Consumption by a Minor   C.R.S. §12-46-112(5) was repealed effective July 30, 1990. Consequently, those eighteen-years of age and older may no longer purchase 3.2 beer.

The sections which make it illegal for a minor to purchase alcohol were changed to C.R.S. §12-47-901(1)(a) & (b) effective July 1, 1997.

C.R.S. §12-46-112(1)(d), which said possession of alcohol by minors was only prohibited in public places, on state property, or in vehicles while on public thoroughfares, was repealed effective July 1, 1997. This is now codified in §§12-47-901(1)(d) and 12-47-901(1)(b).

C.R.S. §§12-46-112(1)(c) and 12-47-128(1)(b), which made it unlawful for a minor to obtain alcohol by any means, were repealed effective July 1, 1997. This law is now codified in §12-47-901(1)(b).

Sale or Gift to a Minor   C.R.S. §§12-46-112(1)(b)(I) and 12-47-128(a)(a), which made it unlawful to sell alcohol to a minor, were repealed effective July 1, 1997. This law is now codified in §12-47-901(1)(a).

C.R.S. §12-47-128(5)(a)(I), which made it unlawful for a vendor to sell alcohol to a minor, was repealed effective July 1, 1997. This law is now codified in §12-47-901(5)(a)(I).

Misrepresentation of Age   C.R.S. §§12-46-112(c) and 12-47-128(1)(b), which made it unlawful for minors to misrepresent their age in attempting to obtain alcoholic beverages, are now codified in §12-47-901(1)(b).

C.R.S. §§12-46-112(1)(g) and 12-47-128(1)(k), which prohibited any person from allowing a minor to use that person's I.D., are now codified in §12-47-901(1)(k).

C.R.S. §§12-46-112(b)(II)(A) & (B) and 12-47-128(5)(II)(A) & (B), which stated that minors who present fraudulent I.D.'s may be lawfully detained by the vendor for questioning and have the I.D. confiscated, are now codified in §12-47-901(5)(II)(A) & (B).

C.R.S. §12-47-128(1)(e), which made it unlawful for any person to buy liquors from one not licensed to sell them, is now codified in §12-47-901(1)(e).

Miscellaneous

C.R.S. §12-47-128(1)(g), which made it unlawful for any person to possess liquors for sale without a license, is now codified in §12-47-901(1)(g).

C.R.S. §12-47-138(1)(d)(I), which prohibited the licensed sale of alcoholic beverages within certain distances of the principal campus of any college or university, is now codified in §12-47-313(1)(d)(I) & (II).

In **Casebolt v. Cowan**, 829 P.2d 352 (Colo. 1992), the court held that Colorado does recognize the doctrine of negligent entrustment as part of its negligence law. Negligent entrustment generally occurs when someone negligently gives a person access to an automobile when a reasonable person would not do so. The court stated that "entrustment of an automobile to one who is likely to operate it under the influence of intoxicating liquors soon after obtaining possession of the vehicle presents an unreasonable risk of physical harm to the entrustee and others" (p. 361).

C.R.S. §§12-46-112(1)(b)(1) and 12-47-128(1)(a), which made it unlawful to sell or provide alcoholic beverages to a visibly intoxicated person, is now codified in §12-47-901(a).

Sale or Gift to an Intoxicated Person

In **Christoph v. Colorado Communications Corp.,** 946 P.2d 519 (Colo. App. 1997), the estate of a passenger who was killed while riding in a car with a driver who had become intoxicated from consuming alcohol he had purchased at a rodeo sued the radio station and the group that sponsored the rodeo. Although the trial court granted summary judgment for the defendants, the decision was reversed on appeal because there was enough circumstantial evidence to let a jury determine whether the defendants "willfully and knowingly" served the driver the alcohol while visibly intoxicated (the "willfully and knowingly" elements are required under dramshop law). He appeared to be sober when he arrived and continued to purchase beer even after he had become extremely rowdy. Therefore, because there was evidence that he may have willfully and knowingly been served while intoxicated, the defendants could be liable.

Dramshop Liability

Similarly, in **Brown v. Hollywood Bar & Cafe,** 942 P.2d 1363 (Colo. App. 1997), the defendant tavern was unsuccessful in getting a jury verdict overturned because there was adequate circumstantial evidence to show that they served a patron, who subsequently was in a car accident, while he was visibly intoxicated. The court also addressed Colorado's $150,000 cap on punitive damages provided in the Dramshop statute and held that the limit only applies as between one licensee and one individual. Therefore, in this case, because there were multiple defendants, each defendant was potentially liable to the plaintiff for $150,000.

Sigman v. Seafood Ltd. Partnership I, 817 P.2d 527 (Colo. 1991), reiterated that C.R.S. §12-47-128.5(1) abolished all common law causes of action against alcohol vendors.

In **Dickman v. Jackalope, Inc.**, 870 P.2d 1261 (Colo. App. 1994), the court stated that "[a] vendor may be held civilly liable only if the vendor knows that he or she is serving alcohol to a person under twenty-one years of age and willfully does so" (p. 1263).

C.R.S. §§12-46-112.5 and 12-47-128.5, which codified social host liability, are now codified in §12-47-801.

Social Host Liability

The Colorado courts have continued to have a high standard for the imposition of social host liability. Unless a social host "willfully and knowingly" serves a minor, the social host generally will not be liable.

In **Charlton v. Kimata**, 815 P.2d 946 (Colo. 1991), a car accident victim brought an action against a social host who provided alcohol to the driver that hit him. The court ruled that C.R.S. §12-47-128.5 (4) prevailed in this case. Therefore, there was no action against the social host under Colorado law because the host did not willfully and knowingly serve a minor.

In **Forrest v. Lorrigan**, 833 P.2d 873 (Colo. App. 1992), Forrest was a guest at a party at the defendant's home. She was injured by a minor driver who had become intoxicated at the party. Marlene Lorrigan had given her eighteen-year-old daughter permission to have the party and the mother knew that alcohol would be present. However, alcohol was neither purchased nor served by the social host defendants. The plaintiff in this case was a passenger in a car and the accident occurred because of the driver's negligence. The lawsuit was filed based on the theory of social host liability.

The court held that the acts of the defendant were not sufficient to constitute willful and knowingly service of alcohol to those under the legal drinking age. A violation of C.R.S. §12-47-128.5 only occurs "when a social host has control over or takes an active part in supplying a minor with alcohol and that providing a home at which alcohol is consumed by minors, without more, does not create liability" (p. 875).

Connecticut

1998 Cumulative Annual Pocket Part

Definition of a Minor

The section which states that a minor is one who is less than twenty-one years of age is now in C.G.S.A. §30-1(12).

Miscellaneous

A 1996 amendment to C.G.S.A. §30-77(b) allows a person of legal age to produce beer for personal or family use up to certain limits specified in the statute. The produced beer shall not be offered for sale.

A 1993 amendment to C.G.S.A. §30-20a imposes a $240 annual fee for a beer license, a $560 annual fee for a university permit for beer and wine, and a $240 annual fee for a university liquor permit.

Definition of Intoxicated Person

While the case of **Coble v. Maloney**, 643 A.2d 277 (Conn. App. 1994), was a Dramshop action where the court held that there was enough evidence to let the jury decide if the tavern unlawfully sold alcohol to an intoxicated person, the case also gave some additional meaning to intoxication. In this case, the defendant tavern argued that just because a patron had a blood alcohol content exceeding .10 and was officially "under the influence" of alcohol according to C.G.S.A. §14-227a, it does not mean that he had reached the point of "intoxication" according to the Dramshop law. The court disagreed and held that the legislative intent was not to give different meanings to those terms.

Dramshop Liability

In **Kelehear v. Larcon, Inc.**, 577 A.2d 746 (Conn. App. 1990), the court specifically set out that the elements of a Dramshop claim are "(1) the sale of intoxicating liquor, (2) to an intoxicated person, (3) who, in consequence of such intoxication, causes injury to the person or property of another" (p. 748). In this case, the court stated that whether or not there was enough evidence that a patron was served while intoxicated was for the jury to decide.

Belanger v. Village Pub I, Inc., 603 A.2d 1173 (Conn. App. 1992) involved an establishment that served alcohol to a driver after the driver was intoxicated. The driver later caused a head-on collision, causing the death of the other driver. The driver registered a blood alcohol content of .313. The court held that the bar was in violation of the Dramshop statute because they served the driver beyond the point of intoxication. In addition, the court held that contributory negligence of the other driver could not be a defense under the Dramshop Act.

One very important case decided by the Connecticut Supreme Court held that adult patrons who furnish alcohol to a minor at a tavern may be responsible for the actions of the minor after he becomes intoxicated.

Social Host Liability

Bohan v. Last, 674 A.2d 839 (Conn. 1996) involved a minor who was furnished alcohol at a bar by some of his friends who were of legal age. After becoming intoxicated, the minor drove his car and subsequently crashed it, killing one passenger. The family of the passenger sued the minor and friends who provided him with the alcohol. Though the court realized that the common law imposes no duty to protect a third person from another, the court held that the friends who provided alcohol to the minor were not immune from liability. The court stated:

> In appropriate circumstances, adults have a duty to refrain from negligently or intentionally supplying alcohol to minors, whether such adults act as social hosts in their homes or as purveyors in a bar, because minors are presumed not to have the capacity to understand fully the risks associated with intoxication. In accordance with well established principles of proximate cause, this common law duty encompass responsibility to innocent third party victims such as Ferro's unfortunate passenger in this case ... Accordingly, we hold further that, unless purveyors of alcohol knew or had reason to know that the person to whom they supplied alcohol was a minor, they had no common law duty to third party victims of minor's intoxication. (pp. 844-845)

In **Cooper v. Delta Chi Housing Corporation of Connecticut,** 674 A.2d 858 (Ct. App. 1996), a minor college student who was injured in a car accident sued various fraternities and sororities for negligently serving him alcohol to the point of intoxication. The defendants asked the court to make the university a defendant in the case for purposes of apportioning liability. However, the court refused to do so because "sovereign immunity barred [the university's] inclusion in this civil action for purposes of apportionment." (p. 861)

Other Cases of Interest

Delaware

1998 Cumulative Annual Pocket Part

According to 4 Del. C. §904(C), if anyone purchases alcohol for a minor, for the first offense, the maximum penalty is a maximum fine of $500, a maximum of 30 days in prison, and a maximum of 40 hours of community service. For subsequent offenses, the fine is $500-$1000, a maximum of 60 days in prison, and a maximum of 80 hours of community service.

Sale or Gift to a Minor

Misrepresentation of Age

A 1995 amendment, 4 Del. C. §904(n), allows a minor to enter a licensed premises as long as the tavern is closed for business and no alcohol is sold. All alcohol must either be removed from the premises or be under lock and key. 4 Del. C. §904(e) which makes it unlawful for a minor to enter a tavern, is still in effect in all situations other than those covered in 4 Del. C. §904(n).

Sale or Gift to an Intoxicated Person

The statute that prohibits the sale or service of alcoholic beverages by a licensed vendor to an intoxicated person is now codified in 4 Del. C. §706. It was formerly in 4 Del. C. §711.

Dramshop Liability

Three cases indicate that the Delaware courts still refuse to impose common law dramshop liability. In **McCall v. Villa Pizza, Inc.**, 636 A.2d 912 (Del. Supr. 1994), McCall became very intoxicated at Villa Pizza one evening so the bouncer decided to have him removed. The bouncer physically and forcibly removed him and left him outside the building. Although it was the policy of the restaurant to call a cab and have an employee wait with the intoxicated person until the cab arrived, the bouncer did not do so. McCall drove his car and was in an accident five miles away, resulting in permanent injuries.

The court refused to hold Villa Pizza liable for a few reasons: (1) No Dramshop law exists in Delaware; (2) The court refused to agree with McCall that Villa Pizza assumed a duty of care by taking physical control of him and breached the duty by leaving him in a worse position; (3) McCall was injured off the premises of Villa Pizza. The court did state that "we recognize that denying recovery in such cases may result in the avoidance by tavern owners of full responsibility for their negligent acts in serving intoxicated persons" (p. 913). Still, the court refused to impose liability.

In **Pakes v. Megaw**, 565 A.2d 914 (Del. Supr. 1989), the court held that there is still no common law or statutory cause of action against tavern owners for injuries as a result of serving alcohol even when the patron is a minor.

Acker v. S.W. Cantinas, Inc., 586 A.2d 1178 (Del. Supr. 1991), involved a bus trip to a Philadelphia Phillies baseball game sponsored by the Santa Fe Bar and Grill Restaurant. The defendant, John Wise, purchased a ticket for the trip where he was served food and beer provided by Santa Fe. When the bus arrived back from the game, he drove his car and collided with another vehicle, causing the death of the passenger in that vehicle. The court refused to hold Santa Fe liable because it is the intent of the state legislature not to have a Dramshop law. The court also refused to impose liability on the bus company.

Social Host Liability

In the **Acker** case, the court also considered whether to hold Santa Fe liable as a social host. They refused to do so because Wise bought four tickets to the event, thereby conferring an economic benefit on Santa Fe. Since Wise conferred this economic benefit on Santa Fe, he was not considered a guest. Therefore, the court held that liability under the social host liability theory was not an option under these circumstances.

Florida

1997 Cumulative Pocket Part

Sale or Gift to a Minor

In **Nieves v. Camacho Clothes, Inc.**, 645 So. 2d 507 (Fla. App. 5 Dist. 1994), a minor and his friend who was of legal drinking age were served alcohol at some establishments. After the minor became ill, he became a passenger in his adult friend's car and they subsequently were in an accident. The minor filed this action against the establishments, alleging that they violated §562.11(1)(a) and §768.125. Although the trial court dismissed the case, it was reversed and remanded on appeal because

> [a] jury may reasonably find that the appellant, a person under twenty-one, was of the class the statute was designed to protect, that his injury was of the type the statute was designed to prevent, and that the violation of the statute, serving alcohol to the appellant, was a proximate cause of his injury. (p. 509)

R. Hughes, Inc. v. Mitchell, 617 So. 2d 767 (Fla. App. 1 Dist. 1993), was a unique case where the appellate court reversed the decision of the jury, holding that there was not enough evidence that the defendant tavern served alcohol in violation of §562.11 and §768.125. In this case, a minor who was at the establishment for several hours died as a result of a fight with another patron.

The court concluded that there was no evidence that the minor was "willfully and unlawfully" served. In reaching their decision the court stated that no one had seen the minor drinking at the bar. Since it was common for him to drink at home, and since he lived in the neighborhood of the tavern, it was possible that he was provided alcohol at a place other than the bar.

In **Bennett v. Godfather's Pizza, Inc.**, 570 So. 2d 1351 (Fla. App. 3 Dist. 1990), an employee of Godfathers left the premises after work with beer he obtained from Godfathers. Later that evening, he was in an automobile accident which injured his two passengers. The court held that Godfathers was not liable for the accident because of the long-standing policy in Florida of no liability in such situations.

Dramshop Liability

Several cases have interpreted the portion of the Dramshop statute that imposes liability for serving alcohol to a habitual drunkard:

In **Ellis v. N.G.N. of Tampa, Inc.**, 586 So. 2d 1042 (Fla. 1991), a man who consumed 20 drinks at a bar later crashed his car and suffered permanent brain damage from the impact. His guardian sued the bar, claiming that the bar knew that he was a habitual drunkard but they served him anyway, a violation of F.S.A. §768.125. The Florida Supreme Court held that the bar could be liable because, according to the statute, knowledge that he was a habitual drunkard is enough to impose liability. If the bar had a history of serving him a substantial number of drinks, this could be enough knowledge to satisfy the requirements of the statute. The court noted that the statute contained different language for serving minors. The statute provides that it is a violation if one "willfully and unlawfully" serves a minor.

The decision in **Ellis** was followed by **People's Restaurant v. Sabo**, 591 So. 2d 907 (Fla. 1991). In this case, the court held that the fact that the tavern had served a person substantial amounts of alcohol on several occasions meant that they could be liable for any injuries subsequently caused by the patron.

In **Roster v. Moulton**, 602 So. 2d 975 (Fla. App. 4 Dist. 1992), the court stated that circumstantial evidence created an issue of fact to determine if the tavern had knowledge that the patron was a habitual drunkard.

In addition, in **Person v. Southland Corporation**, 656 So. 2d 453 (Fla. 1995), the court held that a vendor who sells closed container alcoholic beverages to an alleged habitual drunkard to consume off the premises is not liable under Dramshop.

This rule was also upheld by a federal court in **Williams v. Anheuser-Busch, Inc.,** 957 F. Supp. 1246 (M.D. Fla. 1997), where the court held that the plaintiff's employer did not violate the Dramshop law when they gave him beer as a performance bonus even though they knew he was a habitual drunkard.

Finally, in **Russo v. Plant City Moose Lodge No. 1668**, 656 So. 2d 957 (Fla. App. 2 Dist. 1995), a man struck and killed the plaintiff's husband while attempting to drive his car after consuming alcohol at the Moose Lodge. The court refused to impose liability on Moose Lodge under F.S.A. §768.125 because there was no evidence that he was a habitual drunkard. He visited the Moose Lodge 2-8 times per month with 3-7 beers consumed per visit. He, his wife and his friends all testified that he did not have a drinking problem. Based on this evidence, there was no reason for the Moose Lodge to believe he was a habitual drunkard.

The Florida courts have ruled that an establishment must directly serve a minor to violate the Dramshop statute. For example, **Dixon v. Saunders**, 565 So. 2d 802 (Fla. App. 2 Dist. 1990), involved a situation at a bowling alley where an adult bought a pitcher of beer which he then gave to some minors. Later, the minors were involved in a car accident which left one of them dead. The court held that the bowling alley was not liable because they did not sell or furnish the alcohol to the minors as required by F.S.A. §768.125. The court further held that if the bowling alley did know that the alcohol eventually would be given to the minors, this "passive tolerance" would be a criminal violation under F.S.A. §562.11 (1)(a).

O'Neale v. Hershoff, 634 So. 2d 644 (Fla. App. 3 Dist. 1993), provided a good example of a common situation when liability can be imposed under Dramshop. The court stated that:

if a vendor sells alcohol to minor A, and there are facts putting the vendor on notice that minor A will furnish the alcohol to minor B, then the vendor 'sells or furnishes' alcohol to both A and B within the meaning of the statute. (p. 646)

In **Publix Supermarkets, Inc. v. Austin**, 658 So. 2d 1064 (Fla. App. 5 Dist. 1995), the court held that there is no cause of action in Florida against a vendor who is merely negligent in providing alcohol to a minor who subsequently became involved in a car wreck. The sale must be willful and unlawful to subject a vendor to liability under F.S.A. §768.125.

Social Host Liability

In **Dowell v. Gracewood Fruit Co.**, 559 So. 2d 217 (Fla. 1990), a girl became intoxicated at a company party and struck a pedestrian when she attempted to drive her car. The plaintiff claimed that the company should be liable under F.S.A. §768.125 because they knew she was an alcoholic. The court disagreed and emphasized that there was no social host liability in Florida. F.S.A. §768.125 was enacted to limit vendor liability—not to create social host liability which did not already exist.

However, in **Bardy v. Walt Disney World Co.**, 643 So. 2d 46 (Fla. App. 5 Dist. 1994), a Disney employee became intoxicated at an employee party sponsored by Disney on the Disney premises. Subsequently, he went to his car in the parking lot to lie down. A Disney security guard ordered him to leave despite the employee's protest that he was too drunk to drive. He then proceeded to crash his car and was injured. The court held that Disney was not free from liability because the plaintiff "was an employee of Disney, an invitee on the Disney property for social purposes, and the alcohol he drank had been supplied by Disney" (p. 48). Disney had a duty to refrain from ordering him to drive unless the security guard reasonably believed that the employee could drive safely.

Georgia

1998 Supplement

A 1997 amendment to OCGA §3-3-23 added that it is unlawful for a minor to "attempt to purchase" alcohol.

In **Lee v. State**, 412 S.E.2d 563 (Ga. App. 1991), a policeman arrived at an apartment complex at 1:15 am after hearing complaints of a party. He then proceeded to drive around the complex and found two people hiding. After he realized they were minors who had consumed alcohol, he issued them citations pursuant to OCGA §3-3-23 (a)(2) (the statute which forbids the possession of alcohol by minors). One of the minors argued that his parents had provided him with the alcohol, which if true, would be permissible under OCGA §3-3-23(c) if consumed in the home. However, the court ruled that it was a reasonable conclusion that this was not a true story and that the minors had actually consumed alcohol at the party. Therefore, the citations were upheld.

Possession or Consumption by a Minor

In **Eldridge v. Aronson,** 472 S.E.2d 497 (Ga. App. 1996), a teenager's mother purchased a substantial amount of alcohol at a liquor store which she then served and made available to teenagers for her teenage son's party at her house. A sixteen-year-old who consumed beer at the party was killed that night in an accident. His parents then sued the parents who hosted the party under OCGA §51-1-18(a), which allows custodial parents of a minor to sue anyone who furnishes alcohol to their minor child without their permission. Although the trial court granted summary judgment to the parent hosts, the decision was reversed on appeal.

Sale or Gift to a Minor

The defendants argued that they were not liable because OCGA §51-1-40 precludes recovery by a consumer against a provider. However, the court disagreed because that statute would only apply if the actual consumer brought the action. In this case, because the parents sought their own damages, they were not precluded by §51-1-40. One other interesting development in this case was that the teenage host's father could be liable because he may have "furnished" the alcohol even though he was out of town when the party took place! Because he had knowledge that his wife regularly provided alcohol to teenagers and that he himself often did the same, it was enough evidence to let a jury decide the issue of liability.

OCGA §51-1-40 was enacted and became effective on April 12, 1988. Section (a) provides that the consumption, not the furnishing of alcohol, is the proximate cause of any injury except as provided in (b). Section (b) provides that the alcohol provider could be liable for all injuries to the person or third persons if he willfully, knowingly, and unlawfully furnishes it to a minor, or if he knowingly serves it to a person who is knowingly intoxicated. The furnisher must know that the person will soon be driving a car. Section (c) provides that if a minor presents a false I.D., this could be a rebuttable presumption that the alcohol was not sold willfully, knowingly, and unlawfully. Finally, section (d) provides that a person who occupies a premises that is not licensed to sell alcohol is not liable for the acts of people who drink alcohol on the premises without their consent.

Dramshop Liability

OCGA §51-1-40 was interpreted in several cases:

In **Viau v. Fred Dean, Inc.**, 418 S.E.2d 604 (Ga. App. 1992), Dean was involved in a collision with two vehicles when he was driving under the influence of alcohol. Though he drank alcohol on the premises of FDI, the court held that FDI was not liable because "OCGA §51-1-40(b) does not impose liability upon one who merely furnishes the premises upon which alcohol is consumed. It imposes liability upon one who furnishes the alcohol itself" (p. 606). In addition, the court noted that liability did not attach to FDI because Dean's intoxication was not related to a company sponsored social event.

In a similar case involving a fraternity, **Kappa Sigma International Fraternity v. Tootle,** 473 S.E.2d 213 (Ga. App. 1996), the court held that just because a fraternity sponsors a party where a guest becomes intoxicated and then injures a third party, that is not enough evidence to impose liability on the fraternity. In this case, Kappa Sigma Fraternity hosted a party at a farm at which Clinton Fair, a non-member, was a guest. Although alcohol was available in coolers and a beer keg, Fair only consumed the alcohol he brought to the party himself. Later that night he drove his car and caused an accident which killed Ernest Tootle. The court referred to **Viau v. Fred Dean** and held that the fraternity was not liable for the death under OCGA §51-1-40 because they only provided the premises for the party—not the alcohol that Fair consumed.

Another case in the employment context was **Ihesiaba v. Pelletier,** 448 S.E.2d 920 (Ga. App. 1994), where a limousine driver sued his employer and employees after the employees attacked him while he was driving them home from the office Christmas party. The employer was not liable because, under OCGA §51-1-40, the consumption, not the furnishing of alcohol is the proximate cause.

Steedley v. Huntley's Jiffy Stores, Inc., 432 S.E.2d 625 (Ga. App. 1993), arose out of the same facts as **Koonce** (see Social Host Liability), where the driver sued the store that sold him alcohol. He claimed that he was a minor and the store violated OCGA §51-1-40 because they knew that he would be driving. The court did not impose liability on the store because "a consumer of alcohol, even an underage consumer, may not recover from the provider of that alcohol for injuries resulting from consumption of the alcohol" (p. 626). Further, "the consumer has the last opportunity to avoid the effect of the alcohol, by not drinking or not driving" (p. 626). *See,* **White v. Hubbard**, 416 S.E.2d 568 (Ga. App. 1992), for a similar case.

However, **Griffin Motel Co. v. Strickland,** 479 S.E.2d 401 (Ga. App. 1996), held that §51-1-40 does not preclude a third party who is injured from recovering even though he also consumed alcohol. Therefore, if a third party and a driver of an automobile both consume alcohol, if the third party is injured in a car accident because of the driver's intoxication, the third party may recover.

In **Riley v. H&H Operations, Inc.** 436 S.E.2d 659 (Ga. 1993), the Georgia Supreme Court held that if a person in the exercise of reasonable care should have known that the recipient of alcohol was a minor and would be driving soon, it will be as though the person had actual knowledge under OCGA §51-1-40. This overruled the old common law rule in **Sutter v. Hutchings**, 327 S.E.2d 716 (Ga. 1985), which held that actual knowledge was necessary. This same ruling was upheld in **Taylor v. N.I.L., Inc.**, 470 S.E.2d 491 (Ga. App. 1996), and in **Griffin Motel**. However, the liability only extends to consequences arising from the actions of the actual minor who purchases the alcohol. **Perryman v. Lufran, Inc.**, 434 S.E.2d 112 (Ga. App. 1993) held that a furnisher of alcohol to a minor is not liable under §51-1-40 for the negligent acts of a second minor who becomes intoxicated by those beverages. The federal courts agree that the furnisher of alcohol is not liable for the negligent acts of the second minor. **Jaques v. Kendrick,** 43 F.3d 628 (11th Cir. 1995).

In **Whelchel v. Laing Properties, Inc.**, 378 S.E.2d 478 (Ga. App. 1989), the court held that an employer who hosted a Christmas party at a hotel with an open bar available to its employees could be subject to liability under the Dramshop statute. In this case, a driver was killed in a car accident when she was hit by a car driven by an employee who had become intoxicated at the party.

Social Host Liability

The Georgia courts have placed a duty on social hosts to prevent their guests from driving while intoxicated. In **Pirkle v. Hawley**, 405 S.E.2d 71 (Ga. App. 1991), the court held that:

> Georgia has determined that a social host may be liable to third persons for furnishing alcohol to a guest and that the social host must take some action to prevent the guest from driving once he or she is discovered to be intoxicated. (p. 75)

This case involved an employee who became intoxicated at an office party and later crashed his car into another driver. In this case, the court held that there was enough evidence to let a jury determine if liability should be imposed.

Another social host liability case, **Manuel v. Koonce**, 425 S.E.2d 921 (Ga. App. 1992), involved a sixteen-year-old who invited friends over to his house when he was home alone. One of his friends became intoxicated, which resulted in his girlfriend driving herself home in his vehicle. After she arrived at her house, she yielded the keys to her intoxicated boyfriend, who subsequently crashed his car into a van, killing himself and injuring several people.

The court ruled that the owners of the home were not liable under OCGA §51-1-40 because the alcohol was consumed in their absence and without their consent. Further, the sixteen-year-old was not liable because he did not know the intoxicated person would be driving. When the couple left the house, the girl was driving so there was no reason to know that her intoxicated boyfriend would drive.

Other Cases of Interest

In **Borders v. Board of Trustees, VFW Club,** 500 S.E.2d 362 (Ga. App. 1998), a woman who was injured at a dance by a man who was intoxicated sued VFW, the sponsor of the dance. The trial court dismissed the case, but the appellate court reversed it to let a jury determine whether VFW breached its duty of ordinary care by not removing the man prior to the plaintiff's injury. The record indicated that VFW hired security guards to remove intoxicated patrons and their failure to do so could establish liability on VFW.

Hawaii

1998 Cumulative Supplement

Possession or Consumption by a Minor

The code section which makes it unlawful for a licensee to sell or furnish alcohol to a minor is HRS §281-78(b)(1)(A), rather than 281-78(a)(2)(A), as previously listed.

Sale or Gift to an Intoxicated Person

The code section which makes it unlawful to provide alcohol to an intoxicated person is HRS §281-78(b)(1)(B), rather than 281-78(a)(2)(B), as previously listed.

Dramshop Liability

Cases in Hawaii indicate that the courts will impose Dramshop liability in situations when an innocent third party is injured; however, Dramshop liability in Hawaii is not designed to protect a person who voluntarily becomes intoxicated.

In **Myers v. South Seas Corporation**, 871 P.2d 1235 (Hawaii App. 1992), the court stated the general rule in Hawaii that a tavern owner owes a duty of reasonable care to protect people from being injured by other patrons. However, "an intoxicated and disorderly tavern patron, who participates and is injured during an altercation with another patron, is not within the class of persons protected by the liquor licensing statutes" (p. 1237).

Similarly, in **Winters v. Silver Fox Bar**, 797 P.2d 51 (Hawaii 1990), a minor consumed alcohol at a bar and later lost control of his car and died in a crash. The court refused to impose liability on the bar because "a minor who sustains injury due to his own voluntary intoxication is not within the class of persons protected by the statute" (p. 51).

In **Reyes v. Kuboyama**, 870 P.2d 1281 (Hawaii 1994), a group of minors purchased beer from a store and it was subsequently taken to one of the minor's homes for a party. The alcohol was provided to another minor who later gave a ride to a young lady who had not consumed alcohol. The driver crashed the car which caused permanent injuries to the passenger. The court held that the store could possibly be liable because Hawaii law recognizes the duty "where an innocent third party has been injured by an intoxicated minor other than the minor to whom the liquor was sold, subject to the determination by the [judge or jury]" (p. 1290).

See also, **Reyes v. Kuboyama:** *Vendor Liability for the Sale of Intoxicating Liquors to Minors Under a Common Law Negligence Theory*, 17 U. Haw. L. Rev. 355 (1955).

Social Host Liability

The Hawaiian cases indicate that the courts are not willing to judicially impose social host liability.

Johnston v. KFC National Management Co., 788 P.2d 159 (Hawaii 1990), arose out of an employee Christmas party at Kentucky Fried Chicken and a party afterwards at an employee's home. At both parties, alcohol was consumed. One of the attendees later drove her car and crashed it into a moped, causing permanent injuries to the moped driver. The court refused to impose liability on KFC as the sponsor of the after party because Hawaii does not recognize social host liability for non-commercial suppliers of alcohol.

The fact that Hawaii law precludes social host liability was affirmed in **Wong-Leong v. Hawaiian Indep. Refinery, Inc.**, 879 P.2d 538 (Hawaii 1994). In Wong-Leong, the estates of victims of a car crash caused by an employee's intoxication brought this action against the employer because, prior to the accident, the employee had become intoxicated at a company party on the company premises. The court held that the employer could not be held liable as a social host. However, there was enough evidence to preclude summary judgment to support that the employer could be liable under *respondeat superior* or negligent failure to control.

The Hawaii courts reluctance to judicially impose social host liability was demonstrated in **Faulk v. Suzuki Motor Co. Ltd.**, 851 P.2d 332 (Hawaii App. 1993). In **Faulk**, the court refused to apply social host liability for a wreck that occurred after a guest consumed alcohol at a host's party. This was the decision of the court even though the social host provided the alcohol, knew the guest was drunk, and knew that the guest's driving abilities would be impaired by the consumption of alcohol.

Idaho

1998 Cumulative Supplement

In *Alcohol on Campus*, this statute was incorrectly listed as IC §23-1013. It should be listed as IC §23-1023.

Sale or Gift to a Minor

In **Hickman v. Fraternal Order of Eagles**, 758 P.2d 704 (Idaho 1988), a fraternal organization served alcohol at a party to a person who later drove his car and caused a wreck, killing one person and injuring another. The organization was not liable, partly because the driver consumed a substantial amount of alcohol after the party, and thus, was a superseding cause of the accident.

Social Host Liability

In **Slade v. Smith's Management Corp.**, 808 P.2d 401 (Idaho 1991), a nineteen-year-old male was struck and killed by a vehicle being driven by a man who had become intoxicated at his employer's party where alcohol was served.

The court referred to **Alegria v. Payonk**, 619 P. 2d 135 (Idaho 1980), and held that liability for providing alcohol to an incapacitated person should not be constricted to commercial vendors. In their reasoning, the court stated that:

> [w]hether a glass of intoxicating beverages is placed in the possession of a friend for consumption, or in the possession of a customer also for consumption, makes no difference insofar as the law is concerned if the person to whom the beverage is provided is a driver having the possession of a motor vehicle and it is evident that he may drive it on a public highway. (p. 405)

Thus, Idaho continues to invoke liability on social hosts.

Illinois

1998 Cumulative Annual Pocket Part

The former S.H.A. ch. 43 §131 is now 235 ILCS 5/6-16.
The former S.H.A. ch. 43 §95.05 is now 235 ILCS 5/1-3/05.

Definition of a Minor

The former S.H.A. ch. 43 §134(a), which says a minor cannot purchase alcohol or accept it as a gift, is now 235 ILCS 5/6-20.

Possession or Consumption by a Minor

The former S.H.A. ch. 43 §131, which forbids minors to possess alcohol in public places, is now 235 ILCS 5/6-16(a).

The former S.H.A. ch. 43 §131, which prohibits licensees from selling or delivering alcohol to minors, is now 235 ILCS 5/6-16(a).

Sale or Gift to a Minor

The former S.H.A. ch. 43 §134(a), which says a minor cannot purchase alcohol or accept it as a gift, is now 235 ILCS 5/6-20.

It is interesting to note that in one case where the defendant was convicted of unlawfully delivering alcohol to minors he was placed on conditional discharge for six months, fined $250.00 plus costs, sentenced to ten weekends in jail, and required to perform 100 hours of community service [**People v. Rhodes,** 612 N.E.2d 536 (Ill. App. Dist. 4 1993).]

The former S.H.A. ch. 43 §131, which makes it unlawful to use a false I.D. to purchase alcohol, is now 235 ILCS 5/6-16(a).

Misrepresentation of Age

The former S.H.A. ch. 43 §183(d), which makes it a misdemeanor to misrepresent your age for the purpose of buying alcohol, is now 235 ILCS 5/10-1(e).

The former S.H.A. ch. 43 §134(a), which makes it unlawful to alter an I.D. card, is now 235 ILCS 5/6-20.

Miscellaneous The former S.H.A. ch. 43 §183(a), which makes it unlawful to sell alcohol without a license, is now 235 ILCS 5/10-1(b).

The former S.H.A. ch. 43 §130, which allows state colleges to sell alcohol in convention and conference facilities, is now 235 ILCS 5/6-15.

235 ILCS 5/6-16(c) says it is a class A misdemeanor when anyone allows a gathering at their residence where at least two of the persons present are minors and the following factors apply: a) the occupier of the residence knows that minors will possess or consume alcohol; b) the possession or consumption of alcohol by minors does not fit under one of the exceptions to the law forbidding alcohol use by minors; c) the person knows that a minor leaves the residence intoxicated.

Sale or Gift to an Intoxicated Person The former S.H.A. ch. 43 §183, which makes it unlawful to sell or give alcohol to an intoxicated person, is now 235 ILCS 5/6-16(a).

Dramshop Liability The Dramshop Liability statute is now codified in 235 ILCS 5/6-16(a)

Walter v. Carriage House Hotels, Ltd., 646 N.E.2d 599 (Ill. 1995), was a case that presented a sound historical analysis of the doctrine of complicity as an affirmative defense to a Dramshop claim. In this case, the plaintiff and his friend consumed several alcoholic drinks at a tavern. Later that evening, the friend battered the plaintiff, causing serious injuries. The plaintiff filed this dramshop action against the tavern and sued his friend for battery. The tavern argued that the claim was barred by the doctrine of complicity because the plaintiff actively contributed to the intoxication of the friend.

The trial court disagreed and held that there was enough evidence to send the case to the jury to decide the issue of liability. This case was affirmed on appeal because, complicity is an affirmative defense and the tavern had the burden of proving that the plaintiff actively contributed to his friend's intoxication. The court stated that "[i]n the past, some courts have placed too much reliance on such matters as the plaintiff's accompanying the inebriate to several locations or buying the inebriate one or more drinks" (p. 606).

In another case involving complicity, the court held that the plaintiff must actively contribute to be precluded from recovery. *See also,* **Raithel v. Dustcutter, Inc.**, 634 N.E.2d 1163 (Ill. App. 4 Dist. 1994).

In **Jackson v. Moreno**, 663 N.E.2d 27 (Ill. App. 1 Dist. 1996), the estate of a man who purchased alcohol and was subsequently killed in a car wreck brought this dramshop action against the franchise who sold the alcohol and the company that leased the property to the franchise. The trial court dismissed the suit. However, on appeal it was decided that the plaintiffs did have a claim because the statute imposes liability on "anyone who owns, rents, leases, or permits the occupation of a building or premises knowing that alcohol will be sold there" (p. 29). The defendants had an agreement that the franchise would be able to sell alcohol; therefore, this was evidence that they had control over the situation.

Beukema v. Yomac, Inc., 672 N.E.2d 755 (Ill. App. 1 Dist. 1996), held that as long as the claim of negligence is not based on the serving of alcohol, a common law negligence claim can be brought in the same lawsuit as a dramshop claim.

First America Trust Co. v. McMurray, 620 N.E.2d 447 (Ill. App. 4 Dist. 1993), reiterated the holding in **Puckett v. Mr. Lucky's Ltd.**, 529 N.E.2d 1169 (Ill. App. 4 Dist. 1989), that the dramshop act is the exclusive remedy in situations involving injury to third persons caused by intoxicated tavern patrons and there is no common law cause of action which can be brought against vendors for illegal sales. *See also*, **Flory v. Weaver**, 553 N.E.2d 105 (Ill. App. 4 Dist. 1990).

In **McKeown v. Homoya**, 568 N.E.2d 528 (Ill. App. 5 Dist. 1991), the court disagreed with the plaintiff that it was unconstitutional for the dramshop act to be the exclusive remedy against tavern owners for injuries caused by intoxication. The court also held that "a tavern has no duty to restrain a patron from driving away no matter how intoxicated that individual may be" (p. 530). *See also*, **Krawczyk v. Polinski**, 642 N.E.2d 185 (Ill. App. 2 Dist. 1994).

In **Charles v. Seigfried**, 651 N.E.2d 154 (Ill. 1995), the Illinois Supreme Court held that there is no liability for the sale or gift of alcohol other than is provided in the Dramshop statute. In addition, the court emphasized that "for over one century, this court has construed the Dramshop Act as inapplicable to a social host situation" (p. 159). See also, **Rainey v. Pickera**, 651 N.E.2d 747 (Ill. App. 5th Div. 1995).

Social Host Liability

However in **Cravens v. Inman**, 586 N.E.2d 367 (Ill. 1991), the Illinois Supreme Court left an opening for social host liability. In **Cravens**, the plaintiff's minor daughter was killed in a car accident while a passenger in a car driven by Rita Lenzi. The plaintiff claimed that Lenzi was negligently served alcohol at a party and was negligently allowed to drive while intoxicated.

The trial court dismissed the claims but the decision was reversed on appeal, thereby imposing social host liability. However, the court stated that its decision was limited to these facts and offered no opinion about any other potential factual scenarios where liability may be applied. The **Cravens** decision is limited to:

> [w]here (1) a social host knowingly served alcohol and permits the liquor to be served to youths under eighteen years of age at the social host's residence, (2) the social host permits the minor's consumption to continue to the point of intoxication, and (3) the social host allows the inebriated minors to depart from the residence in a motor vehicle. (p. 367)

Robertson v. Okraj, 620 N.E.2d 612 (Ill. App. 4 Dist. 1993), was a case where the plaintiff was unsuccessful in arguing **Cravens** and is a good indication of just how narrowly the Cravens decision will be applied. In this case, an eighteen-year-old was served alcohol at a party. After becoming intoxicated, the minor was taken home by his roommates and he later died of aspiration of gastric contents.

The court gave a sound analysis of why they did not impose liability. First, "Illinois generally does not recognize a common law cause of action against suppliers of liquor, whether they are commercial suppliers or noncommercial suppliers" (p. 615). Next, "except under the circumstances stated in **Cravens**, social hosts who furnish alcoholic beverages to a guest are not liable if the guest subsequently becomes intoxicated and injures himself or herself" (p. 616).

Finally, the defendant owed no duty to someone "who allegedly voluntarily became intoxicated, left the premises with third persons and subsequently died of an unforeseeable aspiration of gastric contents while he was in his own bed" (p. 616). *See also*,

Fitzpatrick v. Carde Lounge, Ltd., 602 N.E.2d 19 (Ill. App. 1 Dist. 1992), another example of the limited application of **Cravens**.

Other Cases of Interest   **Haben v. Anderson**, 597 N.E.2d 655 (Ill. App. 3 Dist. 1992), involved an initiation ceremony to the Lacrosse Club at Western Illinois University. At this ceremony, an eighteen-year-old "rookie" to the club and others were required to perform various degrading and humiliating activities that were in violation of the Illinois hazing statute and university regulations.

It was a tradition of this ceremony for the rookies to consume large quantities of alcohol, which they did on this night. That evening, the rookie became severely intoxicated and one of the members brought him to his dorm room and left him alone on the floor. The member checked on him on more than one occasion and testified that he heard the rookie "gurgling." The rookie died that night of acute alcohol intoxication with a blood alcohol content of .34.

The rookie's father sued the individual members of the club and the court addressed several issues in holding that they could be liable. The court held that one reason that the members could be liable was that the club carried a high status and the rookies felt pressured to drink. Although they were not specifically required to drink, the pressure to drink was so high that the court found drinking to be a de facto requirement. The court also held that it was the intent of the legislature to prevent this from happening because of the hazing statute. Further, the court held that both the individuals and the organization could be liable in this type of case. Finally, the court held that the members who took the rookie to his dorm room may have liability imposed on him for assuming the duty to protect him and not acting reasonably to prevent further harm.

In **Goodnight v. Piraino**, 554 N.E.2d 1 (Ill. App. 3 Dist. 1990), an eighteen-year-old attended a party where liquor was sold and she was coerced into drinking by her date. She tried unsuccessfully to argue that she was coerced into drinking just like the fraternity pledge was coerced in **Quinn v. Sigma Rho Chapter of Beta Theta Pi Fraternity**, 507 N.E.2d 1193 (Ill. App. 4 Dist. 1987). The court rejected this argument because the claim in **Quinn** was based on two factors: (1) the plaintiff was required to drink, (2) the legislature intended to prevent that type of harm with the enactment of the hazing statute.

Estate of Ritchie v. Farrell, 572 N.E.2d 367 (Ill. App. 3 Dist. 1991), was another case where the plaintiff lost because there was no requirement to drink. In this case, the defendant bought alcohol for a minor. After drinking large amounts of the alcohol, the minor died of acute alcohol intoxication. The court held that the defendant had no duty in this case.

Indiana

1998 Cumulative Annual Pocket Part

Possession or Consumption by a Minor   A 1994 amendment added I.C. 7.1-5-7-7(b), which states that any minor who violates I.C. 7.1-5-5-7(a) (formerly I.C. 7.1-5-5-7, which makes it unlawful for a minor to knowingly possess, or consume or transport alcohol on a highway without a parent), while driving a car can have his license suspended for up to one year. Also, I.C. 7.1-5-7-15 makes it unlawful for a person of legal drinking age to assist a minor to unlawfully possess alcohol.

In cases involving the illegal providing of alcohol to minors or intoxicated persons, the Indiana courts have continued to require that the person be "the active means" by which the alcohol was given. [**Rauck v. Hawn,** 564 N.E.2d 334 (Ind. App. Dist. 1 1996)]. Therefore, a person will generally not violate these statutes if he simply agrees to buy liquor along with the minor or intoxicated person. More affirmative acts are needed.

I.C. 7.1-5-10-14 makes it illegal for a permittee to provide alcohol to a person whom he knows to be a habitual drunkard.

Sale or Gift to a Minor

Sale or Gift to an Intoxicated Person

Dramshop Liability

A 1996 amendment added (c) to I.C. 7.1-5-10-15.5 and states that if a person who is at least twenty-one "suffers injury or death proximately caused by the person's voluntary intoxication, the: (1) person; (2) person's dependents; (3) person's personal representative; or (4) person's heirs; may not assert a claim ... against a person who furnished an alcoholic beverage that contributed to the person's intoxication," unless the other sections of this act apply to the situation.

Fast Eddies v. Hall, 688 N.E.2d 1270 (Ind. App. 1997), analyzed the duty an establishment has to protect its patrons from criminal acts. In this case, three patrons, one female and two males, became intoxicated at a tavern. When the tavern manager saw that the female was intoxicated, she asked one of her friends to remove her from the tavern. Upon this request, one of the males, Lamb, escorted her to the car of the other male, Schooley. Later, Schooley drove the female to his house, where he left her passed out in the car. Later that evening, Lamb drove to Schooley's home and he shot and killed the female. The decedent's estate then sued the tavern, alleging it was negligent per se for violating the Dramshop Act.

The appellate court granted summary judgment in favor of the tavern and specifically addressed three issues. First, the tavern had no duty to protect its patrons from the criminal act because it was not reasonably foreseeable that it would occur. Second, the tavern did not "create" a duty for itself when the manager ordered the female to be taken out of the tavern. A more affirmative act is needed to take on such a duty. Finally, even if the tavern did violate the Dramshop Act by serving its patron while intoxicated, the tavern was not liable because they were not the proximate cause of the injury as required under Dramshop. There were too many intervening acts for them to be the proximate cause.

In **Estate of Cummings v. PPG Industries, Inc.,** 651 N.E.2d 305 (Ind. App. 1995), employees of PPG Industries organized a party at a local tavern. The management of PPG did not play a role in organizing the party but they did contribute money to defray some of the costs. PPG posted notices that minors were not allowed to attend. The tavern was responsible for checking IDs and serving the alcohol. A minor employee attended the party, became intoxicated, and later caused an accident, killing one person and injuring another.

The court refused to impose liability against PPG under Dramshop. Though PPG management appeared to have some control over the party since they stopped it when they learned the accident had occurred, they did not control the supply of alcohol. Further, the employees were not required to attend and the party was held off company property.

In **Thompson v. Ferdinand Sesquicentennial Committee, Inc.,** 637 N.E.2d 178 (Ind. App. 1 Dist. 1985), the plaintiff's minor son became intoxicated at a beer garden and later was killed while driving. The court held that the Dramshop law does not have exceptions for minors. A furnisher of alcohol will only be liable for the injuries if the person served was visibly intoxicated at the time the alcohol was furnished, regardless of age.

Muex v. Hindel Bowling Lanes Inc., 596 N.E.2d 263 (Ind. App. 2 Dist. 1992), arose out of a fight between two people at a bowling alley. The plaintiff sued the bowling alley after being injured in the fight by a bowler who had been served a substantial amount of alcohol by the bowling alley.

The court held that there was not enough evidence that the man was intoxicated when he was served to hold the bowling alley liable under Dramshop. However, citing **Bearman v. University of Notre Dame**, 453 N.E.2d 1196 (Ind. App. 3 Dist. 1983), the court held that the bowling alley had a duty to take reasonable precautions to protect its business invitees from injury caused by acts of intoxicated third persons. The bowling alley had reason to know that some bowlers would become intoxicated and pose a threat to the other bowlers.

In **Jackson v. Gore**, 634 N.E.2d 503 (Ind. App. 1 Dist. 1994), it was a question for the jury whether a waitress at a bar had actual knowledge of the intoxication of a patron who later injured a pedestrian while driving. Also, in **Booker, Inc. v. Morrill**, 639 N.E.2d 358 (Ind. 1994), the court held that circumstantial evidence can be used to show that the alcohol provider knew of the recipient's intoxication.

In another Dramshop case, a passenger became intoxicated after being served alcohol, on an Amtrak train, and was put in jail for his intoxication after the train stopped. While in jail, he attempted to stand several times and sustained brain damage from hitting his head after he fell.

In an attempt to get the case dismissed, Amtrak presented three arguments. First, they argued that his attempts to stand constituted intentional acts for which he was barred from recovery by the Indiana Comparative Fault Act. The court disagreed and stated that his injuries were caused by his falls, not by his attempts to stand. Because the falls were not intentional, the court struck down this argument. Second, Amtrak argued that they had no duty to the passenger after the police arrested him. The court disagreed and stated that "[o]ur courts have never interpreted the Dramshop Act as cutting off a provider's liability to the intoxicated person at the tavern door" (p. 365). Because it was not disputed that they had a duty to stop serving him after he became intoxicated, the court held that the duty continued after he left the tavern.

Finally, the court stated that the results that occurred in this case were foreseeable. [**National Railroad Passenger Corp. v. Everton**, 655 N.E.2d 360 (Ind. App. 1995)].

Social Host Liability

Two important cases were decided in Indiana that involved college fraternities. In **Foster v. Purdue University**, 567 N.E.2d 865 (Ind. App. 3 Dist. 1991), an eighteen year-old fraternity member consumed alcohol that had been provided to him by the fraternity. He then proceeded to dive head first onto a waterslide, was injured, and is now a quadriplegic.

The court refused to impose liability on the furnisher of the beer, the local and national chapters of the fraternity, or the house corporation. Several factors contributed to the court's decision, including the fact that the pledge performed an intentional act, and he was partly responsible because he was part of the organization and participated in the informal decision-making of the fraternity.

Motz v. Johnson, 651 N.E.2d 1163 (Ind. App. 1995) was another Indiana case that involved a fraternity. This case arose out of a sexual assault that occurred at the fraternity house. The fraternity was hosting a party and alcohol was being served. At the party, an alumnus of the fraternity became intoxicated (it is likely that he became intoxicated from his own liquor, rather than from the supply provided by the fraternity) and sexually assaulted a freshman girl.

The local chapter was not liable because there was nothing to put them on alert that the sexual assault would take place. The attack was not a reasonably foreseeable result of the intoxication, so the fraternity had no duty. The victim alleged the national fraternity assumed a duty of controlling the alcohol problem at the local chapter through such means as disseminating alcohol pamphlets.

The court did not find the national fraternity liable and stated that they did not assume a duty to protect the victim. The court stated that "to hold otherwise would discourage the national fraternity from disseminating information discouraging alcohol abuse and rape" (p. 1170). The court also found that the fraternity was not liable under Dramshop because there was no evidence that the fraternity served the plaintiff alcohol while she was visibly intoxicated. The court went a step further and stated that even if the fraternity did violate the Dramshop law, they would only be liable for the sexual assault if it resulted from the intoxication of the alumni member.

[*Author's Note:* The Indiana Supreme Court granted transfer to **Motz v. Johnson** on January 4, 1996. This means that the decision has been vacated. Since the Indiana Supreme Court has not given a written opinion about the case, this case has been included in this supplement only as a reference.]

In **Baxter v. Galligher**, 604 N.E.2d 1245 (Ind. App. 3 Dist. 1992), a social guest at a birthday party brought this action against the host and the two guests who injured his eye while they were "messing around."

First, the court referred to the decision in **Burrell v. Meads**, 569 N.E.2d 637 (Ind. 1991), which stated that under Indiana law, a social guest is considered an "invitee," which requires a landowner to exercise reasonable care while the guest is on the premises. However, the court did not impose liability because the hosts did not furnish alcohol to the guests with knowledge that they were visibly intoxicated. Next, although a landowner has a duty to protect social guests from foreseeable risks, the court held that there was no evidence that the host had knowledge of the horseplay or had breached a duty.

Iowa

1998 Cumulative Annual Pocket Part

Definition of a Minor

The section which says the legal age in Iowa is twenty-one is now in I.C.A. §123.3(19).

Possession or Consumption by a Minor

I.C.A. §123.47A, which gave nineteen and twenty-year-old's permission to possess alcohol in some circumstances, was repealed in 1997.

Miscellaneous

A 1995 amendment to I.C.A. §123.28 deleted the portion of the statute which made it legal to possess open containers in the part of the vehicle inaccessible to the driver.

State v. Rosenstiel, 473 N.W.2d 59 (Iowa 1991), held that the open container law of I.C.A. §123.28 does not apply to a person who is on private property.

Dramshop Liability   A 1997 amendment to I.C.A. §123.92 extended the Iowa Dramshop law to include service to minors. After the amendment, any person injured by an intoxicated person has a right of action for all damages sustained against the vendor who sold or served alcohol to a person the vendor knew or should have known was a minor.

Several Dramshop cases have been reported in Iowa. In **Hobbiebrunken v. G&S Enterprises, Inc.**, 470 N.W.2d 19 (Iowa 1991), a man gave four female college students a ride to a local tavern in his boat. After consuming alcohol at the tavern, the man crashed the boat, killing himself, with the four females surviving. The court did not impose Dramshop liability on the tavern because it is a prerequisite for liability under Dramshop that the tavern knew or reasonably should have known that the driver of the boat was intoxicated.

Hayward v. P.D.A., 573 N.W.2d 29 (Iowa 1997) emphasized that even if an establishment unlawfully serves an intoxicated patron, this unlawful service must be the proximate cause of injury for liability to be imposed. In this case, a sheriff was at the scene of a car crash that killed a young woman who had purchased alcohol from the defendant establishment. While at the scene, the sheriff was struck and killed by another drunk driver. The court held that the defendant establishment which sold alcohol to the deceased woman was not liable for the sheriff's death because it was not the proximate, foreseeable result of the sale.

In **Kelly v. Sinclair Oil Corp.**, 476 N.W.2d 341 (Iowa 1991), the court held that the Dramshop law applies only to establishments where alcohol is "sold and served." Therefore, the convenience store that sold alcohol to an intoxicated driver in this case was immune from a Dramshop action because the alcohol was not served. *See*, **Eddy v. Casey's General Store, Inc.**, 485 N.W.2d 633 (Iowa 1992).

In **Thorp v. Casey's General Stores, Inc.**, 446 N.W.2d 457 (Iowa 1989), a mother of a child who was killed by a drunk driver brought a Dramshop action against several establishments, including the state of Iowa since the driver bought a bottle of whiskey from the state store. The court held that the state could be liable for the acts of the employees who were not immune from liability of violating the alcohol laws. This would fall under the doctrine of *respondeat superior*.

Iowa courts have stressed that the purpose of Dramshop law is to protect innocent parties—not to protect parties who simply injure themselves after they voluntarily become intoxicated. For example, **Cox v. Rolling Golf Course Corp.**, 532 N.W.2d 761 (Iowa 1995) arose out of two friends who spent a day together playing golf, and visiting taverns. After consuming a substantial number of beers throughout the day, they had an automobile accident, with the passenger suffering serious injuries. The passenger sued the golf course and other establishments under the Dramshop Act. The court refused to impose liability because the purpose of the Dramshop Act was to protect "innocent parties who are injured as a result of the intoxication of other persons" (p. 763). Since the plaintiff actively participated in the intoxication, he was precluded from recovery.

It is important to note that the Iowa Dramshop law applies only when the establishment serves an intoxicated person. It does not apply when alcohol is sold merely to a minor. In **Nutting v. Zieger**, 482 N.W.2d 424 (Iowa 1992), the minor plaintiff sued a tavern for injuries he sustained after the tavern had served him alcohol. The court refused to impose liability on the tavern because the Dramshop law does not apply to minors. The court stated that there is a possibility of inconsistent decisions since licensees were preempted from liability in situations involving minors but social hosts were not. *See,* **Hoth v. Meisner,** 548 N.W.2d 152 (Iowa 1996).

In **Summerhays v. Clark**, 509 N.W.2d 748 (Iowa 1993), a holiday party with an open bar was hosted by a tavern owner for his employees. This action arose when an employee became intoxicated at the party, and subsequently had an automobile accident, killing his wife's son. The decedent's father brought this action against the tavern and the owner of the tavern as an individual.

Social Host Liability

The court did not impose liability on the tavern because the alcohol was given away and thus, it did not meet the "sold and serve" requirement of the Dramshop law. The court had noted in a previous decision of **Paul v. Ron Moore Oil Co.**, 487 N.W.2d 337 (Iowa 1997), that the legislature intended to narrow the scope of the Dramshop Act when a 1986 amendment changed the language of the statute from "sell or give" to "sold and served." Further, the court did not hold the owner liable as an individual because I.C.A. §123.49(1)(a) was enacted to end social host liability as was previously imposed in **Clark v. Mincks**, 364 N.W.2d 226 (Iowa 1985).

Notwithstanding the language in the above paragraph, it appears that a social host could be liable for improperly serving alcohol to a person whom the host knows to be a minor. In **Bauer v. Cole**, 467 N.W.2d 221 (Iowa 1991), after attending a New Years Eve party, a minor was injured in a one vehicle accident. The minor driver of the vehicle was served alcohol at the party. The court refused to impose liability on the parents who hosted the party because "plaintiffs must show that defendants acted with knowledge in supplying beer to [the driver]" (p. 224).

In **Sage v. Johnson**, 437 N.W.2d 582 (Iowa 1989), a minor who was seriously injured in a diving accident after becoming intoxicated sued the parents who hosted the party and furnished the alcohol. The court held that:

> a minor injured as a result of consuming alcoholic beverages furnished in violation of Iowa Code §123.27 is not necessarily precluded from pursuing a claim against the person furnishing the alcohol, but that such a claim is subject to the comparative fault provisions of Chapter 668. (pp. 584-585)

Snyder v. Fish, 539 N.W.2d 197 (Iowa App. 1995), continued the rule that mere permission for a beer party is insufficient to give rise to liability. There must be an affirmative act.

Another "affirmative act" case also held that a minor may be liable under social host liability for serving alcohol to another minor. **Fullmar v. Tague**, 500 N.W.2d 432 (Iowa 1993), involved events surrounding a high school graduation party where a keg of beer was provided to minors in attendance. After leaving the party, an eighteen-year-old passenger was killed in a car wreck when he was a passenger in one of the cars. The driver had consumed beer at the party and had a blood alcohol content of .149.

The court refused to impose liability on the parents of the party host under I.C.A. §123.47 because they neither hosted the party nor were present where the people gathered. "A plaintiff must prove the defendant's knowing and affirmative delivery of the beer to the underage person" (p. 434). The mother was not liable despite the fact that she gave her son a $65 check to the local gas station where the beer was purchased. However, the minor did not escape liability despite his argument that since this was a "help yourself" beer party he did not affirmatively deliver the beer.

The court distinguished this from **DeMore by DeMore v. Dieters,** 334 N.W.2d 734 (Iowa 1993), because the minor

> bought the beer, provided the cups, and joined in the party, all the while knowing (and observing) that underage friends were drinking from the keg. The fact that Jim did not personally fill his guest's beer glasses does not minimize his affirmative conduct. (p. 436)

Further, the court held that "the legislature intended to prevent minors, as well as adults, from unlawfully supplying to an underage person" (p. 437).

Kansas

1997 Cumulative Supplement

Possession or Consumption by a Minor

In K.S.A. 41-727 the legislature increased the fines for those who violate this statute who are at least eighteen but less than twenty-one to a minimum of $200.

Sale or Gift to a Minor

Mills v. City of Overland Park, 837 P.2d 370 (Kan. 1992), involved a minor who drank alcohol he had purchased from various liquor stores and then proceeded to drink at an indoor soccer game. At the game, he became involved in a disturbance, after which the police let him go without arresting him. He then left the game in an intoxicated condition and was found frozen to death in a ditch the next morning.

The court did not impose liability on any of the defendants. The court held that K.S.A. 41-715 was intended to regulate the sale of liquor and not intended to impose civil liability. The court further held that K.S.A. 21-3610 which makes it unlawful to furnish alcohol to a minor, was "not to have been intended to impose civil liability for injuries or death sustained by a minor as a result of having become intoxicated" (p. 371).

Sale or Gift to an Intoxicated Person

See, **Mills v. City of Overland Park** (above).

Social Host Liability

Kansas has still not imposed social host liability. A case that involved a similar concept arose out of an employment context. In **Thies v. Cooper**, 753 P.2d 1280 (Kan. 1988), an employee drank six or seven beers that were provided by the employer in the employee lounge. He then drove his vehicle and struck and killed a pedestrian. The court addressed the question whether

> an employer who makes available [alcohol] in uncontrolled amounts to its employees on the employer's premises may be held liable for all foreseeable consequences of its acts and omissions including torts committed by employees while driving home from the workplace in an intoxicated condition. (p. 1281)

The court held that "an employer is liable for the tortious acts of his employee only under special circumstances" (p. 1281). The court found no special circumstances in this case so no liability was imposed.

Other Cases of Interest

McGee by and through McGee v. Chalfant, 806 P.2d 980 (Kan. 1991), arose out of a group of people who dropped off an intoxicated person at his car, who then proceeded to drive, and collided with another vehicle, injuring the passenger. The court held that "a person who allows an intoxicated person to drive but does not otherwise exercise control over the intoxicated person has assumed no duty to third persons and is not liable for injuries subsequently caused by the intoxicated driver" (p. 985).

Kentucky

1996 Cumulative Supplement

Research did not reveal any new cases or statutory changes.

Louisiana

1999 Cumulative Annual Pocket Part

LSA-RS §4.91.1-14.91.5 were repealed by the legislature in 1995. Now there are similar provisions contained in LSA-RS §14.93.10 et seq. According to LSA-RS §14.93.10, public possession does not include:

Possession or Consumption by a Minor

(a) the possession or consumption of any alcoholic beverage: (i) For an established religious purpose. (ii) When a person under 21 years of age is accompanied by a parent, spouse, or legal guardian 21 years of age or older. (iii) For certain medical purposes. (iv) In private residences. (b) The sale, handling, transport, or service in dispensing of any alcoholic beverage pursuant to lawful ownership of an establishment or to lawful employment of a person under 21 years of age by a duly licensed manufacturer, wholesaler, or retailer of beverage alcohol.

LSA-RS §14.93.12 makes it unlawful for a minor to purchase or publicly possess alcohol. The penalty is a maximum fine of $100 and/or 6 months in prison.

In an opinion of the attorney general, Op. Atty. Gen. No. 96-407, Dec. 10, 1996, it was held that off-campus fraternities are not within the definition of "private residence." Therefore, it does not fall under one of the exceptions to 14:93.10 which would allow minors to possess alcohol on the premises.

LSA-RS §14.93.11 states that an unlawful sale to a minor

Sale or Gift to a Minor

is the selling or otherwise delivering for value any alcoholic beverage to any person under twenty-one years of age unless such person is the lawful owner or lawful employee of an establishment to which the sale is being made and is accepting such delivery pursuant to such ownership or employment. Lack of knowledge of the person's age shall not be a defense.

To violate this section carries a maximum fine of $100 and/or imprisonment for up to 6 months.

LSA-RS §14.93.13 makes it unlawful to purchase alcohol on behalf of a minor except for the minor's parent, spouse, or legal guardian. To violate this section carries a maximum fine of $100 and/or imprisonment for up to 30 days.

The case of **Gresham v. Davenport**, which was discussed in the 1990 supplement to *Alcohol on Campus* has been decided on appeal by the Louisiana Supreme Court. [537 So. 2d 1144 (La. 1989)]. The court decided four issues:

First, the court held that there was enough evidence to support the finding of the trial judge that the boy who jerked the steering wheel was the cause of the accident.

Second, the court concluded that the conduct of the girl who hosted the party was a cause-in-fact of the accident because, had the boy not been provided with the beer, he would not have jerked the wheel.

Third, though the girl's providing of beer was the cause of the accident, the court held that she did not have a duty to refrain from providing beer to the other minor. The court was careful to limit the holding to these circumstances and specifically stated that it is not impossible for there to be a situation where a minor would owe a duty to refrain from providing alcohol to another minor.

Finally, the court rejected "the plaintiff's contention that absolute liability be imposed on a minor who serves intoxicating liquor to another minor" (p. 1148).

Miscellaneous

In 1992, LSA-RS §26:90(15) was enacted which prohibits an establishment from selling alcohol at a price fixed on an "all you can drink" basis after 10:00 pm.

In **Persilver v. Louisiana Department of Transportation**, 592 So. 2d 1344 (La. App. 1 Cir. 1991), the court held that a police officer fulfilled his duty to prevent a bar patron from driving while intoxicated when he took the patron's keys and gave them to a friend, even though the patron regained possession of his keys, drove his car, and was in an accident. The police officer had no duty to anticipate these events after he gave up the keys to another person who was not intoxicated.

Vaughan v. Hair, 645 So. 2d 1177 (La. App. 3 Cir. 1994), held that the employer who permitted employees to drink on their business premises was not liable for the accident caused by an intoxicated employee after he left work. The reason for this was that the employee did not begin drinking until after work and he was not on a company mission at the time of the accident.

Dramshop Liability

Cases interpreted by the Louisiana state courts have supported the decisions of the First Circuit Court of Appeals of Louisiana in **Chausse v. Southland Corp.**, 400 So. 2d 1199 (La. App. 1 Cir. 1981), by imposing liability on establishments for the sale of alcohol to minors.

Hopkins v. Sovereign Fire & Casualty Ins. Co., 626 So. 2d 880 (La. App. 3 Cir. 1993), involved a head-on collision between a truck and some intoxicated minors who had purchased alcohol. The court held that Dramshop immunity does not protect a store that provides alcohol to minors. Further, liability for the vendor "cannot be avoided where the quantity of items so purchased by a minor makes it clear that those items are likely to be consumed by more than just the immediate purchasers" (p. 886). With regard to the minor who illegally purchased the alcohol and then provided it to the other minors, the court imposed no liability. The court held that "LSA-RS §14:91.1 was not intended to impose upon one minor a duty not to give beer to another" (p. 888).

Similarly, in **Edison v. Walker**, 573 So. 2d 545 (La. App. 1 Cir. 1991), a pedestrian who was struck by a vehicle driven by a minor who was served alcohol at a bar filed suit against the bar. The court held that the bar might be liable because LSA-RS §9:2800.1 "does not relieve the seller or furnisher of alcohol to minors or third persons injured by minors due to the effects of alcohol" (p. 546).

There have been a few Louisiana cases that interpreted the meaning of the phrase "affirmative act" as required under Dramshop law.

In **Mills v. Harris**, 615 So. 2d 533 (La. App. 3 Cir. 1993), the estate of a passenger who was killed as a result of a minor driver's intoxication filed a wrongful death action. The establishment who served the alcohol was not liable because serving alcohol is not an affirmative act which would impose liability. *See also*, **Gregor v. Constitution State Insurance Co.**, 534 So. 2d 1340 (La. App. 4 Cir. 1988).

Bertrand v. Kratzer's Country Market, 563 So. 2d 1302 (La. App. 3 Cir. 1990), gave some guidelines as to what behavior would rise to the level of being an affirmative act that would result in liability. This case arose when the parents of a fifteen-year-old bicyclist who was killed by a drunk driver sued the tavern that served the driver alcohol before the accident. The court refused to impose liability. "A retailer who sells or serves alcoholic beverages to an intoxicated person may face criminal penalties . . . but [the statute] does not create a civil cause of action" (p. 1304). "rmitting someone to leave an establishment in an intoxicated condition is not a violation of the duty to avoid affirmative acts increasing 'the peril of intoxication'" (p. 1394). An example the court gave of an affirmative act would be to eject a drunk person onto a busy highway.

In **Bourgeois v. Puglisi**, 615 So. 2d 1047 (La. App. 1 Cir. 1993), the court refused to impose liability on a tavern whose patron became intoxicated and caused a collision. The court held that "the duty not to sell, serve, or furnish alcoholic beverages to [patron] does not include within the ambit of its protection the risk that [patron] would injure a third person off the premises" (p. 1049).

In **Schulker v. Roberson**, 676 So. 2d 684 (La. App. 3 Cir. 1996), a motorist injured in a car wreck brought this action against several parties, including the intoxicated driver who caused the wreck and the bar where he was served alcohol. The plaintiff argued that since the bar hired security guards they had assumed a duty to protect the motoring public from intoxicated patrons. The court disagreed and stated that it was not within the tavern's duties to prevent intoxicated patrons from driving their vehicles.

Spears v. Bradford, 652 So. 2d 628 (La. App. 1 Cir. 1995), involved an accident that occurred between two vehicles, both driven by people who had consumed alcohol at a party. The mother of the girl who hosted the party was sued.

Social Host Liability

The court stated that "[t]he law imposes no absolute liability against the provider of alcohol; rather, a duty risk analysis is applied" (p. 632). The court further stated that "[c]learly, an adult has a duty not to purchase alcohol for or furnish alcohol to a minor" (p. 632). Further, "under LSA-CC articles 2315 & 2316, the sellers or servers of alcohol also have a duty to avoid performing an affirmative act which increases the peril of an intoxicated person" (p. 632). However, the court did not impose liability on the mother because the evidence revealed that she did not serve alcohol at the party.

In **Hollis v. City of Baton Rouge**, 593 So. 2d 388 (La. App. 1 Cir. 1991), the plaintiff went to the defendant's house where he was served two alcoholic drinks. The plaintiff then proceeded to drive home and had a wreck on the way, permanently paralyzing him. The court refused to impose liability on the host after applying LSA-RS §9:2800.1. The guest was not forced to drink the alcohol, nor was he falsely represented that the drinks contained alcohol. This case continued the general theme in the Louisiana courts of being reluctant to impose liability in a situation where an adult simply did not act responsibly.

Maine

1998 Cumulative Pocket Part

Miscellaneous

M.R.S.A. 28-A § 163 was enacted to require that a person may not hold a BYOB function without obtaining a permit from the Bureau of Liquor Enforcement. The permit must be applied for at least 24 hours in advance and there is a $10.00 fee for each day the function is held. The applicant must bring proof that the sponsor is at least twenty-one-years-old. Further, "the BYOB sponsor may not allow any minor not employed by the BYOB sponsor or not accompanied by a parent, legal guardian, or custodian . . . to remain at the premises of a BYOB function." [28A M.R.S.A. § 163(4)]. The sponsor may not allow a minor to possess or consume alcohol on the premises of the function. Further, the sponsor may not allow a visibly intoxicated person to consume alcohol on the premises.

The law also gives law enforcement officers the right to enter the premises to investigate whether the sponsor is in compliance. Any sponsor who is not in compliance may be fined between $100-$300. The fine for the second offense is $200-$500, and for the third offense and subsequent offenses is $500.

Dramshop Liability

In **Swan v. Sohio Oil Co.**, 618 A.2d 214 (Me. 1992) a passenger in a car was seriously injured when the minor driver crashed the car into a utility pole. The parents of the passenger filed suit. After the plaintiffs dismissed the driver as a defendant in the suit the court held that 28 A M.R.S.A. § 2512 prevented them from maintaining an action against the server of alcohol. *See also*, **Douglass v. Kenyon Oil Co., Inc.**, 618 A.2d 220 (Me. 1992).

Social Host Liability

Peters v. Saft, 597 A.2d 50 (Me. 1991), arose out of an accident at a party where alcohol was served. The plaintiff filed suit after he received a serious spinal cord injury as a result of being pushed into a pool by an intoxicated guest. The plaintiff argued that the $250,000 cap on damages was unconstitutional. The court disagreed and ruled that the cap was constitutional because the legislature had a rationale basis for the cap to be enacted.

Other Cases of Interest

In **Albano v. Colby College**, 822 F. Supp. 840 (D. Maine 1993) a twenty-year-old college student who sustained severe head injuries while he was on a trip with the college's tennis team sued Colby College and the tennis coach for negligence. The team was in Puerto Rico, where the drinking age is eighteen, and Albano injured his head after consuming enormous amounts of alcohol. The court held that neither the coach nor the college had a legal duty to prevent the injury. The court noted that Albano was an adult who voluntarily chose to drink, the injury did not take place on the campus of Colby College, and the college did not supply the alcohol. The court also decided not to apply the doctrine of in loco parentis, in part because the doctrine has eroded over the years.

Maryland

1998 Replacement Volume

Definition of a Minor

The definition of "consumer" was incorrectly listed in *Alcohol on Campus*. It should be listed as Md. Ann. Code art. 2B § 1-102(a)(b).

The section which makes it unlawful for a licensee to sell or otherwise furnish alcohol to minors in now codified in art. 2B §12-108.

Possession or Consumption by a Minor

In **Boyd v. Board of Liquor License Commission for Baltimore City,** 692 A.2d 1 (Md. App. 1997), the court analyzed a licensee's defense of "due caution" when it sells alcohol to a minor. Under this defense, if the establishment unlawfully sells alcohol to a minor, it is a defense if they used "due caution" to establish that the person was not a minor. However, the court did note that according to art. 2B §12-108, this defense only is available if the minor is not a Maryland resident.

Sale or Gift to a Minor

Md. Ann. Code art. 27 §400 makes it is unlawful for a person to misrepresent their age when buying alcohol.

Md. Ann. Code art. 27 §400B makes it illegal to use identification with a false age.

Misrepresentation of Age

The section which makes it unlawful to drink on public property is now codified in art. 2B §19-202.

Md. Ann. Code art. 27 §401B requires a possessor of a keg of beer to register the keg according to the provisions in Md. Ann. Code art. 2B §21-106. It also makes it unlawful for anyone under the age of twenty-one to consume from the keg.

Miscellaneous

The section which makes it unlawful for a licensee to sell alcohol to an intoxicated person is now codified in art. 2B §12-108.

Sale or Gift to an Intoxicated Person

Maryland has continued to refuse to judicially impose Dramshop liability. In **Moran v. Foodmaker, Inc.**, 594 A.2d 587 (Md. App. 1991), the plaintiff drove her car to visit a friend at her friend's house. After she parked her car, she went to get something from the trunk. As she was doing so, another car drove into the rear of her car, pinning her between the two vehicles. As a result of this accident, the plaintiff suffered serious injuries. The driver had just left a local tavern where he had consumed alcohol to the point that his blood alcohol content was .19%.

Dramshop Liability

The court refused to hold the tavern liable even though they had continued to serve him after he was visibly intoxicated. The court stated that "[M]aryland remains aligned with the small minority of states which take a rigid and unenlightened approach to the issue of civil liability for commercial vendors of alcoholic beverages" (pp. 590-591).

In **Valentine v. On Target**, 686 A.2d 636 (Md. App. 1996), the court affirmed the long-standing rule in Maryland that " the law recognizes no relation of proximate cause between the sale of liquor and a tort committed by a buyer who has drunk the liquor" (p. 642).

Massachusetts

1998 Cumulative Annual Pocket Part

A 1994 amendment to M.G.L.A. 138 §34A provides that any minor who attempts to purchase alcohol will have their driver's license suspended for ninety days.

Possession or Consumption by a Minor

In **Bennett v. Eagle Brook Country Store**, 557 N.E.2d 1166 (Mass. 1990), the plaintiff sued a tavern for negligence in serving alcohol to a patron who later drove his car and struck the plaintiff. The court refused to hold the business liable even though they vi-

Sale or Gift to an Intoxicated Person

olated provisions of M.G.L.A. 138 §69, which makes it unlawful for a licensee to sell alcohol to an intoxicated person. Even though this is a criminal penalty, "the statute does not expressly grant an independent ground for civil liability" (p. 1168). Since there was not enough evidence to establish negligence, the business was not liable.

Dramshop Liability

Tobin v. Norwood Country Club, Inc., 661 N.E.2d 627 (Mass. 1996), arose out of a family reunion held in a party room of a country club where alcohol was served. A minor female who attended the party consumed a substantial amount of alcohol. After getting into an argument with her date, she proceeded to walk home and was struck and killed by a passing car. Her blood alcohol content was .229.

The court held that the country club was liable because when an establishment serves liquor with teenagers present "the situation is so fraught with foreseeable risk that a business that is in a position to control or reduce that risk has a duty to do so" (p. 633). This is the law even without an actual "hand to hand" serving of the minor. "The duty is breached when the establishment knew or reasonably should have known that it was furnishing alcohol to minors" (p. 633). Though the club was liable, the court ruled that their liability could be reduced by the amount the girl negligently contributed to her own injuries.

In **Kirby v. LeDisco**, 614 N.E.2d 1016 (Mass. App. Ct. 1993), two victims who were assaulted by an intoxicated tavern patron filed suit against the tavern, alleging negligence. The court refused to impose liability on the tavern because, even though they served the assailant eight beers, it did not support the inference that the tavern was put on notice that it was serving alcohol to an intoxicated person.

It appears that the Massachusetts courts require that a provider of alcohol have some degree of control over the alcohol in order for liability to be imposed. In **O'Sullivan v. Hemisphere Broadcasting**, 520 N.E.2d 429 (Mass. 1996), the plaintiff was injured when her car was struck by a driver who had consumed beer at a promotional event sponsored by the defendants, Metro, Miller, and WBCN. The court refused to hold the defendants liable because the defendants did not control nor did they have the right to control the distribution of free beer.

In **Vickowski v. Polish American Cit. Club**, 664 N.E.2d 429 (Mass. 1996), a pedestrian injured by a drunk driver brought a negligence action against the tavern that had served alcohol to the driver. The court refused to impose liability because there was no evidence that the tavern knew or had reason to know they were serving an intoxicated person.

This can be contrasted with **Gottlin v. Graves**, 662 N.E.2d 711 (Mass. App. Ct. 1996), where it was held to be rational for a juror to conclude from the evidence that the bartender would have known the driver was intoxicated. In that case the tavern and driver were liable for an accident that occurred when the driver "had drunk one beer on the way to the tavern, consumed draft beers and two shots of Jack Daniels while at the tavern, and finally, was served one beer 'for the road'" (p. 714).

Social Host Liability

In **Cremins v. Clancy**, 612 N.E.2d 1183 (Mass. 1993), a group of teenagers brought some beer to the defendant's house and consumed it. Later, one of the teenagers caused a car wreck. The court refused to hold the defendant liable as a social host even though he provided the atmosphere for drinking. The defendant did not control the alcohol supply so he was not liable as a social host. *See* also, **Makynen v. Mustakangas**, 655 N.E.2d 1284 (Mass. App. Ct. 1995), which held that a social host has no ability to control the liquor supply when it belongs to the guest.

In **Hamilton v. Ganias**, 632 N.E.2d 407 (Mass. 1994), a nineteen-year-old guest filed suit against social hosts, seeking redress for injuries suffered by the guest from an accident. The court refused to impose liability and stated that:

> [t]his case is different from cases in which an innocent third party is injured by the negligence of an intoxicated guest. The reasons for establishing social host liability to a third person injured by the negligence of an intoxicated guest in certain circumstances simply do not apply to the claim of an intoxicated guest who injures himself. (p. 408)

This case applied the principles of **Manning v. Nobile,** 582 N.E.2d 942 (Mass. 1991), where the court held that a social host had no duty to an adult guest who became intoxicated by the voluntarily consumption of alcohol and subsequently injured himself while negligently driving a car.

In **Wallace v. Wilson**, 575 N.E.2d 1134 (Mass. 1991), guests at a party, where the host's mother was present, assaulted and battered some uninvited persons who were on the premises. The court held that the mother was not liable even though she knew the guests were consuming alcohol because she owed no duty to those uninvited persons.

Michigan

1998 Cumulative Annual Pocket Part

Possession or Consumption by a Minor

The section which allows a minor to consume alcohol if the minor is enrolled in a class offered in an academic building and taught by a faculty member of an accredited institution of post secondary education where consumption is a necessary part of the course is now codified in M.C.L.A. §436.33b(11).

In **Brown v. Jones**, 503 N.W.2d 735 (Mich. App. 1993), five minors each contributed money to buy a fifth of schnapps to celebrate a birthday. Subsequently, one of the minors had a car wreck after drinking the alcohol. First, the court refused to impose liability on the passengers for negligence because there is generally no duty to protect a person from the conduct of a third person. Next, the court ruled that M.C.L.A. §436.33a, which says that alcohol shall not be furnished to minors, did not apply to the minor passengers.

In **Town & Country Lanes, Inc. v. Liquor Control Commission**, 446 N.W.2d 335 (Mich. App. 1990), the court held that a bowling alley could be liable for furnishing alcohol to a minor even though the alcohol he drank was from a pitcher properly purchased by an adult.

Sale or Gift to a Minor

In **Lamson v. Martin,** *after remand,* 549 N.W.2d 878 (Mich. App. 1996), the defendant purchased alcohol for a minor who subsequently became intoxicated and crashed his vehicle, killing the plaintiff's son. The court, when interpreting M.C.L.A. §436.33(1) (the statue making it unlawful to sell alcohol to a minor), held that a reasonable jury could have found that the defendant made a "diligent inquiry" as to the age of the person for whom she purchased alcohol. When the defendant had asked the minor why she could not purchase alcohol for herself, the minor replied that she had to work late. Further, the court affirmed that M.C.L.A. §436.33(1) applies to all persons—not just licensed establishments. In addition, lack of knowledge of age can sometimes be a defense.

Misrepresentation of Age The section which makes it unlawful to use a false I.D. to purchase alcohol is now codified in M.C.L.A. §436.33b(2).

Miscellaneous Section 436.33a, which gave the court the authority to impound a vehicle of a minor who transported alcohol in it, was repealed effective April 1, 1997.

The attorney general of Michigan issued an opinion which says that when a banquet hall corporation and restaurant corporation with common owners conduct business in the same building, the banquet hall, which does not sell alcohol, need not be licensed under the Michigan Liquor Control Act. [Op. Atty. Gen. 1997, No. 6963].

Definition of an Intoxicated Person **Miller v. Ocampaugh**, 477 N.W.2d 105 (Mich. App. 1991), stated that "[a] person is visibly intoxicated when the person's intoxication would be apparent to an ordinary observer" (p. 109). See also, **Heyler v. Dixon,** 408 N.W.2d 121 (Mich. 1987). Visible intoxication may be proven by circumstantial evidence. *See also*, **Dines v. Henning**, 459 N.W.2d 132 (Mich. App. 1990).

Dramshop Liability In **Tennile v. Action Distributing Co.,** 570 N.W.2d 130 (Mich. App. 1997), the court held that the dramshop act only applies to retailers. Thus, since the dramshop act is the "exclusive" remedy arising out of the furnishing of alcohol by a licensee, it is the exclusive remedy only when a retailer is the defendant. Consequently, if the defendant is a wholesale supplier of liquor, as in this case, the plaintiff may bring other claims other than the one under dramshop.

While **Rogalski** (see "Social Host Liability") refused to extend tort liability to a social host for intentional torts, Michigan courts have reached the opposite conclusion under the Dramshop statute. In **Weiss v. Hodge,** 567 N.W.2d 468 (Mich. App. 1997), a tavern patron who was allegedly served alcohol while he was visibly intoxicated assaulted a man who had arrived at the tavern to pick up his girlfriend. The court held that the Dramshop statute is not limited to the negligent acts of a patron. Unlike the social host liability context, the Dramshop statute does allow a Michigan licensee to be held liable for the intoxicated torts of the intoxicated patron.

In **Dhuy v. Rude**, 465 N.W.2d 32 (Mich. App. 1990), the plaintiff was injured while a passenger in a car being driven by a minor who consumed alcohol purchased from the defendant's store. The plaintiff and other minors had contributed money which they then gave to the driver to purchase the alcohol. The court did not allow the plaintiff to recover under Dramshop and gave two primary reasons for this decision. First, since the plaintiff contributed money towards the purchase of the alcohol, he was not an innocent party as required for recovery under Dramshop. Second, the plaintiff argued that since the driver was not visibly intoxicated when the plaintiff contributed the money, that he did not contribute to the unlawful purchase of alcohol. The court disagreed with this argument and stated that the question of visible intoxication was immaterial since the driver was a minor and the purchase would have been illegal regardless of his state of sobriety or intoxication.

Pollard v. Village of Ovid, 446 N.W.2d 574 (Mich. App. 1989), arose out of a wedding reception where a minor who was served alcohol to the point of intoxication subsequently crashed his car into a wall, killing his adult passenger. The estate of the passenger sued the hosts of the wedding reception, claiming that they knew alcohol was served to the minor.

The court refused to impose liability because the law was not intended to protect a non-innocent injured third party. Because the decedent actually participated in the minor's intoxication, recovery was precluded. **Arbelius v. Poletti**, 469 N.W.2d 436 (Mich. App. 1991), overruled part of **Pollard** and held that the non-innocent party doctrine applies only to dramshop actions, and not to actions for common law negligence.

In addition, **Larrow v. Miller**, 548 N.W.2d 704 (Mich. App. 1996), held that one who supplies illegal drugs and participates in that person's intoxication is barred by the non-innocent party doctrine. In this case, the estate of a passenger who was killed in a car wreck with an intoxicated driver was barred from recovery because the passenger supplied marijuana to the driver and contributed to the intoxication.

Dobson v. Maki, 457 N.W.2d 132 (Mich. App. 1990), arose out of a party where minors were charged an admission fee to drink from kegs of beer. One of the guests became intoxicated and subsequently was in an automobile accident. The court refused to impose dramshop liability on the store that sold the kegs because in a 1986 amendment to the dramshop statute, "the legislature clearly deleted the provision for indirect sales to minors, while leaving intact liability for indirect sales to visibly intoxicated persons" (p. 134). Therefore, because the store did not directly sell the alcohol to the minor plaintiffs, no liability was imposed.

Social Host Liability

Rogalski v. Tavernier, 527 N.W.2d 73 (Mich. App. 1995), placed a limit on what is foreseeable in the social host liability context. This case was brought by the plaintiff in an attempt to hold social hosts liable for serving alcohol to minors who subsequently became involved in an altercation where a minor was stabbed and killed. The court refused to impose liability. The court stated that a subsequent stabbing is unlike the situation in **Longstreth v. Gensel,** 377 N.W.2d 804 (Mich. 1985) (the original case which established social host liability in Michigan), which involved an automobile accident. The court stated that "criminal or violent acts are not foreseeable results of the serving of alcohol to minors and, therefore, cannot serve as a basis for social host liability" (p. 76).

Minnesota

1998 Cumulative Annual Pocket Part

Sale or Gift to a Minor

A 1989 amendment in Section 340A.503, subd.2 added a prohibition against knowingly permitting the use of a person's license by a minor for the purchase or attempt to purchase alcoholic beverages. Further, a 1989 amendment added a clause in subdivision 6 that provides for the defense that "the defendant reasonably and in good faith relied upon representations of proof of age" in selling alcohol to a minor.

A 1990 amendment in Section 340A.503, subd.1 added a sentence making consumption of alcohol in the household of the parent or guardian with consent an affirmative defense if proven by a preponderance of the evidence. Additionally, the 1990 amendment in subdivision 3 makes possession of alcohol, by persons under age 21, at a place other than the household of a parent or guardian a rebuttable presumption of intent to consume it at a place other than the household of a parent or guardian.

Sale or Gift to an Intoxicated Person

In **Jewett v. Deutsch**, 437 N.W.2d 717 (Minn. App. 1989) the plaintiff's wife was killed as a result of a car accident with Dale Welker, who had been drinking for four hours prior to the accident. According to testimony, Welker had consumed between 10-15 beers at the tavern owned by Deutsch ("Bob's Tavern").

The plaintiff brought an action against Welker and Deutsch, alleging negligence and illegal sale of intoxicating liquor. The court began by noting that Minnesota Statute Sect. 340A.502 (1986) prohibits the sale of alcoholic beverages "for the use of an obviously intoxicated person" (p. 720). According to the court, "[t]he standard for determining whether a person is obviously intoxicated is whether exercising reasonable powers of observation, one sees or should see that the buyer is intoxicated" (p. 720).

In reaching the conclusion that Bob's Tavern was liable for a violation of Section 340A.502, the court noted that Welker's blood alcohol content was .27 one hour after the accident. Further, the court noted that the officer who arrived on the scene of the accident testified that Welker was obviously intoxicated. Finally, the court considered the testimony of a toxicologist that Welker would have shown signs of obvious intoxication while at Bob's Tavern.

Dramshop Liability

In **Lefto v. Hoggsbreath Enterprises,** 567 N.W.2d 746 (Minn. App. 1997), the court held that the fiance of a man who was injured in a car accident, the cause of which was the driver being served alcohol in violation of the dramshop law, could recover against the tavern under dramshop. In their reasoning, the court noted that the Dramshop Act allows a "spouse, child, parent, guardian, employer, or other person" who is injured to recover. In this case, the fiance qualified as "an other person."

In **Wagner v. Schwegmann's South Town Liquor, Inc.,** 485 N.W.2d 730 (Minn. Ct. App. 1992) the plaintiffs, parents of the decedent, brought suit against the respondent for an illegal sale of alcoholic beverages pursuant to Minn. Stat. Sect. 340A.801 (1988). A friend of the decedent testified that he bought a keg of beer from Schwegmann's while the decedent was present. The purchaser at this time was eighteen years of age. He showed the respondent a Minnesota identification card bearing his picture, but the name and birth date of his twenty-two-year-old brother. The purchaser filled out a receipt, but did not sign it. Later that evening, the decedent consumed beer from the keg, became intoxicated, and was involved in an automobile accident early the next morning. The court remanded the case, holding that the respondent could use the defense that it reasonably relied upon the purchaser's proof of age when it sold the keg of beer to him.

Further, in **Weber v. Au**, 512 N.W.2d 348 (Minn. Ct. App. 1994), the plaintiff police officer brought suit under Sect. 340A.801, subd. 1 against Au's bar. A minor who had been drinking at Au's bar began a fight outside the bar. A policeman arrived on the scene, chased the minor, and suffered a knee injury. The gist of the complaint against Au's bar was that "but for" the bar's contributing to the minor's drunkenness, the policeman never would have suffered the knee injury because he would not have had to chase the minor. Noting that the Supreme Court had rejected this "but for" analysis, [See **Kryzer v. Champlin American Legion No. 600**, 494 N.W.2d 35, 37 (Minn. 1992)] the court held that the police officer's lawsuit under Sect. 340A.801, subd. 1 could not be maintained because he "failed to allege that any intoxication of the minor contributed to the cause of [the officer's] injuries" (p. 351).

Similarly, in **Kryzer v. Champlin American Legion No. 600**, 494 N.W.2d 35 (Minn. 1992), the plaintiff brought suit against the bar for injuries she suffered to her wrist as a result of being forcibly removed from the bar. The plaintiff alleged that the bar had sold her liquor while she was obviously intoxicated and that as a result of this sale, she suffered a wrist injury when she had to be removed from the bar.

The court reiterated the time-tested rule that "a claimant seeking recovery pursuant to the civil damage act must show that the defendant illegally sold intoxicating liquor which caused intoxication and "that such intoxication was the proximate cause of plaintiff's injuries" (p. 36). Thus, the court held that the bar was not liable because the employee's conduct in removing the plaintiff from the bar "does not provide any causal connection between the intoxication and the injury" (p. 37).

More recently, the Court of Appeals of Minnesota expounded upon the scope of the Civil Damages Act, Minn. Stat. Sect. 340A.801, subd. 1 (1994) in **Englund v. MN CA Partners/MN Joint Ventures**, 555 N.W.2d 328 (Minn. App. 1997). In **Englund**, the plaintiff was a motorcyclist who was injured in a car crash with a woman who had purchased drinks at a hotel bar and later consumed them after leaving the premises.

The court first noted that the sale of alcohol constitutes an "illegal sale" under the act if : "(1) the sale violates a provision of the liquor act, Minn. Stat. Ch. 340A (1994 & Supp. 1995); and the violation is substantially related to the purposes of the civil damage act" (p. 330). The court held that "a vendor violates the on-sale provision of the liquor act, Minn. Stat. Sect. 340A.404, when it fails to operate as a reasonable vendor, acting in good faith to sell liquor to be consumed only on the licensed premises" (p. 332). The court remanded the case for a determination of whether the hotel bar had acted reasonably in its sale of liquor. Finally, the court held that a violation of the on-sale provision is substantially related to the purposes of the civil damages act.

Social Host Liability

In **Vanwagner v. Mattison**, 533 N.W.2d 75 (Minn. App. 1995) the minor, plaintiff, was injured in a car accident after consuming alcohol at a party hosted by the defendants. The minor plaintiff brought a negligence action against the defendants for furnishing alcohol to him. The defendants argued that the plaintiff's own negligence should be compared to their negligence in accordance with the comparative fault statute, Minn. Stat. Sect. 604.01 (1992).

The court agreed, stating that "the [defendants'] argument that social hosts should not be subject to a higher standard of liability than commercial vendors appears sound" (p. 80). Thus, the court held that "the common law actions permitted under subdivision 6 of Section 340A.801 do not involve absolute liability and are therefore subject to comparative fault" (p. 80). Because the minor was more at fault than the defendants, the court held for the defendants.

Similarly, the Court of Appeals of Minnesota discussed the application of Section 340A.801, subd. 6 (1990) in **Siltman v. Tulenchik**, 1995 WL 6426 (Minn. App.). In Siltman, the plaintiff brought a personal injury action against the minor defendant. The plaintiff alleged that the defendant negligently furnished alcohol to a minor in violation of Minnesota statutes. The plaintiff argued that subdivision 6 represented a legislative intent for subdivision 1 to include a cause of action against both social hosts and commercial vendors.

The court disagreed, stating, among other things, that "years of case law interpret subdivision 1 as allowing a cause of action only against commercial vendors" (p. 1). Finally, the court affirmed its previous holding in **Holmquist,** 367 N.W.2d at 470-72 that Section 340A.503, subd. 2(1) (1990) "preempts any cause of action against a social host for negligently furnishing alcohol to a minor" (p.2).

Mississippi

1998 Cumulative Supplement

Sale or Gift to a Minor The 1995 amendment to Miss. Code §67-3-53 makes it unlawful for the employer of a permit holder to sell beer and light wine to any person under twenty-one years of age.

Misrepresentation of Age Miss. Code §67-1-81 no longer contains a reference that it is unlawful for a person to misrepresent their age. However, it remains unlawful under §67-3-70(2).

Miscellaneous In **Maine v. Office Depot, Inc.**, 914 F. Supp. 1413 (S.D. Miss. 1996), the plaintiff administratrix brought a wrongful death action against Office Depot for allowing a minor to photocopy a doctored driver's license. The minor subsequently used the copy of the doctored driver's license to buy alcohol. The plaintiff claimed that Office Depot's negligence in allowing the minor to make the copies proximately caused the death of the plaintiff's decedent who was killed while riding in the intoxicated minor's car. In holding that Office Depot was not liable for this death, the court surveyed various Mississippi cases involving alcohol related injuries and concluded that:

> [t]he Mississippi Supreme Court, absent some statutory requirement to do so, has been reluctant to extend liability in alcohol related injury cases to persons who are not directly involved in causing the injury. The Court further finds that, if presented with the question of imposing liability upon Office Depot in this case, the Mississippi Supreme Court would decline to impose such liability under the common law. (p. 1419)

Missouri

1998 Cumulative Annual Pocket Part

Possession or Consumption by a Minor A 1994 amendment to Section 311.325 creates the presumption that a sealed container describing its contents as intoxicating liquor does indeed contain intoxicating liquor. The burden of proof is on the minor that the container does not contain intoxicating liquor. Now, the mere fact that a minor is served beer with a brand label is sufficient to prove that it contains 3.2% alcohol.

The restrictions under Section 311.310 which make it unlawful to provide alcohol to minors, do not apply to the situation where liquor is supplied to a minor for medical purposes.

Miscellaneous In **Kelley v. Supervisor of Liquor Control, State of Missouri**, 823 S.W.2d 147 (Mo. App. 1992), the court upheld the suspension of a liquor license after the licensee failed to check a minor's identification when selling beer to him. In its decision, the court noted that a court reviewing a liquor license suspension is not required to make an independent assessment of whether the licensee acted in good faith in the sale of beer to a minor.

The court in **Elliot v. Kessler**, 799 S.W.2d 97 (Mo. App. W.D. 1990) affirmed the rule that the new Dramshop Act could not be applied retroactively to preclude suits that arose before the effective date of the new act.

In **Shelter Mut. Ins. Co. v. White**, 930 S.W.2d 1 (Mo. App. W.D. 1996) an intoxicated driver crashed his pickup truck into another pickup truck, severely injuring the other driver and killing his fiance. The parents of the late fiance brought an action against the passengers in the truck of the intoxicated driver. The plaintiffs claimed that these passengers were negligent in that they supplied the driver with beer while he was driving and encouraged him to drive at excessive speeds.

In holding that the defendants were not liable for furnishing alcoholic beverages to the driver, the court confirmed the rule of Section 537.053 (1994) that "[t]he consumption of alcoholic beverages, rather than the furnishing of alcoholic beverages, [is] the proximate cause of injuries inflicted upon another by an intoxicated person" (p.2). However, the court did conclude that the passengers could be liable for encouraging the driver to drive under the influence of alcohol and to ignore traffic signs.

Social Host Liability

Missouri continues to refuse to extend liability to social hosts who provide alcohol to minors. **Smith v. Gregg**, 946 S.W.2d 807 (Mo. App. 1997), involved a high school graduation party where those in attendance each contributed $3.00 to drink from a keg of beer. One of those in attendance was assaulted by another minor who had consumed beer from the keg. He then sued the hosts of the party and the guest of honor for his injuries under several theories of liability. The court refused to impose liability because under Missouri law a social host is not civilly liable for damages when they serve alcohol to minors. Further, the defendants were not liable for negligent supervision of the party because there were not enough facts to indicated that a special relationship to create such a duty existed between the defendants and the plaintiff. Finally, the defendants were not liable for not providing security because they had no ability to control the assailant, nor was there any evidence to suggest it was necessary for them to control him.

Other Cases of Interest

In **Nisbet v. Bucher**, 949 S.W.2d 111 (Mo. Ct. App. 1997), a college freshman joined St. Pat's Board, Inc., a campus organization responsible for organizing the annual campus St. Patrick's Day festivities and whose membership included fraternity members. The student (whose name was Michael) was required to participate in an initiation ceremony which included the coerced chugging of excessive amounts of alcohol. The initiation was conducted in two places, both owned by two different fraternities. Michael eventually became unconscious from too much alcohol consumption and began secreting fluids from his nose and mouth. The members left him unattended face down on the floor and delayed getting him appropriate medical attention. Michael died two days later. The fraternities, St. Pat's Board, and individual members were sued for the wrongful death of the student.

The court first noted that traditionally Missouri law does not find a social host liable for furnishing alcohol to an individual who is eventually injured. However, the court determined that the defendants could be liable because the situation appeared to be one where the student was pressured to drink and the membership was conditioned upon his drinking. The court noted that:

> We recognize that Michael could have avoided the situation by walking away from the initiation activities. In that respect, Michael's actions could be construed as voluntary. Yet, as the petition alleges, participation in the initiation activities was a

prerequisite for membership on the St. Paul's Board. If great social pressure was applied to Michael to comply with the membership 'qualifications' of the St. Pat's Board, he may have been blinded to the danger he was facing. In other words, his will to drink or not drink may have been overborne by the requirements to achieve membership on the St. Pat's Board and by the pressure he was receiving from the defendants.

Montana
1997 Replacement Volume

Possession or Consumption by a Minor

MCA 45-5-624(a) makes it unlawful for a minor to possess or consume alcohol.

Misrepresentation of Age

The former MCA 16-3-301(3) is now codified as MCA 16-3-301(4).

Sale or Gift to an Intoxicated Person

The former MCA 16-3-301(2)(b) is now codified as MCA 16-3-301(3)(b).

Other Cases of Interest

In **Peschke v. Carroll College,** 929 P.2d 874 (Mont. 1996), a campus cafeteria employee was shot by an intoxicated person who had just been ejected from a campus chapel by the priest. The employee and her family sued the college, claiming the college was negligent because the priest failed to warn others or inform campus security that he had ejected this person who he knew had a gun. At trial, the plaintiff presented substantial evidence regarding the inadequacies of the campus security; this evidence was rebutted by the college with evidence indicating how effective the campus security was. The jury returned a verdict in favor of the college, finding they were not negligent, and this verdict was upheld by the Montana Supreme Court.

Nebraska
1997 Supplement

Definition of a Minor

The section which states that a minor is a person below the age of twenty-one is now codified in §53-103(24).

Sale or Gift to a Minor

In **Pelzek v. American Legion**, 463 N.W.2d 321 (Neb. 1990), a minor who paid admission to a party where she was served alcohol sued the hosts for injuries she sustained in a car accident after she became intoxicated. The court refused to impose liability because the Nebraska legislature repealed the Dramshop liability statute in 1935. Further, selling alcohol to a minor is not the cause of the injuries. The cause "is the negligent operation of an automobile" (p. 323).

Miscellaneous

State v. Lesiak, 449 N.W.2d 550 (Neb. 1989), held that "voluntary intoxication is not a defense to a crime, unless an accused is intoxicated to such an extent that he is incapable of forming the requisite element of criminal intent" (p. 552).

Dramshop Liability

In **Schroer v. Synowiecki**, 435 N.W.2d 875 (Neb. 1989), a tavern owner was sued by the representatives of a customer who was killed in a car chase which was the culmination of an altercation that began in the tavern. The plaintiffs claimed that the tavern owner was liable because of a duty to protect the patrons from harm caused by third persons.

The court did not impose liability on the tavern because the law does not require a tavern owner to possess extraordinary foreseeable powers. Further, even if the tavern breached a duty, this negligence was not the proximate cause of the chase. Finally, the court did not impose liability under Neb. Rev. St. §53-180, the section which makes it unlawful to procure alcohol for minors, because that statute does not create a duty to third parties.

Nevada
1998 Cumulative Supplement

At least two cases have demonstrated that Nevada continues to adhere to the old common law rule for Dramshop liability. **Hinegardner v. Marcor Resorts**, 844 P.2d 800 (Nev. 1992), involved a minor who was served alcohol at an establishment and then drove his car under the influence and crashed it into another car, injuring the plaintiff. The court refused to impose liability on the establishment because Nevada adheres to the old common law rule that the serving of alcohol is not the proximate cause of the injury. "Individuals, drunk or sober, [are] responsible for their own torts" (p. 802).

Dramshop Liability

Snyder v. Viani, 885 P.2d 610 (Nev. 1994), reaffirmed the principles of **Hinegardner**. The facts in this case are similar except that the intoxicated minor was killed in the accident and his estate sued the tavern. Once again, the court emphasized that Nevada follows the common law rule and imposed no liability on the tavern.

New Hampshire
1997 Cumulative Supplement

RSA 175:1 XLIX states that a minor is a person under the age of twenty-one. See also, RSA 507-F:1(VI).

Definition of a Minor

RSA 175:8-a, which makes it unlawful for a minor to possess alcohol, was recodified in 1990 to RSA 179:10.

Possession or Consumption by a Minor

The legislature passed RSA 175:10-a in 1996, which states that a minor who possesses alcohol with the intent to purchase and takes a substantial step towards the purchase is guilty of a violation.

RSA 175:6 which makes it unlawful to sell alcohol to minors, was recodified in 1990 to RSA 179:5. RSA 175:6-b, which requires the seller to request identification of a purchaser whose age is in question, was recodified in 1990 to RSA 179:8. Similarly, RCA 175:6-a is now RCA 179:7.

Sale or Gift to a Minor

In **State v. Zeta Chi Fraternity**, 696 A.2d 536 (N.H. 1997), a fraternity was convicted of criminal charges of selling alcohol to minors and of prostitution. The case arose from a rush party held at the fraternity house where strippers were hired by the fraternity and beer was available from a soda machine in the apartment portion of the house. On appeal, the New Hampshire Supreme Court affirmed both counts of the conviction. Although the fraternity argued that they did not control the beer machine and thus, did not cause the beer to be sold, the court rejected this argument. An interesting and important part of this case is that the court admitted the minutes of past fraternity meetings into evidence for the jury to see. The reason for admitting these minutes was to "counter the impression" created by the fraternity when they introduced their risk management policy into evidence. The minutes demonstrated proof that the fraternity frequently violated their own policy.

Misrepresentation of Age

RSA 175:7, which makes it unlawful for a minor to misrepresent his age, was recodified in 1990 to RCA 179:9.

Miscellaneous

The former RSA 180:1, which makes it unlawful to transport illegally obtained alcoholic beverages, is now RSA 179:2.

In an opinion by the attorney general, it was stated that when an officer is confronted with a situation involving underage transportation of alcohol, if the officer fails to make an arrest it is a breach of statutory duty. [1994 Op. Atty. Gen. 4.]

Sale or Gift to an Intoxicated Person

This section, which makes it unlawful to provide alcohol to an intoxicated person, was recodified in 1990 to RSA 179:5.

Definition of Intoxicated Person

According to RSA 175:1 XXXVIII, an "intoxicated individual" is one "whose mental or physical faculties are impaired as a result of drug or alcohol use so as to diminish that person's ability to think in a manner in which an ordinary, prudent and cautious person in full possession of his faculties and using reasonable care, would act under like circumstances." See also, RSA 507-F:1(IV).

Social Host Liability

In some important decisions, the New Hampshire Supreme Court gave some guidance as to when social host liability may be imposed. In **Hickingbotham v. Burke**, 662 A.2d 297 (N.H. 1995), a minor who was injured in a car wreck after being served alcohol at a party sued the hosts to recover for his injuries. First, the court considered whether to impose liability under RSA 179:5 and determined that no civil right of action is granted to a plaintiff under this section. Next, for the first time in New Hampshire, the court considered whether they should recognize social host liability based upon principles of common law negligence. The court concluded that "a plaintiff who is injured as a result of a social host's service of alcohol may maintain an action against that social host, so long as the plaintiff can allege that the service was reckless" (p. 301). The court added that principles of common law negligence would apply and whether the guest is a minor is a factor to be considered in determining whether or not the serving of the alcohol is reckless.

In a similar case, **MacLeod v. Ball**, 663 A.2d 632 (N.H. 1995), a minor college student was injured when he became intoxicated and fell off a bridge while he was pretending to jump. He sued the individuals who provided the alcohol to himself and three other students. The court, citing **Hickingbotham**, held that no liability would be imposed under RSA 179:5. However, if the plaintiff could prove the delivery of the alcohol was reckless, the defendant would be liable.

New Jersey

1998 Cumulative Annual Pocket Part

Possession or Consumption by a Minor

A 1991 amendment to Section 2C:33-15 raised the minimum fine for a violation of this section from $100 to $500.

A 1995 amendment to Section 2C:33-17 makes it a penalty under this section to entice or encourage a minor to drink alcohol.

A 1991 amendment to Section 33:1-81 increased the minimum fine for a minor to enter a licensed establishment to purchase alcohol from $100 to $500.

Cassanello v. Luddy, 695 A.2d 325 (N.J. Sup. Ct. 1997), is an example where a tavern breached its duty of ordinary care. This case arose when two patrons were served alcohol at a tavern to the point of intoxication. At one point in the evening, they got into a scuffle with the plaintiff which was then broken up by a security guard. Later, when the plaintiff left the tavern, the two patrons chased down his vehicle and fractured his skull by striking him with an axe hammer.

The court held that the tavern was negligent in several ways, primarily in that they continued to serve the intoxicated patrons even after the security guard had broken up the scuffle. Also, the security guard was negligent when he failed to call the police after the plaintiff asked him to do so. As a final matter, the court noted that under these circumstances, it was fair to place a legal duty on the tavern "to take reasonable measures to safeguard the plaintiff when he leaves the premises." (p. 328).

At least two New Jersey cases have used the doctrine of comparative fault to reduce, or bar, a plaintiff's recovery as a result of the plaintiff negligently contributing to his own injuries. In **Lee v. Kiku Restaurant**, 603 A.2d 503 (N.J. 1992), a restaurant patron, along with the car driver, was served alcohol while intoxicated. The passenger sued the establishment after he was injured in a subsequent car accident. The court held that the doctrine of comparative fault would apply. The court held that they would "apportion fault between the patron and the tavern based on the extent to which each party's negligence contributed to the plaintiff's injuries" (p. 510). *See also,* **McGovern v. Koza's Bar & Grill**, 604 A.2d 226 (N.J. Super. L. 1991).

Fisch v. Bellshot, 640 A.2d 801 (N.J. 1994), was a case similar to **Lee**. The jury found the defendant 75% negligent after she consumed alcohol at a bar and later died in an accident. Because of her negligence, the court dismissed her estate's suit against the bar.

In **Wagner v. Schlue,** 605 A.2d 294 (N.J. Super. 1992), the court held that a party can be liable if they do not prevent an intoxicated person from driving and that intoxicated person injures himself. In this case, the defendant relinquished the intoxicated plaintiff's car to her and the plaintiff was later injured when she crashed her car into a pole. The court noted that it would have taken very little effort for the defendant to prevent the plaintiff from driving and when putting forth that effort "is weighed against the potential disastrous consequences of allowing a drunken driver on the public highways, the scales tip heavily in favor of imposition of the duty." (p. 396).

In **Componile v. Maybee**, 641 A.2d 1143 (N.J. Super. L. 1994), an adult guest attended a party where an admission price was charged and alcohol was served. The guest sued to recover for injuries he sustained after being punched and kicked by another party guest. First, the court reemphasized the rule from **Kelly** v. **Gwinnell**, 476 A.2d 1219 (N.J. 1984), that a social host who serves liquor to a guest can be liable for injuries that the guest inflicts on third persons as a result of driving. However, the court did not impose liability in this case because the **Kelly** rule applies only when the guest drives. The court noted:

Sale or Gift to a Minor

Sale or Gift to an Intoxicated Person

Dramshop Liability

Social Host Liability

A social host may only be directly liable to minors and to third persons injured in automobile accidents. A social host is not liable to anyone else injured as a result of the social host's serving of intoxicating beverages to a guest. (p. 1147)

Dower v. Gamba, 647 A.2d 1364 (N.J. Super. A.D. 1994), involved two minors who were injured in an automobile driven by an intoxicated driver. The minors and driver had come from a party where alcohol was available to the guests in a baby pool. The court concluded that although N.J.S.A. 2A:15-5.6a applies to social hosts who "provide" alcohol, this does not require that the host directly serve the alcohol. Therefore, having beer available through a common source such as a baby pool could rise to the level of "providing" alcohol; as a result, liability may be imposed.

Apparently, the New Jersey courts will set a fairly high standard as to what constitutes a host. In **Kollar v. Lozier**, 669 A.2d 845 (N.J. Super. A.D. 1996), the estate of a man who was killed in a motorcycle wreck after being chased by the police sued, among others, his employer. After the company softball game, the decedent and other members of the company became intoxicated at the tavern; this was followed by the police chase that lead to the fatality. The court did not impose liability on the employer because the "employer was not a host within the meaning of the social host liability principles" (p. 851). The employer did not pay for the food, had no control over the alcohol, and it was not a company function.

In addition, in **Brett v. Great American Recreation, Inc.**, 652 A.2d 774 (N.J. Super. A.D. 1995), thirteen college friends, ages 20-21, spent the weekend at a winter resort condominium owned by the uncle of one of the students. Five of the students were seriously injured when they went for a toboggan ride at night. Some of the students were drinking, but the court refused to hold the owner's niece liable because, "there was no evidence that [she] served the beer, much less that she served it to anyone that was visibly intoxicated" (p. 780).

Although the above cited cases did not enforce social host liability, at least one case has held a parent liable for the consequences of a party when the parent was not even at home when the party was held. **Witter by Witter v. Leo**, 635 A.2d 580 (N.J. Super. A.D. 1994), involved a sixteen-year-old who had a party when his mother was out of town. After drinking five beers, a sixteen-year-old guest injured himself when he attempted to jump into the pool from the roof.

In this suit against the mother of the host, the court ruled that

[p]arents have a duty to provide for reasonable supervision of their minor child if it is reasonably foreseeable that, in their absence, the child will invite friends to a beer party at which one of the minor guests will become intoxicated and thereby injure himself. (p. 582)

See also, **Morella v. Machu**, 563 A.2d 881 (N.J. Super. A.D. 1989).

New Mexico

1998 Replacement Pamphlet

Definition of a Minor

The statute which says a minor is a person who is under the age of twenty-one is now codified in N.M.S.A. §60-7B-1.

Possession or Consumption by a Minor

A 1991 amendment to N.M.S.A. §60-7B-10 eliminated the $100 penalty and substituted it with a provision that a violation of this section will be punished pursuant to N.M.S.A. §31-19-1. This same substitution was made in N.M.S.A. §60-70-9.

The statute which makes it unlawful for a minor to buy, attempt to buy, receive or possess alcohol is now codified in N.M.S.A. §60-7B-1 subd. C.

A 1991 amendment states that a violation of N.M.S.A. §60-7B-8 is now a petty misdemeanor.

Misrepresentation of Age

In **Murphy v. Tomada Enterprises, Inc.**, 819 P.2d 1358 (N.M. App. 1991), the estate of a car passenger sued the tavern which served the driver and passenger after they were already intoxicated and were subsequently in an accident. The estate claimed that the tavern was liable under N.M.S.A. 41-11-1(B), New Mexico's Dramshop statute. The tavern claimed that they were not liable because they did not dispense the alcohol to the passenger in a reckless manner. However, the court stated that

Dramshop Liability

> we construe subsection B as relating only to injury to a patron to the extent that it is proximately caused by the patron's own intoxication, not by the intoxication of another patron ... Liability of defendant could be predicated on defendant's serving liquor to [the driver]. (p. 1360)

New York

1999 Cumulative Annual Pocket Part

A 1991 amendment to McKinney's Alcoholic Beverage Control Law §65(1) makes it an affirmative defense for a seller of alcohol to reasonably rely on a college identification card that states that the buyer of alcohol is at least twenty-one-years old.

Sale or Gift to a Minor

Section 65-6 was rewritten and is in effect from January 1, 1999 until January 1, 2002. It is still a violation of the law for a minor to misrepresent his age to purchase alcohol. However, the new law specifies the penalties for each offense. Most interestingly, for third and subsequent violations, not only does the minor have to pay a fine of up to $700 and perform up to thirty hours of community service, but he must also be tested by an appropriate agency for alcoholism.

Misrepresentation of Age

Burkhard v. Sunset Cruises, Inc., 595 N.Y.S.2d 555 (A.D. 2 Dept. 1993), stated that "[e]vidence that a person has consumed alcohol and has the odor of alcohol on his or her breath, is not conclusive proof of intoxication ... since the effect of alcohol may differ greatly from person to person" (p. 555) (quoting **Senn v. Scudieri**, 567 N.Y.S.2d 665 (A.D. 1 Dept. 1991).

Miscellaneous

Numerous Dramshop cases have been reported in the last several years. Many of these cases centered around the issue of whether the person served was visibly intoxicated. In **Romano v. Stanley**, 643 N.Y.S.2d 238 (A.D. 3 Dept. 1996), summary judgment was not granted for a tavern in this Dramshop action because there was not enough evidence that the decedent was not intoxicated. In **Donato v. McLaughlin**, 599 N.Y.S.2d 754 (A.D. 3 Dept. 1993), the tavern was not liable for an accident caused by a driver because the driver was not visibly intoxicated when the tavern served him alcohol.

Dramshop Liability

In **Nehme v. Joseph**, 554 N.Y.S.2d 642 (A.D. 2 Dept. 1990), the plaintiff did not win in this Dramshop action where his wife was killed by a car driven by someone who had become intoxicated at a tavern. The court stated that the plaintiff did not meet its burden of proof because "[i]t is incumbent upon a plaintiff who charges a violation of the Dramshop Act to offer evidence that the party to whom liquor was sold acted or appeared to be intoxicated at the time of the sale" (p. 643).

In **Martinez v. Camardella**, 558 N.Y.S.2d 211 (A.D. 3 Dept. 1990), the court held that a golf course could be liable under Dramshop for injuries that occurred in a car accident after the driver had become intoxicated at a reception at the golf course. Witnesses observed the driver at the five hour reception with a drink in his hand on numerous occasions. Therefore, there was enough evidence for a jury to conclude that he was apparently intoxicated.

Some important decisions have made it known that the alcohol must be directly sold to the subject of the litigation for liability to be imposed. **Sherman v. Robinson**, 591 N.Y.S.2d 974 (Ct. App. 1992), involved a minor who presented false identification to a convenience store and purchased a large quantity of alcohol. Subsequently, he provided alcohol to a minor driver and a minor passenger of a car. After becoming intoxicated, the driver and passenger were seriously injured in a car accident. They sued the convenience store for their injuries, claiming that the store should be liable under common law and Dramshop for the injuries since they indirectly provided the alcohol to the minors who were in the accident. The court disagreed and stated that a prerequisite to liability under McKinney's General Obligations Laws §11-100 and §11-101 is to provide alcohol unlawfully "to that person" (p. 976).

In **Dodge v. Victory Markets, Inc.**, 606 N.Y.S.2d 345 (A.D. 3 Dept. 1993), a group of minors pooled their money together to buy beer. Later, one of the intoxicated minors seriously injured himself in a car accident. In the minor's suit against the seller of beer, he stated several claims. First, the court held that the seller was not liable under common law negligence because "they fall squarely within the age-old rule which precludes recognition of a common law cause of action against providers of alcoholic beverages in favor of persons . . . who are injured as a result of their own voluntary intoxication" (p. 348). Next, the court held that a violation of §65 "does not create a private right of action" (p. 348). Further, the court held that §11-100 and §11-101 "extends only to injuries perpetrated by the *very minor* to whom the unlawful sale or furnishing of alcohol was made" (p. 348).

Stevens v. Spec Inc., 637 N.Y.S.2d 979 (A.D. 3 Dept. 1996), arose from an altercation in a bar where an independent contractor sound system worker struck the plaintiff with a beer bottle. The bar was not liable under Dramshop because the worker was not visibly intoxicated. In addition, the bar was not liable for negligence because "there is no duty to protect against an occurrence which is extraordinary in nature and which, therefore, the restaurant could not reasonably have been expected to anticipate" (p. 981).

In **Beyrle v. Finneron**, 606 N.Y.S.2d 467 (A.D. 4 Dept. 1993), the plaintiff sued a bartender under Dramshop, alleging that the bartender's serving of alcohol contributed to her subsequent injuries. The court disagreed because "there is no reasonable or practical connection between the alleged unlawful sale of alcohol to the patron and plaintiff's resulting injuries" (p. 467).

In another Dramshop action, **Fishman v. Beach**, 625 N.Y.S.2d 730 (A.D. 3 Dept. 1995), the court held that the restaurant's duty to prevent harm from occurring to patrons "was limited to conduct on the premises which it had the opportunity to control and of which it was reasonably aware" (p. 732). Therefore, in this case, the restaurant's duty did not extend to an altercation which occurred at least sixty feet off the premises without some evidence that the restaurant had knowledge of the altercation. In addition, **Strassner v. Saleem**, 594 N.Y.S.2d 559 (Sup. 1993), stated that "it is well-settled that the duty to control or supervise an intoxicated guest does not extend beyond one's premises" (p. 560).

In **Allen v. County of Westchester**, 567 N.Y.S.2d 826 (A.D. 2 Dept. 1991), the wife of a man who was killed after he became intoxicated at a Christmas party filed a claim for wrongful death under Dramshop. The court did not impose liability because the husband simply drank too much at the party and, had he survived, he would not have had a claim for himself. Similarly, **Rann by Rann v. Hamilton**, 599 N.Y.S.2d 51 (A.D. 2 Dept. 1993), stated that "[o]ur courts have declined to impose liability upon dispensers of alcoholic beverages for the injuries caused by voluntarily intoxicated customers" (p. 52).

At least one case has held that a sale is required for actual liability to be imposed. In **Custen v. Salty Dog, Inc.**, 566 N.Y.S.2d 348 (A.D. 2 Dept. 1991), the court held that the restaurant could not be liable under Dramshop for injuries suffered by an employee after she became intoxicated at the restaurant. She did not pay for the alcohol so there was no "sale" as required by §11-101.

Slocum v. D's & Jayes Valley Restaurant, 582 N.Y.S.2d 544 (A.D. 3 Dept. 1992), gave some meaning to the term "procure," which was necessary because a person does not have a claim under Dramshop "where the injured party procured the alcoholic beverage for another whose intoxication caused the accident" (p. 544). In this case, the court held that "procure includes using one's own money to purchase alcohol from another, contributing money to the purchase of alcohol, and giving away alcohol to another after purchasing it with one's own funds" (p. 545).

In **Senn v. Scudieri**, 567 N.Y.S.2d 665 (A.D. 1 Dept. 1991), the plaintiff filed suit under Dramshop for injuries she suffered in a car wreck when riding with a driver who was intoxicated. Her claim failed because there was no enough evidence that the restaurant had violated §65 of the Alcoholic Beverage Control Law when they served the driver alcohol. He neither appeared nor acted intoxicated at the time of the sale.

McCawley v. Carmel Lanes, Inc., 577 N.Y.S.2d 546 (A.D. 3 Dept. 1991), stated that McKinney's Alcoholic Beverage Control Law §11-101(1) allows a plaintiff to recover punitive damages, damages for the loss of future support, and funeral expenses.

Social Host Liability

In **Lane v. Barker,** 660 N.Y.S.2d 194 (A.D. Sup. Ct. 1997), the plaintiff sued the hosts of a party after he was injured by one of the party guests who became intoxicated at the party. The plaintiffs sued the party host and his parents under General Obligations Law §11-100 and common law negligence. First, although the parents knew that minors would be drinking alcohol at the party, the court held that they were not liable under §11-100 because that statute requires a person to "furnish" or "procure" alcohol to be liable. The court did note, however, that their son could be liable because he did furnish and procure the alcohol. As far as the negligence claim, the court held that both the parents and son should be liable because landowners have a duty to act reasonably.

In a similar case, **Rust v. Reyer,** 670 N.Y.S.2d 822 (N.Y. 1998), a minor hosted a party at her house when her parents were out of town. A high school fraternity then convinced her to let them bring kegs of beer to the party and to charge an admission fee which she and the fraternity would share. A party guest who was struck in the face by another guest sued the party host, alleging that she unlawfully furnished alcohol to minors as prohibited by §11-100. Even though the fraternity provided the beer, the court held that the host could still have "furnished" the beer in violation of §11-100 because she chose to participate in the scheme with the fraternity. In short, she should be liable because she played an indispensable role in furnishing the alcohol and was more than just an innocent bystander.

In **Jacobs v. Amodeo**, 618 N.Y.S.2d 120 (A.D. 3 Dept. 1994), the estate of a minor who was killed in his automobile after attending a keg party brought this action under McKinney's General Obligations Laws §11-100 and §11-101. They argued that, although the three kegs were not sold directly to the minor, the large quantity should have been notice to the store that it would be consumed by others who were either minors or intoxicated.

The court disagreed and quoted **Sherman v. Robinson**, that "[n]othing in the General obligations Law imposed upon defendant a duty, merely because a quantity of alcoholic beverages was purchased, to investigate possible ultimate consumers" (p. 121). See also, **Dalrymple v. Southland Corp.**, 609 N.Y.S.2d 284 (A.D. 2 Dept. 1994).

Reickert v. Misciagna, 590 N.Y.S.2d 100 (A.D. 2 Dept. 1992), addressed the issue of whether a parent can be liable under McKinney's General Obligations Law §11-100 when they are not at home but injuries result from underage drinking on their property. This case involved an eighteen-year-old plaintiff who went to a friends house whose parents were away. The minors drank beer, some of which was provided by the plaintiff. He later dove into the pool, hit his head on the bottom, and is now paralyzed.

The court did not hold the host's parents responsible because it was the intent of the legislature in enacting §11-100 that the furnisher of alcohol must be aware of his actions. Since the parents were not aware that underage drinking was going on and they did not furnish the alcohol , they were not liable. Similarly, **MacGilvray v. Denino**, 540 N.Y.S.2d 449 (A.D. 2 Dept. 1989), held that §11-100 "does not encompass liability based upon mere knowledge of alcohol consumption" (p. 450).

In **Cole v. O'Tooles of Utica, Inc.**, 643 N.Y.S.2d 283 (A.D. 4 Dept. 1996), a group of minors purchased and consumed alcohol at a tavern and later at a function sponsored by the fire department. Later that same evening they attended a house party where they contributed money to purchase two kegs of beer. After the party, three minors were in a car wreck, killing two and injuring one.

The court held that the owner of the house where the party occurred was not liable because "he was not at home at the time of the party, that he did not have advance knowledge that the party was going to be held, and that the injuries occurred off the premises under his control" (p. 287). However, there was enough evidence for a claim to be stated against the tavern and festival operator under §11-101.

In **Schrader v. Carney**, 586 N.Y.S.2d 687 (A.D. 4 Dept. 1992), the court held that the language of §11-100(1) "plainly states that any person providing a minor with alcoholic beverages may be held liable" (p. 690). Therefore, since there is no age limitation, a minor could be held liable for providing another minor with alcohol.

Other Cases of Interest In **Smith v. West Rochelle Travel Agency, Inc.**, 656 N.Y.S.2d 340 (N.Y. App. 1997), a seventeen-year-old was killed when he voluntarily jumped off of a cruise ship while on a spring break trip sponsored by a travel agency. The court refused to hold the travel agency liable for the death because, among other reasons, the fact that the minor jumped off the ship was such a superseding and abnormal event that the travel agency should not be held responsible.

In **Oja v. Grand Chapter of Theta Chi Fraternity**, 667 N.Y.S.2d 650 (Sup. Ct. Tompkins County, 1997), a father sued the national chapter of Theta Chi fraternity and individual fraternity members for his son's alcohol related death during a hazing ritual. In this case, the father alleged that as a condition of membership in the fraternity, pledges were commanded to drink liquor at an accelerated rate. During the ritual, Binaya Oja, a fraternity pledge, drank excessive amounts of liquor until he repeatedly vomited in garbage cans placed in the immediate vicinity. He eventually became unconscious, was left unattended by the fraternity members, and died of alcohol poisoning. The father sued the national chapter and individual fraternity members under the state's anti-hazing statute and negligence.

The court initially noted that New York courts generally refuse "'to recognize a common-law cause of action against providers of alcoholic beverages in favor of persons injured as a result of their own voluntary intoxication.'" However, the court refused to dismiss this case and held that there was enough evidence to let a jury decide whether there should be liability. The court stated that if "the evidence shows that the drinking was imposed upon the pledges, and that their obedience was extracted as an express or implied condition of membership," the fraternity would be liable for Oja's death. The court expressed that liability could attach to the fraternity if drinking were found to be a "de facto requirement" of initiation. In other words, if it appears to the jury that drinking was an implied condition of membership, the fraternity could be liable even if drinking was not officially required.

North Carolina

1997 Cumulative Supplement

Possession or Consumption by a Minor

While research did not reveal a statute that specifically forbids the possession or consumption of alcohol by a minor, G.S. §18B-300(a) states that a person twenty-one-years-old or older can purchase, possess, and consume alcohol. Thus, the opposite should be true—a minor should not be allowed to purchase, possess, and consume alcohol.

Dramshop Liability

The North Carolina Dramshop statute requires that an individual must be an "aggrieved party" as defined by the statute in order to recover. The definition of this term under the statute specifically excludes those who "aided or abetted in the sale or furnishing to the underage person." [N.C.G.S. §18B-120]. A North Carolina appellate court addressed what constitutes "aiding and abetting" in the case of **Estate of Darby v. Monroe Oil Co.**, 488 S.E.2d 828 (N.C. App. 1997). The case involved a group of minors who became intoxicated and were killed in a single car crash. Although Darby did not contribute any money to purchase the alcohol, he did drive the group to the convenience store to purchase the alcohol and later allowed one of the intoxicated minors to drive. Thus, the court concluded that Darby's estate could not recover because Darby aided and abetted in the purchase of alcohol so he was not an aggrieved party as defined by the statute.

In **Sorrells v. M.Y.B. Hospitality Ventures**, 435 S.E.2d 320 (N.C. 1993), the court held that it was not "reasonably foreseeable that the plaintiffs would suffer severe emotional distress upon learning that their son had been killed in a one-car accident after he was negligently served alcohol at the defendant's place of business" (p. 321). Consequently, the defendants were not held liable for compensating the plaintiffs for this emotional distress.

Social Host Liability

An important case demonstrated the danger involved when an employer adopts policies that are not properly enforced. **Peal by Peal v. Smith**, 444 S.E.2d 673 (N.C. App. 1994), aff'd, 457 S.E.2d 599 (N.C. 1995), involved a fatal automobile accident which was caused by an employee of a construction company after consuming beer at the work site. Beer was consumed by ten or twelve employees at the worksite with the knowledge of supervisors even though there was a written policy which stated that no person under the influence of alcohol or drugs would be allowed on the site. At trial, the jury found the company and individual liable for $2,250,000. On appeal, the construction company argued that this was a social host liability case and that they were not liable because they did not provide the alcohol.

The court disagreed and said that this was not a social host liability case and held that it was a case of common law negligence. The court stated that "[t]he conduct by the corporation, *in violating its own policy*, provided evidence that the corporation failed to exercise ordinary care to protect plaintiff and her family from the very results that the policy intended to prevent" (p. 679) (*Emphasis added*). Because the corporation knew that beer drinking occurred, this knowledge could provide enough evidence to prove that they did breach a duty.

Hart v. Ivey, 420 S.E.2d 174 (N.C. 1992), arose from an accident that occurred after a group of minors attended a party where they paid $2.00 to drink from the supply of beer that was provided. After the party, an eighteen-year-old crashed his car into another vehicle, causing serious injury to the plaintiff. First, the court held that the hosts of the party were not liable under NCGS §18B-302 because "the purpose of the section is to restrict the consumption of alcohol by those under twenty-one years of age and it was not adopted for the protection of the driving public" (p. 177). *See also,* **Estate of Mullis v. Monroe Oil Co.**, 488 S.E.2d 830 (N.C. App. 1997). However, the court did state that the hosts could be liable under common law negligence because they "were under a duty to the people who travel on the public highways not to serve alcohol to an intoxicated individual who was known to be driving" (p. 178).

Canady v. McLeod, 446 S.E.2d 879 (N.C. App. 1994), involved a roofer who drank alcohol provided to him by the house owner. Subsequently, he fell off the roof and died. The court held that the house owner was not liable because the evidence was not sufficient to show that the house owner was substantially certain that the alcohol would cause injury. In addition, the court found the roofer to have been contributorily negligent.

In **Camalier v. Jeffries**, 460 S.E.2d 133 (N.C. 1995), an employee who consumed alcohol at a company party crashed his car into another vehicle, causing the death of the driver. The host of the party and the company were not liable because there was no evidence that they knew or should have known that the employee was intoxicated.

Other Cases of Interest

In **Wilson by Wilson v. Bellamy**, 414 S.E.2d 347 (N.C. App. 1992), a girl claimed that she was sexually assaulted at a fraternity party on the night she joined her new sorority. Alcoholic beverages were served by the fraternity. Although there was conflicting testimony, the plaintiff claimed that she was sexually assaulted by several members. Among the numerous claims she filed against the fraternity and individual fraternity members, the plaintiff claimed the fraternity was negligent in the management of the party. The court stated that it did not matter if the fraternity was negligent because "the plaintiff admitted that she voluntarily consumed half a bottle of champagne, at least five or six beers, and a shot of Southern Comfort liquor" (pp. 359-360). Because of this behavior, the plaintiff was held to be contributorily negligent as a matter of law and did not prevail on any of her negligence claims.

North Dakota

1997 Pocket Supplement

N.D.C.C. §5-01-08 specifies that minors cannot consume alcoholic beverages other than during a religious service. In addition, a minor cannot be under the influence of alcohol, nor may a minor manufacture alcohol.

Possession or Consumption by a Minor

In **Anderson v. K.S.**, 500 N.W.2d 603 (N.D. 1993), the court held that even though a minor went to a house where she knew alcohol was present and remained at the house for thirty minutes, there was not enough evidence to convict her of unlawful possession of alcohol. Her presence alone, without control over the alcohol, was insufficient. The minor must exercise some degree of control over the alcohol.

In **Zueger v. Carlson,** 542 N.W. 2d 92 (N.D. 1996), the North Dakota Supreme Court held that the Dramshop statute does not eliminate the common law liability of tavern owners. For the first time in North Dakota, the court in this case held that a tavern owner has the duty to protect its patrons from assaults by third persons. The plaintiffs in this case were injured in a fight at a tavern and the court concluded that the tavern may have breached its duty of reasonable care. The fact that the attacker was a violent person who had been involved in previous altercations at the tavern may have made the fight foreseeable. If so, the tavern would be liable.

Dramshop Liability

In **Aanenson v. Bastien**, 438 N.W.2d 151 (N.D. 1989), two friends were served alcohol at a bar and were injured when one crashed his motorcycle into the other. The result was this Dramshop claim by the friend who was hit. The tavern claimed that the plaintiff should not be allowed to recover because he actively contributed to the intoxication of his friend. The court disagreed because "it is the accepted practice of those who find sociability in taverns . . . to take turns purchasing those drinks. That being the likely and customary practice it would seem to defeat the objective of the Dramshop Act" (p. 161).

Born v. Mayers, 514 N.W.2d 687 (N.D. 1994), involved an employee who took a client to a bar where he purchased drinks until the client became intoxicated. Later, at a friend's house, the client punched another man in the face, which eventually caused the man to suffer a stroke. The court concluded that N.D.C.C. §5-01-06.1, the social host liability statute, could apply to the employee and his employer because they provided alcohol to the client after he was intoxicated. According to the statute, a claim is not limited to those who professionally sell alcohol.

Social Host Liability

Ohio

1998 Pocket Part

Sale or Gift to a Minor   **Lape v. Rose**, 621 N.E.2d 173 (Ohio App. 12 Dist. 1993), stated that a party's "intoxicated condition should not automatically disqualify her as one to whom a duty is owed and who is to be protected from injuries and damages caused by the sale of intoxicating beverages to a minor" (p. 715). Thus, the law still places a duty not to sell alcohol to a minor even if the minor is intoxicated.

Dramshop Liability   **Tillett v. Tropicana Lounge & Restaurant**, 610 N.E.2d 453 (Ohio App. 9 Dist. 1991), stated that:

> [a] civil cause of action may be sustained against a liquor permit holder or his employee when 1) a noticeably intoxicated person 2) is knowingly served alcohol, and 3) negligently injures another, 4) away from the premises, 5) as the proximate result of his or her intoxication. (p. 454)

Ohio seems to follow the lead of many other states by not allowing a person to state a Dramshop claim as a result of his or her own voluntary intoxication. **Smith v. The 10th Inning, Inc.**, 551 N.E.2d 1296 (Ohio 1990), involved a tavern patron who was served alcohol and subsequently crashed his car after he became intoxicated. He sued the tavern for serving him the alcohol after he was intoxicated. The court held that:

> [a]n intoxicated person has no cause of action against a liquor permit holder under R.C. §4301.22(B) where the injury, death or property damage sustained by the intoxicated patron off the premises of the permit holder was proximately caused by the patron's own intoxication. (p. 1296)

See also, **Hosom v. Eastland Lanes, Inc.**, 595 N.E.2d 534 (Ohio App. 10 Dist. 1991), for a similar ruling. *See also*, **Fifer v. Buffalo Cafe,** 601 N.E.2d 601 (Ohio App. 6 Dist. 1991).

However, in **Northcutt v. Grilliot,** 1997 WL 464785 (Ohio App. 2 Dist. 1997), an Ohio appellate court held that a minor does have a cause of action against an establishment for injuries caused by his or her own intoxication. The court was careful to stress, however, that they could not predict whether the Ohio Supreme Court would make such a distinction. In fact, other Ohio appellate courts have refused to do so by holding that even minors do not have a cause of action against the provider for their own injuries when they voluntarily become intoxicated. [**Steed v. Chances Entertainment, Inc.,** 1996 WL 488850 (Ohio App. 5 Dist. 1996)].

In **Stillwell v. Johnson**, 602 N.E.2d 1254 (Ohio App. 1 Dist. 1991), two people, one of them sixteen years of age, drank alcohol at a picnic and then subsequently caused an accident, killing a pedestrian. The court held that:

> a permit holder may be liable to third parties injured off the premises by one of its customers if the permit holder knowingly sold an intoxicating beverage in violation of R.C. §4301.69(A), prohibiting the sale of beer or intoxicating liquor to an underage person. (p. 1257)

Thus, the sponsors of the picnic could be liable for their actions.

Cummins v. Rubio, 622 N.E.2d 700 (Ohio App. 2 Dist. 1993), was a lawsuit filed against a tavern customer and owner for injuries sustained by a patron from a knife fight in the parking lot. The court refused to impose liability on the tavern because it had no ownership interest in the shopping center parking lot and thus, no right to control. Further, there was not enough evidence that the tavern served the patron when he was visibly intoxicated, a necessity under the Ohio Dramshop law.

In **Horwath v. Smith,** 683 N.E.2d 846 (Ohio App. 1996), an Ohio appellate court refused to hold a social host liable when he provided alcohol to his fiance who later intentionally caused injuries to the plaintiff. The court noted that public policy says that the one who consumes the alcohol must be primarily responsible for his or her own behavior.

Social Host Liability

In **Stevens v. United Auto Workers, Local 1112,** 673 N.E.2d 930 (Ohio App. 1996), a car passenger who suffered injuries in an accident that was caused by a driver who had consumed alcohol at a union fundraiser brought this action against union members. Although there was alcohol available at the fundraiser, the court refused to hold the union liable because there was no evidence that the union actually sold or served alcohol to the driver who caused the accident.

In **Williams v. Veterans of Foreign Wars**, 650 N.E.2d 175 (Ohio App. 2 Dist. 1994), a minor who drank keg beer provided at a wedding reception sued the hosts of the reception and the establishment for injuries he sustained in a car accident. The court stated that "one who consumes beer without the express or implied permission of either owner, or the social host providing the beer to guests, has not been furnished the beer within the contemplation of R.C. §4301.69(A)" (p. 178).

In **Huston v. Konieczny**, 556 N.E.2d 505 (Ohio 1990), a minor attended a New Years Eve party at the home of a friend whose parents were out of town but had given him permission to have people over to the house. The minor filed this lawsuit for injuries he sustained when another intoxicated minor from the party crashed into his automobile. The court held that there was enough evidence so that a jury may find the parents liable because the parents gave permission for the gathering, they knew or should have known that alcohol would be present, and there was no parental supervision. Thus, this case sends a strong signal that adults should be wary of giving minors permission to have social gatherings out of their presence.

Prest v. Delta Delta Delta Sorority, 686 N.E.2d 293 (Ohio App. 1996), was a case where a twenty-year-old college student attended a "Derby" party at the Sigma Chi fraternity at Ohio State University. He and a member of Delta Delta Delta sorority left the party in an intoxicated state and then went to the Delta Delta Delta house where they snuck up on the rooftop. At approximately 4:00 a.m., the young man had fallen asleep and he rolled off the roof where he fell to his death. His estate brought this wrongful death action against the local and national chapters of Delta Delta Delta and Sigma Chi. However, the case was dismissed because a national office has no duty to control the actions of the local chapter. Further, the local groups were not liable because a rooftop is an "open and obvious" danger so it did not require the fraternity to warn about the danger that it carries with it.

Other Cases of Interest

In **Malone v. Miami University,** 625 N.E.2d 640 (Ohio App. 1993), a Miami employee went to lunch with his supervisors and the employee consumed alcohol at the lunch. That afternoon, he continued to consume alcohol at work although his supervisors were unaware of this. When he clocked out he appeared to be intoxicated, and after he refused his supervisor's offer to drive him home, he drove himself and crashed his car into the plaintiff. The plaintiff sued Miami University, but the court refused to impose liability. Specifically, the court held that employers do not "have a duty to protect an employee who has become intoxicated, without encouragement or assistance from his employer, against the likelihood that he will have an automobile collision on the way home from work." (p. 642).

Oklahoma
1999 Cumulative Annual Pocket Part

Sale of Gift to an Intoxicated Person

In **Ohio Casualty Insurance Co. v. Todd,** 813 P.2d 508 (Okl. 1991), the plaintiff sued a tavern for injuries he incurred in a one car accident after he was served alcohol at the tavern. The plaintiff argued that the tavern should be civilly liable because they served alcohol to him after the point of intoxication as prohibited by 537(A)(2). However, the court refused to impose liability because the legislature did not intend for 537(A)(2) "to protect the intoxicated adult who, by his own action, causes injury to himself." (p. 510). Oklahoma law only protects innocent third parties who are injured as a result of a tavern serving an intoxicated patron. [*See* **Brigance v. Velvet Dove Restaurant,** 725 P.2d 300 (Okl. 1986)]. The court also held that the tavern was also not liable under common law because "the duty of the tavern does not extend to an adult customer who voluntarily consumes intoxicants and is injured." (p. 510).

Dramshop Liability

Under Oklahoma Dramshop law, whether alcohol is served to a minor or an adult is a critical distinction to make. In **Busby v. Quail Creek Golf & Country Club**, 885 P.2d 1326 (Okl. 1994), an eighteen-year-old attended a party at a country club where almost all of those in attendance were minors. All guests were checked for identification, and those who were of legal drinking age were marked with an "X" on the back of their hands. Apparently, the plaintiff was marked with an unauthorized marker, and thus, gave the impression that she was of legal drinking age. After consuming alcohol, she fell off a second floor balcony and was seriously injured. Her blood alcohol content was .21. Even though she violated the law by illegally purchasing alcohol, the court held that the country club could be liable for her injuries. The court noted:

> The fact that the minor violated the law when purchasing or consuming beer does not prevent a cause of action because as between the seller and the minor, it is the seller who is the responsible party in the action. (p. 1334) "Minors are incompetent . . . to deal responsibly with the effects of alcohol" (p. 1334).

See also, **Mansfield v. Circle K Corp.**, 877 P.2d 1130 (Okl. 1994).

Esther v. Wiemer, 859 P.2d 1140 (Okl. App. 1993), reemphasized the rule in **Ohio Casualty Ins. Co. v. Todd**, 813 P.2d 508 (Okl. 1991), "that a tavern owner's duty does not extend to an adult customer who voluntarily becomes intoxicated and is injured" (p. 1142).

In **Grantham v. Tulsa Club, Inc.**, 918 P.2d 410 (Okl. App. 1996), a guest at a company Christmas party became intoxicated at the party and crashed his car, killing himself and seriously injuring the plaintiffs. The court refused to hold the club, where the party was held, liable under Dramshop "because there was no evidence that [the driver] was noticeably intoxicated when [the club] served alcohol to him" (p. 412).

Tomlinson v. Love's County Stores, Inc., 854 P.2d 910 (Okl. 1993), said that a commercial vendor could be liable for selling beer to minors that is consumed off the premises. In this case, the court held that the seller of alcohol could be liable for an accident involving three minors who drank beer while driving around the town. However, the duty not to sell alcohol to minors may be rebutted if the seller reasonably believed that the buyer was of legal drinking age after checking his identification.

In **Sanders v. Crosstown Market, Inc.**, 850 P.2d 1061 (Okl. 1993), a sixteen-year-old bought beer from a grocery store for guests at a party he was hosting at his parent's home. A seventeen-year-old drank the beer, became intoxicated, and crashed her car. She claimed that the grocery store was liable because selling beer to the sixteen-year-old was negligence per se because they knew he was a minor. The court refused to impose liability on the grocery store because the injury was "so remote from the sale of beer . . . as to prevent her from being within the class [Oklahoma law] was designed to protect" (p. 1063).

Social Host Liability

In **Kellogg v. Ohler**, 825 P.2d 1346 (Okl. 1992), the plaintiffs tried to recover from parents when an accident occurred after a gathering with alcohol at their home while they were away on vacation. The court did not even address the issue of social host liability on the parents because "[i]n order to be considered a social host some degree of control is necessary" (p. 1348). In this case, the parents were out of town and did not even know about the gathering. Further, the minor who was staying at the house and who had purchased the alcohol was not liable because he had no control over who drank the alcohol or how much of it that they drank. Even though the court did not address the issue of social host liability, three justices indicated that there is no social host liability in Oklahoma. In the subsequent case of **Battles v. Cough,** 947 P.2d 600 (Okl. Civ. App. 1997), an Oklahoma appellate court specifically stated that "Oklahoma has not adopted social host liability." (602)

Oregon
1998 Supplement

The maximum fine for violating ORS §161.635 has been raised from $500 to $1,000.

Misrepresentation of Age

ORS §472.310 was repealed in 1995. However, §471.410(1) continues to make it unlawful to provide alcohol to a visibly intoxicated person.

Sale or Gift to an Intoxicated Person

In **Fulmer v. Timber Inn Restaurant and Lounge,** 954 P.2d 201 (Ore. App. 1998), a plaintiff who was injured after he was served substantial amounts of alcohol argued that the establishment who served him was negligent per se under §471.410(1). However, the court rejected this argument because it had already been rejected by the Oregon Supreme Court in a prior case. [See **Hawkins v. Conklin,** 767 P.2d 66 (Ore. 1988)].

Some Oregon cases have noted that the intent of the Dramshop law is not to give claims to individuals injured as a result of their own intoxication. In **Plattner v. VIP's Industries, Inc.**, 768 P.2d 440 (Ore. App. 1989), the court held that "the legislative history of ORS §30.950 indicates that its purpose is to confine the judicially created liability of alcohol servers to third parties" (p. 442). *See also*, **Hunt v. Evenhoff**, 829 P.2d 1051 (Ore. App. 1992).

Dramshop Liability

Fugate v. Safeway Stores, Inc., 897 P.2d 328 (Ore. App. 1995), stated that in a negligence action, the plaintiff has the burden of proving that a beer seller's negligent sale to the party who caused the accident "was a substantial factor in causing her injuries" (p. 331). However, it does not have to be the only cause. The "substantial factor" rule was applied in **Smith v. Harms**, 865 P.2d 486 (Ore. App. 1993), where four minors who were socializing together decided to buy some beer. The plaintiff and another of the minors went into the store to purchase the beer and were not asked to produce identification. After drinking the beer, the plaintiff crashed his car and is now a paraplegic. The court held that the plaintiff did not have a negligence claim against the store because he illegally purchased the beer which was deemed to be a substantial factor in the cause of the accident.

Other Cases of Interest

Sparks v. Warren, 856 P.2d 337 (Ore. 1993), was an action brought against Sigma Chi Fraternity and the University of Oregon for an assault by one of its members. The defendant drank several beers at the fraternity house that were provided to him by an older member of the fraternity. Later that evening, he assaulted the plaintiff. The plaintiff claimed that the fraternity was negligent for several reasons, including lack of supervision of the party and providing alcohol to minors. The court ruled for the fraternity because the plaintiff did not prove that the assault that occurred was a foreseeable risk.

Pennsylvania

1998 Cumulative Annual Pocket Part

Sale or Gift to a Minor

Some interesting cases have arisen in this area. **Conner v. Duffy**, 652 A.2d 372 (Pa. Super. 1994), held that: "[i]n order for an injured plaintiff to recover for a violation of 47 P.S. §4-493, he must prove that: 1) the tortfeasor was served alcoholic beverages while visibly intoxicated; and 2) this violation of the statue proximately caused his injuries" (p. 373). *See also*, **McDonald v. Marriott Corp.**, 564 A.2d 1296 (Pa. Super. 1989).

In **Com v. Tau Kappa Epsilon**, 609 A.2d 791 (Pa. 1992), arose when an undercover member of the State College Bureau of Police Services investigated eleven off-campus fraternity houses to determine if minors were being served alcohol. At the trial, the fraternities were convicted of 47 P.S. §4-493(1), the statute which forbids serving alcohol to minors. However, these convictions were overturned "because the Commonwealth failed to prove beyond a reasonable doubt that the beverages contained one half of one percent or more of alcohol by volume," (p. 793) as required by law.

In **Herr v. Booten**, 580 A.2d 1115 (Pa. Super. 1990), the estate of a college student who died of acute ethanol poisoning with a blood alcohol content of .64 sued the decedent's roommates for furnishing the alcohol. The court held that even though the alcohol was provided to the decedent on the eve of his twenty-first birthday, the actions of the roommates still amounted to negligence per se. Further, the court held that the roommates may be held liable for failing to exercise reasonable care to prevent the decedent from suffering further harm after he consumed the alcohol.

Dramshop Liability

Reilly v. Tiergarten Inc., 633 A.2d 208 (Pa. Super. 1993), began when the minor plaintiff purchased alcohol from several establishments. Later that evening, he was in an argument with his father and chased him with a knife. When the police arrived, he refused to give up the knife and eventually was shot in the abdomen and the pelvis. The plaintiff then filed this Dramshop action against the establishments that had served him the alcohol. Although there is a duty to not sell alcohol to minors and the establishments involved in this case breached this duty, the court held that they were not negligent because the knife attack and the subsequent shooting "were not the natural and probable results of [the defendant's] failure to comply with the Dramshop Act" (p. 210). Therefore, because adequate cause was not established, the court concluded that there could not be negligence.

Also, in **Johnson v. Harris**, 615 A.2d 771 (Pa. Super. 1992), the owners of a drinking establishment were not liable under Dramshop for injuries caused by one of their patrons because there was no evidence that the patron was served alcoholic beverages while she was visibly intoxicated. *See Also*, **Hiles v. Brandywine Club**, 662 A.2d 16 (Pa. Super. 1995) (holding that patron must be visibly intoxicated for recovery under Dramshop). **Detwiler v. Brumbaugh**, 656 A.2d 944 (Pa. Super. 1995), held that employees of a licensed establishment may be held liable under Dramshop.

In **Holpp v. Fez, Inc.**, 656 A.2d 147 (Pa. Super. 1995), a police officer sued a tavern for injuries he sustained when he went to the tavern on a call to assist with an altercation that had broken out at the tavern. First, the court held that the police officer could not recover because Pennsylvania follows the "fireman's rule," which states that a police officer or fireman cannot recover from the owner of land from injuries sustained in connection with official duties. Second, the tavern was not liable under Dramshop because the plaintiff could not identify the patrons who were served alcohol after the point of intoxication.

In **Kapres v. Heller**, 640 A.2d 888 (Pa. 1994), a nineteen-year-old college student who was struck by a car after he became intoxicated brought this social host liability action against the hosts of the parties where he was served alcohol. The court held that the minor party hosts could not be held liable under a theory of social host liability because "one minor does not owe a duty to another minor regarding the furnishing or consumption of alcohol" (p. 891).

Social Host Liability

Goldberg v. Delta Tau Delta, 613 A.2d 1250 (Pa. Super. 1992) arose out of the stabbing death of a college student. The decedent, a student at Robert Morris College, went to the campus of Carnegie Mellon University to visit a friend. A third friend joined them and they proceeded to drink alcohol and smoke marijuana together. After leaving a fraternity party, where they had consumed more alcohol, the "third friend" stabbed the decedent. The court held that the friend could not be liable under a social host liability theory because he was a minor. Even if he could be found liable, he did not contribute to the intoxication enough for it to be considered a "substantial factor" in the furnishing of the alcohol to a minor. This "substantial factor" element was part of the test for social host liability set out in **Jeffries v. Commonwealth**, 537 A.2d 355 (Pa. Super. 1988).

In **Orner v. Mallick**, 639 A.2d 491 (Pa. Super. 1994), a minor who became intoxicated after being served alcohol at several graduation parties brought this action to recover for serious injuries he sustained when he fell down a hotel ramp. The court did not impose liability because the minor did not establish that the host's breach of duty by serving alcohol to a minor was the cause of the injuries.

Booker v. Lehigh University, 800 F. Supp. 234 (E.D. Pa. 1992), was a case where the university was alleged to have assumed a

Other Cases of Interest

duty when it enacted a comprehensive social policy for student organizations. In this case, a nineteen-year-old Lehigh sophomore sued the university after she injured herself while walking home after attending a series of fraternity parties where she was served excessive amounts of alcohol. Lehigh had implemented a social policy which required several things for a party host to do before hosting a party. For instance, the host was responsible for ensuring that only those twenty-one years of age and older were served alcohol; the host had to hire security guards to check I.D.'s; and the host had to register each party with the university, although the registration form specifically stated that the registration did not constitute university approval.

Among other things, the plaintiff argued that the university undertook a duty to protect minors by implementing the social policy and they failed in this duty because many fraternities did not comply with the policy. The court found in favor of the university and noted that the policy was nothing more than a list of guidelines that the university wanted the fraternities to follow. The terms of the policy placed the responsibility for compliance on the fraternities and it specifically said that it did not constitute approval by the university.

A similar case was decided by the Superior Court of Pennsylvania. In **Millard v. Osborne,** 611 A.2d 715 (Pa. 1992), the court refused to hold the college liable for the death of a student who became intoxicated at a fraternity party just because the college had a specific alcohol policy. The court noted that "[a] college may not 'control' the behavior of its students as may have been possible in the past." (p. 721).

Rhode Island

1997 Pocket Supplement

Misrepresentation of Age

In 1989, the Rhode Island legislature enacted G.L. §3-8-6.2, which provides that a person may not use an identification card in an unlawful manner. Among other things, a person may not "knowingly permit any unlawful use of his or her Rhode Island identification card." [G.L. §3-8-6.2(6)]. Nor may a person "aid or assist another to fraudulently obtain a Rhode Island identification card." [G.L. §3-8-6.2(7)]. Any violation of this section constitutes a misdemeanor.

Dramshop Liability

In **Smith v. Tully**, 665 A.2d 1333 (R.I. 1994), a police officer who responded to a call to seize an intoxicated patron at a tavern, sued the tavern for injuries he sustained in an altercation with the patron. The court held that the police officer could not recover because Rhode Island follows the common law rule that police officers cannot recover in this situation because it is their job to assume these types of risks. Even though G.L. §3-14-7-(2) provides that a defendant "who recklessly serves liquor to a visibly intoxicated individual is liable for damages proximately caused by that individual's consumption of the liquor," the court held that G.L. §3-14-9 allows common law defenses in Dramshop actions. Since the "policeman's rule" is a common law defense, the police officer was not allowed to recover.

Social Host Liability

Two important cases decided by the Supreme Court of Rhode Island suggest that Rhode Island will not likely judicially impose social host liability in the near future. The language of the opinions clearly indicate that the court will defer to the legislature to make that decision should they choose to do so.

Ferreira v. Strack, 652 A.2d 965 (R.I. 1995), was the first time the Rhode Island Supreme Court addressed the concept of social host liability and whether a host owes a duty to an innocent third party who was injured as a result of a guest's intoxication. This case involved some pedestrians who, on Christmas Eve, were injured by a drunk driver who had attended a party at the home of the defendants. The driver, who had consumed a substantial amount of alcohol before he attended the party, was not officially invited but had heard about the party through word of mouth. Apparently, he was not served alcohol at the party but he did help himself to a beer from the refrigerator.

The court held that if Rhode Island were to recognize social host liability, it was the duty of the legislature to adopt it. Since there is no statutory social host liability in Rhode Island, the court held that the hosts had no duty to protect the pedestrians. Further, the court believed that the driver was not even considered a social guest in this situation. Since he was not invited to the gathering, his status was more like a trespasser. However, even if we was an official social guest, since Rhode Island does not recognize social host liability, the court refused to hold the hosts' liable.

In **Vater v. HB Group**, 667 A.2d 283 (R.I. 1995), some party guests sued the party host for injuries they sustained in a car accident after the party. The court did not impose liability on the host of the party because Rhode Island "has never adopted social host liability" (p. 283). Further, the court stated that it "declines to adopt the doctrine of social host liability at this time" (p. 283).

South Carolina

1997 Pocket Part

Possession or Consumption by a Minor

Code §20-7-370 was repealed in 1996. In addition, Code §20-7-380 was also repealed. However, Code §20-7-8920 and §20-7-8925 which became effective July 1, 1996, make it illegal for a minor to purchase or possess alcohol.

Sale or Gift to a Minor

The following changes in codification became effective on January 1, 1997:
   Former Code §61-13-290 now codified as Code 61-6-4080.
   Former Code §61- 9-40(A) now codified as Code §61-4-50.
   Former Code §61-9-410 now codified as Code §61-4-580.

In **Norton v. Opening Break of Aiken, Inc.**, 462 S.E.2d 861 (S.C. 1995), a tavern allowed one of its employees to use the premises for a party after the tavern was closed. A minor brought beer to the party and drank it along with some alcohol that was provided to him at the party. That evening, the minor was in a car accident which killed the driver of the other car. The decedent's estate sued the tavern, alleging that they violated the statute which prevents minors from drinking alcohol in a licensed premises. The court held that the tavern's violation of the statute constituted negligence per se. Similarly, **Whitlaw v. Kroger Co.**, 410 S.E.2d 251 (S.C. 1991), held that:

   §§61-9-40 and 61-9-410 give rise to civil liability if the plaintiff
   can establish negligence per se. After establishing negligence per

se, the plaintiff must then prove that the violation of the statute was causally linked, both in fact, and proximately, to the injury. (p. 253)

This same analysis was reemphasized in **Steele v. Rogers**, 413 S.E.2d 329 (S.C. App. 1992), where the court held that there was enough evidence to send the case to the jury. In **Steele**, a minor was accidentally shot in the leg when he and his friends were drinking alcohol they had purchased from an establishment. The court held that whether this injury was a foreseeable result of selling beer to minors was a jury question.

In **Jamison v. The Pantry, Inc.**, 392 S.E.2d 474 (S.C. App. 1990), the court held that there was enough evidence to send this case to the jury where a convenience store sold beer to some minors and the driver was killed in a car wreck after he became intoxicated. The court, in determining there was enough evidence to send it to the jury, noted:

> It was reasonably foreseeable that a nineteen-year-old who was sold a case of beer by a convenience store in violation of statutes would consume a portion of the beer, would become intoxicated, would drive an automobile, would collide with another vehicle, and would injure or kill someone. (p. 477)

Jamison was referred to by the court in **Daley v. Ward**, 399 S.E.2d 13 (S.C. App. 1990). In **Daley**, the court held that a purpose of the statute which makes it unlawful to serve alcohol to an intoxicated person "is to protect not only the individual served in violation of the statute, but also the public at large, from the possible adverse consequences" (p. 15). Thus, an innocent third party injured as a result of a tavern serving an intoxicated person has a cause of action.

Misrepresentation of Age

The statutes pertaining to this section can now be found in Code §20-7-8925 and §61-4-60.

Miscellaneous

The former Code §61-5-20, which makes it unlawful to transport liquor in the passenger compartment of a car if the seal has been broken, is now codified as Code §61-6-4020. The former Code §61-9-87, which says that beer and wine may never be transported in open containers in an automobile, is now codified as Code §61-4-110. The former Code §61-5-30, which says it is unlawful to possess or consume alcohol on a premises where the owner has forbidden it, is now codified as Code §61-6-4710.

Sale or Gift to an Intoxicated Person

The statutes pertaining to this section can now be found in Code §61-4-580, §61-6-1500, and § 61-6-2220.

Ever since the case of **Christiansen v. Campbell,** 328 S.E.2d 351 (S.C. App. 1985), South Carolina courts have allowed an intoxicated person to recover from a tavern for injuries if the tavern served him after he was intoxicated. However, the Supreme Court of South Carolina overruled **Christiansen** in **Tobias v. Sports Club, Inc.,** 504 S.E.2d 318 (S.C. 1998). South Carolina joined the majority of jurisdictions by holding that "South Carolina does not recognize a first party cause of action against the tavern owner by an intoxicated adult predicated on an alleged violation of S.C. Code Ann. §§[61-6-2220 and 61-4-580(2)]." (p. 319).

The rationale for this is that "public policy is not served by allowing the intoxicated adult patron to maintain a suit for injuries which result from his own conduct." (p. 320). However, the intoxicated patron may still bring a negligence claim against the tavern which the tavern may defend by asserting defenses such as comparative negligence and assumption of risk.

In **Crolley v. Hutchins**, 387 S.E.2d 716 (S.C. App. 1989), a bar patron consumed at least four drinks at the tavern. When he tried to order another drink, he was refused service because of his intoxicated state. He subsequently caused such a commotion that the police came and arrested him for disorderly conduct. That night he attempted to hang himself in the jail cell and suffered brain damage as a result. His blood alcohol content was .272%. He claimed that the tavern was negligent per se for violating the statute which makes it unlawful to serve alcohol to an intoxicated person.

The court refused to impose liability because the attempted suicide was too remote of an event to hold the tavern liable. In a negligence action, proximate cause is one of the four necessary elements and it was not present in this case.

South Dakota

1998 Pocket Supplement

In 1990, SDCL 35-9-1.1 was enacted. This statute makes it a class 2 misdemeanor to sell or give alcohol to a person between 18-21 years-of-age unless it is in the presence of a parent or guardian or for medical purposes.

Sale or Gift to a Minor

In 1991, SDCL 35-9-1.2 was enacted. This states that any person charged with violating SDCL 35-9-1 or SDCL 35-9-1.1 can offer as a defense that they made a reasonable attempt to verify the minor's age.

As a result of a 1990 amendment, a class 2 misdemeanor is now punishable by a fine of $200 or 30 days in jail, or both.

Sale or Consumption by a Minor

In **Wildboer v. South Dakota Junior Chamber of Commerce,** 561 N.W.2d 666 (S.D. 1997), the Harrisburg chapter of the South Dakota Chamber of Commerce sponsored a "poker" charity event which required participants to visit various taverns where they received a playing card at each one. Two of the participants drank alcohol at some of the taverns and were subsequently in a car crash which killed them both and severely injured and disfigured the fifteen-year-old driver of the other vehicle. The fifteen-year-old's parents sued the South Dakota Chamber of Commerce and the taverns. First, the court held that the South Dakota Chamber of Commerce was not liable because it was the local chamber of commerce which planned the event. As for the taverns, the court held they were not liable because §35-4-78 clearly states that "there is no civil liability to sellers of alcoholic beverages for the furnishing of alcoholic beverages to persons who are 'obviously intoxicated.'" (p. 671).

Dramshop Liability

On remand, the South Dakota Supreme Court in **Baatz v. Arrow Bar**, 452 N.W.2d 138 (S.D. 1990), held that there would be no liability imposed on the tavern or its employees. The facts of this case can be found in *Alcohol on Campus, 1990 Update.*

Tennessee

1998 Supplement

T.C.A. §39-6-929 has been repealed. However, it is still unlawful for an adult to furnish or buy alcohol for a minor under §57-5-301(d)(2).

Sale or Gift to a Minor

Miscellaneous	T.C.A. §39-6-905, which made it unlawful "for any person to buy for another any intoxicating liquor from any person," has been repealed.
Dramshop Liability	In **Larue v. Lake Incorporated,** 966 S.W.2d 423 (Tenn. App. 1997), a Tennessee appellate court construed that for §57-10-102 to apply, the plaintiff has the burden to prove beyond a reasonable doubt that the defendant "sold" alcohol to a minor or intoxicated person. Thus, if there is not conclusive evidence that alcohol was "sold," there is no liability. In addition, the court noted that when the defendant argues the defense of comparative negligence, it is usually best to let the jury decide what percentage each party is negligent.

In **Cook v. Spinnaker's of Rivergate, Inc.**, 878 S.W.2d 934 (Tenn. 1994), a minor sued the restaurant that served her alcohol for injuries she sustained in a car accident after leaving the restaurant. The court held that the restaurant was negligent per se since they violated the Tennessee statute that makes it illegal to sell alcohol to a minor or a person who is visibly intoxicated. In addition, if the restaurant wanted to use the defense of contributory negligence, they had to prove the minor's negligence was the proximate cause of her injuries.

Kirksey v. Overton Pub, Inc., 804 S.W.2d 68 (Tenn. App. 1990), involved a twenty-seven-year-old who died as a result of a bet with a friend that he could not consume ten "Zombie" alcoholic drinks in 1 hour. After consuming the drinks, his friends brought him to an apartment where he died the next morning of acute alcohol intoxication.

First, the court held that the friend who made the bet with him could not be liable under 57-4-203 (the statute which makes it unlawful for a vendor to sell alcohol to an intoxicated person) because the legislature only intended that the tavern be liable for serving alcohol to visibly intoxicated patrons. The bettor would not be liable even if he had conspired with the bar to serve stronger drinks. Further, the court held that the bettor was not responsible for the decedent's condition after he became intoxicated. In addition, the court held that the jury was able to take into consideration the fact that the decedent had been smoking marijuana. Finally, the court held that the defendant could use assumption of risk and contributory negligence as defenses.

In **Worley v. Weigels**, 919 S.W.2d 589 (Tenn. 1996), the parents of a minor who was injured in a car wreck while riding with an intoxicated driver sued the store which sold the beer consumed by the minor driver. Neither of the minors purchased the beer. The court held that "[s]ince the purchaser in this case did not consume the beverages purchased, the accident was not caused by purchaser's consumption of the beverage. Therefore, there is no liability on the seller" (p. 593). As far as the store selling the alcohol to the minor who provided the alcohol to the accident victims, the court found no liability under the Dramshop statute because "an action will not lie against a seller of intoxicating beverages unless it is proved beyond a reasonable doubt that the seller knew that the purchaser was a minor and sold intoxicating beverages to him or her anyway" (p. 593).

In **Rollins v. Winn Dixie**, 780 S.W.2d 765 (Tenn. App. 1989), a group of minors purchased alcohol from two establishments and became intoxicated while driving around the town. Subsequently, they were in an accident which killed the driver and some of passengers. A surviving passenger and deceased passenger's estate filed this suit against Winn Dixie and Pal's Package Store for serving alcohol to minors. The court held that the plaintiffs were familiar with the use of alcohol and with its effects on a person's ability to drive and that they were aware that [the driver] was intoxicated shortly before the accident. Therefore, their decision to continue to ride with [the driver] was contributory negligence which, as a matter of law, prevents them from recovering against either Winn Dixie or Pal's Package Store. (p. 769)

McIntyre v. Balentine, 833 S.W.2d 52 (Tenn. 1992) arose out of an automobile accident as a result of a motorist's consumption of alcohol. The court held that Tennessee used the modified comparative fault system. Under this system, a negligent plaintiff may still recover so long as the plaintiff's negligence was less than the defendant's negligence.

Texas

1999 Cumulative Annual Pocket Part

A 1997 amendment to §106.02 says that a minor who has been convicted of violating this section three times is subject to a fine of between $250 and $2,500, a maximum of 180 days in jail, or both. In addition, the minor can be required to perform community service. Regardless if the minor has a prior conviction under this section, his license may be suspended.

Possession or Consumption by a Minor

A 1993 amendment to V.T.C.A. Alcoholic Beverage Code §106.06(a) removed "knowingly" and added an element of "with criminal negligence." Now it reads that "a person commits an offense if he purchases an alcoholic beverage for or gives or makes available an alcoholic beverage to a minor with criminal negligence."

In a 1993 amendment to V.T.C.A. Alcoholic Beverage Code §106.13 the legislature substituted "with criminal negligence" for "knowingly."

Sale or Gift to a Minor

The same penalties listed in "Possession or Consumption by a Minor" also apply to violations of this section.

Misrepresentation of Age

Venetoulias v. O'Brien, 909 S.W.2d 236 (Tex. App. Houston 14th Dist. 1995), involved a woman who was at a bar with some friends. While at the bar, the president of the bar's holding company said he would make sure the woman got a ride home if she would agree to drink with him. The woman agreed and subsequently consumed approximately fifteen drinks and became visibly intoxicated. After refusing to go to a party with the president, he put her in her car and placed her keys, which he had been holding, in the ignition. She proceeded to drive and was in an accident. The jury found the president and the company liable for $57,500 in actual and punitive damages. This verdict was upheld on appeal, in large measure because the bar violated the Dramshop law by serving her after the point of intoxication. In addition, the president did not exercise reasonable care by putting her in the car and placing the keys in the ignition while she was intoxicated.

Dramshop Liability

The doctrine of comparative fault is used in Texas. Basically, this doctrine compares the plaintiff's negligence with that of the defendant. If the plaintiff is more than fifty percent at fault, he cannot recover. Two important cases give a good example of how the doctrine works and the exception to the doctrine that is applied in cases involving punitive damages. **Smith v. Sewell**, 858 S.W.2d 350 (Tex. 1993), held that an individual who is provided alcohol in violation of the Dramshop law and is injured may have a cause of action against the provider of the alcohol. This is a departure from the historical rule that a person who voluntarily becomes intoxicated cannot sue for his own injuries. The rationale for this is that the Dramshop Act is premised on the alcohol provider's conduct—not the conduct of the recipient or third party. Therefore, an individual can recover for his own injuries arising from his voluntary intoxication. However, the court did hold that this recovery is limited by the Comparative Responsibility Act under §33.011. "Thus, an intoxicated person suing a provider of alcoholic beverages for his own injuries under Ch. 2 will be entitled to recover damages only if his percentage of responsibility is found to be less than or equal to fifty percent" (p. 356).

I-Gotcha, Inc. v. McInnis, 903 S.W.2d 829 (Tex. App. Fort Worth 1995), involved a minor who was served alcohol at a topless bar without showing identification and who subsequently was killed while driving under the influence. The jury awarded damages of $225,000 to each parent and $30,000 to her surviving brother. In addition, $1,500,000 in punitive damages were awarded to the parents and $30,000 in punitive damages were awarded to the brother. The verdict was upheld on appeal because there was sufficient evidence for a jury to conclude that the bar served minors and did not act responsibly. The court also held that the principles of comparative fault do not apply to a claim for punitive damages although it does apply to a Dramshop claim.

The meaning of the term "provider" as stated in the Dramshop Act was given some meaning in **Moore v. Shoreline Ventures, Inc.**, 903 S.W.2d 900 (Tex. App. Beaumont 1995). In this case, the court held that a tavern that permitted an intoxicated person to use its restroom, but did not provide him with any of the alcohol that lead to his intoxication, could not be liable under Dramshop for injuries the driver caused in a subsequent wreck. The tavern was not a "provider" of alcohol as required by the statute.

The Texas Supreme Court, in **Southland Corp. v. Lewis**, 940 S.W.2d 83 (Tex. 1997), addressed the issue of

> whether a community provider of alcoholic beverages can be liable for injuries allegedly caused by an intoxicated driver when the producer sold alcohol to a passenger in the vehicle and the driver did not purchase or consume any of the alcohol. (p. 84)

This case involved a driver who had consumed alcohol, then he drove his passenger to a convenience store to buy additional alcohol. Shortly thereafter, the driver caused an accident. The court refused to impose Dramshop liability on the convenience store because

> [c]hapter 2 imposes liability only when a provider serves alcohol to an obviously intoxicated individual, and the intoxication of that individual proximately causes harm . . . Under this standard, the sale of alcohol to a passenger cannot be the cause in fact of an accident unless the passenger caused the accident by interfering with the operation of the car. (p. 85)

In **Donnell v. Spring Sports, Inc.**, 920 S.W.2d 378 (Tex. App. Houston 1st Dist. 1996), a softball player who was severely injured in a fight with the opposing team sued the softball park for his injuries. First, the court held that the park was not negligent in not providing security guards because their presence probably would not have prevented the fight since it happened so quickly. In addition, the court refused to hold that the park was negligent per se for serving alcohol to obviously intoxicated adults.

In **Pena v. Neal, Inc.**, 901 S.W.2d 663 (Tex. App. San Antonio 1995), the estates of a driver and passenger who were killed

322

in a car collision with a drunk motorist sued the convenience store under Dramshop where the motorist was supposedly served alcohol after the point of intoxication. The trial court granted summary judgment in favor of the store but this decision was reversed on appeal. The appellate court reversed the decision based on two primary issues. First, although § 106.14 provides a safe harbor provision where employees can escape liability if they take certain educational steps to prevent these situations from happening, there was a dispute of fact as to whether the store in this case abided by this provision. Second, there was enough evidence to let a jury determine whether the store served the motorist and, if so, whether she was obviously intoxicated at the time.

Graff v. Beard, 858 S.W.2d 918 (Tex. 1993), was a case where the Texas Supreme Court had to decide whether to impose "a common law duty on a social host who makes alcohol available to an intoxicated adult guest who the host knows will be driving" (p. 918). The Supreme Court overturned the decision of the appeals court and declined to impose liability in this situation.

Social Host Liability

There were two reasons for this decision. First, the guest is in a much better position than the host to monitor his own consumption of alcohol. Second, the guest ultimately makes the decision of whether or not he will drive while intoxicated no matter how much the host persuades him not to do so. This case involved the traditional social host liability situation where the plaintiff crashed his car after becoming intoxicated at a party by drinking alcohol provided by the host.

Ryan v. Friesenhahn, 911 S.W.2d 113 (Tex. App. San Antonio 1995), was an important case in establishing a duty under common law negligence between an adult social host and a minor guest. In this case, a minor held an open "BYOB" party at his parent's home with their consent. A minor female was killed in an accident after she left the party. Her parents subsequently brought a wrongful death action against the parents whose son hosted the party.

First, the court held that since the party was a violation of the statute making it unlawful to sell alcohol to minors, this could constitute negligence per se. Next, the court interpreted that the legislature intended that the adult social host would be liable in this situation where minors are served. The court stated that:

> a jury could find that the [adult social hosts] ... allowed open invitations to a beer bust at their house and they could foresee, or reasonably should have foreseen, that the only means of arriving at their property would be by privately operated vehicles; once there, the most likely means of departure would be by the same means. That adults have superior knowledge of the risks of drinking should be apparent from the legislature's decision to allow persons to become adults on their eighteenth birthday for all purposes but the consumption of alcohol. (p. 118)

After **Ryan**, Texas Supreme Court addressed the issue of social host liability in **Smith v. Merritt**, 940 S.W.2d 602 (Tex. 1997). In **Smith**, the court held that there was no social host liability where a host serves alcohol to a person who is at least eighteen-years-of age. However, the court specifically noted that this decision did not overrule **Ryan.** Thus, the logical conclusion is that until the Texas Supreme Court says otherwise, social host liability only applies to when alcohol is served to minors below the age of eighteen.

In **Barfield v. City of Houston**, 846 S.W.2d 399 (Tex. App. Houston 14th Dist. 1992), plaintiffs who were attacked and injured on the streets outside the coliseum where they had just attended a

Other Cases of Interest

concert sued the concert promoters and the concert security company. The court did not impose liability because, even though alcohol was served at the concert, the defendants had no duty to protect the plaintiffs from the criminal acts of third parties in a public area they had no duty or right to control.

Utah

1998 Supplement

Definition of a Minor

The section which defines a minor as a person under the age of twenty-one is now codified in §32A-1-105.

Possession or Consumption by a Minor

The section which makes it unlawful for a minor "to purchase, attempt to purchase, solicit another person to purchase, possess, or consume" alcohol is now codified in §32A-12-209(1).

Sale or Gift to a Minor

The section which makes it a class A misdemeanor for anyone to sell or otherwise furnish alcohol to a minor is now codified in §32A-12-2-3(1). The exception for physicians who provide alcohol for medicinal purposes and for parents who provide alcohol to their children is in §32A-12-203(3).

In **State v. Souza**, 846 P.2d 1313 (Utah App. 1993), the defendant appealed his jury trial conviction of supplying alcohol to minors in violation of Utah Code Section 32A-12-203 (1991). The defendant and another gentleman picked up two minor girls in a van in which there was beer. One of the girls testified that the defendant never actually handed a beer to them but "appeared to be going along with that" (p. 1316). The defendant thus argued that he did not "otherwise furnish or supply" alcohol to a minor in violation of §32A-12-203 (1991).

In response, the court upheld the defendant's conviction because such a conviction under 32A-12-203 (1991) merely requires that "an accused have some control of that alcohol, know that he or she was making it available to a minor, and intend or be reckless to the fact that the minor would accept it" (p. 1322).

Misrepresentation of Age

The statute which makes it unlawful for minors to misrepresent their age in order to obtain alcohol is now codified in §32A-12-209(2). The section which makes it a class B misdemeanor for anyone to transfer their own I.D. card to a minor to aid the minor in the purchase of alcohol is now in §32A-1-301.

Sale or Gift to an Intoxicated Person

The section which makes it unlawful for anyone to "sell, offer to sell or otherwise furnish or supply" alcohol to a person who is "apparently under the influence of alcoholic beverages ... or drugs ... is now codified in §32A-12-204.

Dramshop Liability

The Utah Dramshop statute is now codified in §32A-14-101.

In **Reeves v. Gentile**, 813 P.2d 111 (Utah 1991), the plaintiff, an injured pedestrian, brought suit against a tavern owner under Utah Code §32A-14-1 ("the Dramshop Act") for injuries sustained when he was struck by a car driven by a patron of defendant's bar. The defendant first argued that the evidence was insufficient for a jury to find that she "directly gave, sold, or otherwise provided liquor to [the patrons]" (p. 114). In response, the court noted that there was no dispute concerning the fact that the patrons had consumed beer while on the premises. Thus, "it was not unreasonable for the jury to find by a preponderance of the evidence that [the bar] provided beer" (p. 115) to the intoxicated patrons.Next, the defendant argued that the trial court erred in failing to instruct the jury that it could apply the doctrine of comparative negligence to the dramshop defendant. The court dismissed this argument because "the clear intent of the legislature was to compensate innocent third parties by making dramshop owners strictly liable without regard to the finding of fault, wrongful intent, or negligent conduct on their part" (p. 116). However, the court did rule that the trial court should have "compared the negligence of the intoxicated person to the person seeking recovery" (p. 117). According to the court, "the injured parties should not be allowed to recover regardless of their own conduct" (p. 118).

In **Brinkerhoff v. Forsyth**, 779 P.2d 685 (Utah 1989), the plaintiffs brought suit against the bartender of a state-owned club under the Dramshop Act for serving intoxicating beverages to an individual who later drove and killed a young woman. The court ruled that the bartender, a state employee, was exempt from liability under Section 32-11-2, a predecessor to the current Dramshop Act.

In **Horton v. Royal Order of the Sun**, 821 P.2d 1167 (Utah 1991), the plaintiff brought an action against two private clubs for personal injuries he suffered as a result of his involuntary intoxication. Apparently, the employees of both establishments continued to serve alcoholic beverages to the plaintiff despite the fact that he was obviously intoxicated. While at one of the clubs, the plaintiff passed out and fell, hitting his head. The plaintiff argued that Utah's Dramshop Act, granted him a cause of action against both of these clubs.

However, the court affirmed its recent holding in **Beach v. University of Utah** that "third persons may recover under the Dramshop Act for injuries suffered at the hands of the intoxicated person but that the Act does not give a cause of action in strict liability to the intoxicated person" (p. 1169) [citing **Beach**, 726 P.2d 413 at n.3]. For a similiar ruling, *see* **Richardson v. Matador Steak House, Inc.** 948 P.2d 347 (Utah 1997).

The Supreme Court of Utah in **Stephens v. Bonneville Travel, Inc.,** 935 P.2d 518 (Utah 1997), held that the Dramshop law can be applied to noncommercial social hosts in some situations. In this case, the plaintiffs sued the Beehive Travel Agency after a Beehive customer became intoxicated after consuming liquor provided at the agency and he then crashed his car into the plaintiffs. The court looked to the plain language of the statute and held that the Dramshop act imposes liability on anyone who provides "liquor" to those listed in the Act as opposed to beer or other alcoholic beverages. Thus, a person who serves "liquor" in a noncommercial setting, i.e., a social host, can be liable under dramshop. However, if they serve alcoholic beverages other than liquor, they would not be liable. The court noted that Utah is the only state with a dramshop act that imposes different standards of liability depending on the type of alcoholic beverage served.

Social Host Liability

Vermont

1997 Cumulative Pocket Supplement

Sale or Gift to a Minor   In **State v. Stanislaw**, 573 A.2d 286 (Vt. 1990), the defendant was charged with involuntary manslaughter because he furnished a minor with alcohol, which thereby caused her death. The minor succumbed to alcohol poisoning after drinking approximately three quarters of a bottle of rum. A witness testified that the defendant had purchased the bottle of rum for the minor. The defendant argued for a dismissal of the charges due to lack of probable cause. The court rejected this argument, stating that "[t]hese facts and circumstances were sufficient to warrant a reasonable and prudent person to conclude that the defendant had committed involuntary manslaughter by unlawfully furnishing a minor with alcohol with death resulting" (p. 292).

Dramshop Liability   The Supreme Court of Vermont discussed the remedies available to the parents of an individual who is killed by a drunk driver in **Clymer v. Webster**, 596 A.2d 905 (Vt. 1991). In **Clymer**, the parents of the decedent brought claims under the Dramshop Act and the Wrongful Death Act against both the driver and the commercial vendors who sold alcohol to the driver of the car that ultimately killed their daughter. The court noted that the decedent would have been able to bring an action under the Dramshop Act if she had survived. Thus, the court held that the decedent's parents could recover damages under the Wrongful Death Act.

In **Kelley v. Moguls, Inc.**, 632 A.2d 360 (Vt. 1993), the Supreme Court of Vermont expounded upon the scope of the Dramshop Act. In **Kelley**, the court held that a licensed vendor may be liable for the death of a drunk driver who had been drinking at the licensed vendor's establishment prior to the fatal accident. The court held that the common law negligence action against the licensed vendor was not preempted by the Dramshop Act. In making this decision, the court noted that "both consumption and furnishing may be causative factors of an alcohol-related injury or death" (p. 363).

In **Swett v. Haig's, Inc.**, 663 A.2d 930 (Vt. 1995), the plaintiff sued a tavern after she was seriously injured by a drunk driver. The plaintiff alleged that, prior to the accident, the tavern served liquor to the driver despite his intoxicated state. The court began with the premise that "[t]he Dramshop Act preempts common-law negligence actions that come within its scope" (p. 931). However, the court noted that this preemptive effect was limited and held that "the injured motorist may bring a common law negligence action against the intoxicated driver" (p. 931).

The Supreme Court of Vermont discussed the liability of franchisers under the Dramshop Act in **Carrick v. Franchise Associates, Inc.**, 671 A.2d 1243 (Vt. 1995). In **Carrick**, the plaintiffs brought an action against the franchiser of a restaurant which allegedly over served an individual who later drove and killed their decedent. The court affirmed the trial court's grant of summary judgment for the defendants because "there [was] no allegation that defendants ever had possession of the alcoholic beverages that were served . . ." (p. 1244).

A 1991 amendment to 7 VSA §657 added the provision that the state attorney general may require a person charged with violating this statute to attend an alcohol and driving program at the person's own expense.

Virginia

1998 Cumulative Supplement

NOTE: The Virginia legislature repealed everything in Title 4 of the state code effective October 1, 1993. While there were very few substantive changes made in the alcohol laws, the information below can be used as a guide to learn where the alcohol laws are now codified.

This information may now be found in Code §4.1-305. Also, a 1996 amendment added "or attempt to purchase or possess" following "purchase or possess."

Possession or Consumption by a Minor

A Virginia appellate court has held that a minor may be charged with possession of alcohol even if the minor does not have physical possession of the alcohol at the time of the arrest. **Hale v. Commonwealth**, 478 S.E.2d 710 (Va. App. 1996), was a case of first impression in Virginia. In this case, the court charged a minor with possession of alcohol based on evidence that he drank alcohol prior to his arrest. The court held that "use of a substance necessarily implies [its] possession" (p. 712). The minor's eyes were bloodshot, the police officer smelled alcohol on the minor's breath, and the minor admitted that he had consumed one beer that day. Based on the evidence, though he had no alcohol in the car, the court held that this case had enough evidence to constitute possession of alcohol.

Code §4.1-304 makes it unlawful to sell alcohol to a person under the age of twenty-one.

Sale or Gift to a Minor

A 1996 amendment added Code §4.1-305 B, which makes it a class C misdemeanor for a person under twenty-one-years-old to present false identification to purchase alcoholic beverages. A violation of this section may result in a fine of at least $500 or 50 hours of community service. In addition, the minor's driver's license may be expired for up to one year.

Misrepresentation of Age

Code §4.1-304 makes it unlawful to sell alcohol to an intoxicated person.

Sale or Gift to an Intoxicated Person

"Intoxicated means a condition in which a person has drunk enough alcoholic beverages to observably affect his manner, disposition, speech, muscular movement, general appearance or behavior" [Code §4.1-100].

Definition of Intoxicated Person

Code §4.1-308 makes drinking or offering a drink to another in a public place a misdemeanor. The same exceptions listed under this section in the *1990 Update* to *Alcohol on Campus* apply.

Miscellaneous

Washington

1999 Cumulative Pocket Supplement

Possession or Consumption by a Minor

Two Washington appellate courts have held that a minor may be charged with possession of alcohol even if the minor does not have physical possession of the alcohol at the time of the arrest. **State v. Dalton**, 865 P.2d 575 (Wash. App. Div. 3 1994), held that "[t]he presence of liquor in one's system does not constitute possession per se because the person's power to control, possess, use or dispose of its ends upon assimilation" (p. 576). However, the court did state that "evidence of assimilation is circumstantial evidence of prior possession" (p. 576). In this case, the court affirmed defendant's conviction of possession of alcohol because his slurred speech, blood shot eyes, and alcohol breath was sufficient evidence that he had possessed alcohol.

In **State v. Walton**, 834 P.2d 624 (Wash. App. Div. 1 1992), the court upheld the defendant's conviction for being a minor in possession of alcohol based on his age, his admission that he had consumed alcohol at a party, and the police officer's testimony that he could smell alcohol on the minor's breath.

In **State v. Shawn P.**, 859 P.2d 1220 (Wash. 1993), the court held that the Washington statute that revokes driving privileges of juveniles ages thirteen to eighteen who consume or possess alcohol does not violate the equal protection clause of the United States Constitution.

Sale or Gift to a Minor

RCWA 66.44.300 makes it a misdemeanor for anyone to invite a minor to a tavern, to provide him or her alcoholic beverages at the tavern, or to mislead the tavern owner as to the age of the minor.

Schooley v. Pinch's Deli Market, Inc., 912 P.2d 1044 (Wash. App. Div. 2 1996), involved a group of minors who consumed beer at a pool party. The defendant was a commercial vendor who sold beer to one of the minors without asking for proof of age. Subsequently, an eighteen-year-old female consumed from that supply of beer, then dove head-first into the shallow end and is now a quadriplegic.

The court held that the commercial vendor could be liable for the injuries because the events that happened were foreseeable. The female was a member of the protected class to whom the vendor owed a duty of care. The court stated that three social policies were relevant in this decision. First, the law should prevent minors from the negligence of adults. Second, commercial vendors should be held accountable for their negligence. Third, the law should "compensate those foreseeably put at risk by a defendant's negligent conduct" (p. 1049). Therefore, the protected class is not limited to the actual purchaser of alcohol. The Washington Supreme Court affirmed this decision [**Schooley v. Pinch's Deli Market**, 951 P.2d 749 (Wash. 1998)]

In **Crowe v. Gaston**, 951 P.2d 1118 (Wash. 1996), a minor purchased alcohol from an establishment; he then subsequently gave the alcohol to some other minors who accompanied him. One of the minors, Crowe, was injured after he accepted a ride with one of the intoxicated minors and the car swerved off the road. In his suit against the establishment, the court referred to **Schooley** and held that Crowe should be protected by the statute.

Misrepresentation of Age

RCWA 66.20.200 makes it unlawful "for the owner of a card or identification to transfer the card to any other person for the purposes of aiding such person to procure alcoholic beverages from any licensee or store employee."

RCWA 66.24.570 was enacted in 1996 and authorizes "a license for sports entertainment facilities to be designated as a class R license to sell beer, wine, and spirits at retail, for consumption upon the premises only" [RCWA 66.24.570(1)]. "A sports entertainment facility includes a publicly or privately owned arena, coliseum, stadium, or facility where sporting events are presented for a price of admission." [*Authors Note:* Presumably, this section does not apply to the University of Washington since RCWA 66.44.190 forbids the sale of alcohol on the campus except at the faculty club.]

Miscellaneous

A 1998 amendment to RCWA 66.44.200 created a $500 fine if any person under the influence of liquor purchases or consumes liquor at a licensed establishment. In addition, every establishment must post this law in a conspicuous location until July 1, 2000.

Sale or Gift to an Intoxicated Person

Washington is one of several states that refuse to reward a person who is injured as a result of voluntary intoxication. **Estate of Kelly by and through Kelly v. Falin**, 896 P.2d 1245 (Wash. 1995), held that "a commercial vendor owes no duty of care to patrons who suffer injuries as a result of their intoxication" (p. 1250). The court held that this "decision recognizes that while commercial vendors have a duty to minors and innocent bystanders, no duty arises when intoxicated adults harm themselves" (p. 1249). The rule otherwise "fosters unresponsibility and rewards drunk driving" (p. 1250).

Dramshop Liability

In **Rinks v. Bearss**, 921 P.2d 558 (Wash. App. Div. 1 1996), a twenty-year-old defendant became intoxicated after drinking beer at several places. That evening, a minor friend bought more beer for them at a supermarket, which was also named as a defendant in this case. Early the next morning, the minor attempted to drive his vehicle and he crashed it into another car, killing a person and injuring that individual's wife, who filed this lawsuit. The court found "no logical or principled basis for excluding [the innocent motorists] from the protected class. If the injuries were foreseeable at the time of the negligent sale of alcohol to a minor, legal redress should be allowed" (p. 560). Since the store sold a large quantity of beer to a minor, it is reasonable to believe that the accident was foreseeable.

In **Williams v. Kingston Inn, Inc.**, 792 P.2d 1282 (Wash. App. 1990), although "a commercial purveyor of alcoholic beverages owes a duty not to furnish intoxicating liquors to a person who is obviously intoxicated," (p. 1284) the court in this case held that the tavern was not liable based on the lack of evidence of the patron's intoxication.

In **Hanson v. Friend**, 824 P.2d 483 (Wash. 1992), the parents of a fifteen-year old who drowned in a lake brought this action against the adults who had furnished him with alcohol. The court held that:

Social Host Liability

> [u]nder RCWA 66.44.270(1), it is a criminal act for any person, including a social host, to furnish liquor to a minor. Pursuant to this statute, social hosts owe a duty to exercise ordinary care not to furnish liquor to a minor. A minor may maintain an action against a social host where this duty is breached, and the injuries sustained by the minor are proximately caused by the breach. (p. 488)

Although the court held that the adults may be liable, the claim could be reduced by the minor's own negligence and could be barred if the minor was more than 50% at fault.

In **Reynolds v. Hicks**, 951 P.2d 761 (Wash. 1998), a minor consumed alcohol at a wedding reception and was in an automobile accident that night which severely injured the plaintiff. The plaintiff sued the hosts of the reception, alleging that they negligently served alcohol to minors. Specifically, the plaintiff argued that R.C.W. §66.44.270, which makes it unlawful to supply alcohol to minors, established a duty of care owed by the hosts to the plaintiff. Although **Hanson** established that a minor who is injured as a result of being served alcohol by a social host can sue the host, Washington does not extend this same treatment to a third party who is injured by the intoxicated minor. The court did note, however, that the third party could sue a commercial vendor in the same situation.

The court in **Webstad v. Stortini**, 924 P.2d 940 (Wash. App. Div. 2 1996), stated that "Washington also does not recognize a duty creating liability for a social host who provides intoxicating liquor to an intoxicated guest" (p. 948). Also, in **Cox v. Malcolm**, 808 P.2d 758 (Wash. App. 1991), the court held that "Washington has thus far declined to extend liability to purely social hosts" (p. 763). The holding of these cases suggests that an intoxicated adult may not bring a social host liability claim. However, under **Hanson**, it appears that a minor can.

Houck v. University of Washington, 803 P.2d 47 (Wash. App. 1991), involved an eighteen-year-old student at the University of Washington who attended a non-university sponsored drinking party in a residence hall room. Later that evening, on the way to a dance held in the residence hall, the student was seriously injured when he and his friends stopped the residence hall elevator between floors and pried open the doors. The student was injured when he fell down the elevator shaft when he attempted to jump to the next floor. The residence hall policy allowed drinking by those of legal age in the privacy of their rooms. The policy also stated that the residents were required to abide by all laws of the city and state. At trial, the jury returned a verdict in favor of the university, but this decision was reversed on appeal.

The court held that since officials of the university knew about these ongoing elevator pranks and the ongoing student drinking, that it raised "a question of fact as to whether the university was negligent in failing to act on that knowledge" (p. 52). The court reversed on this issue and stated that the university did not need actual knowledge of the student's intoxication to have a duty. However, there were other issues in this case where the court ruled in favor of the university. First, the court held that in this case, the university had "no common law duty to prevent students from drinking" (p. 53). The court cited **State v. Chrisman**, 676 P.2d 419 (1984), and noted that the dormitory rooms were private residences and not under the control of the university. The court also rejected the student's claim of premises liability.

Other Cases of Interest

Fairbanks v. J.B. McLoughlin Company, Inc., 929 P.2d 433 (Wash. 1997), did not reveal any new changes in the law; it did, however, indicate how easy it is at times for a case to survive the preliminary procedural matters and at least make it to the jury. In this case, an employee was provided alcohol at a company banquet and she later crashed her car into the plaintiff. The plaintiff sued the company, alleging they negligently furnished alcohol at the banquet. Even though several witnesses testified that the employee appeared sober at the banquet, the Washington Supreme Court held that this case should go to the jury to decide the issue.

Washington, D.C.

1998 Supplement

Possession or Consumption by a Minor

The section which makes it unlawful for a minor to possess alcohol is now codified as D.C. Code § 25-130(a).

Sale or Gift to a Minor

The sections which makes this unlawful were incorrectly listed in *Alcohol on Campus*. The pertinent sections are 25-121(a)(b) and 25-130.1(b).

Misrepresentation of Age

D.C. Code § 25-121(d)(1) was amended to state that a licensee shall refuse service to anyone without valid identification. D.C. Code § 25-121(d)(2) provides that this identification must be "issued by an agency of government." D.C. Code § 25-121(d)(3) has been deleted.

The penalties for violating D.C. Code § 25-130(a) have been amended. Now, for the first offense, driving privileges can be suspended for 90 days. For the second offense, they can be suspended for 180 days. For the third offense, driving privileges can be suspended for one year.

West Virginia

1998 Cumulative Supplement

Possession or Consumption by a Minor

A 1993 amendment added W. Va. Code §60-7-12a(a), which makes it a misdemeanor for a minor to "order, pay for, share the cost of, or attempt to purchase [consume or possess] any intoxicating beer, wine, or alcoholic liquors purchased from a licensee." The former W. Va. Code §60-7-12a(a) is now section (b) and carries a $500 fine instead of a $50 fine and maximum jail time of 72 hours.

A 1993 amendment added W. Va. Code §60-8-20a(a) which provides that "any person under the age of twenty one years who purchases, consumes, sells, possesses, or serves wine or other alcoholic liquor is guilty of a misdemeanor." Conviction can result in a $500 fine or a maximum of 72 hours in jail.

Miscellaneous

Haba v. Big Arm Bar & Grill, Inc., 468 S.E.2d 915 (W. Va. 1996), held that when a plaintiff's negligence exceeds that of defendant's negligence, the plaintiff's claim is barred by the doctrine of comparative negligence.

Dramshop Liability

In **Bailey v. Black**, 394 S.E.2d 58 (W. Va. 1990), the widow of a man who was killed in a car accident by a drunk driver brought this action against the tavern who served the drunk driver alcoholic beverages. In addition, the drunk driver sued the tavern for her own injuries suffered in the crash. The court interpreted W. Va. Code §60-7-12 (which makes it illegal to serve an intoxicated person) to mean that the tavern could be liable for the death of the innocent party and the injuries of the drunk driver. The court held that both parties were in the class that the statute was designed to protect.

In **Anderson v. Moulder**, 394 S.E.2d 61 (W. Va. 1990), a beer distributor sold a keg of beer to a seventeen-year-old. That evening, the youth died in a car crash when he was a passenger in a car driven by another minor who had also consumed from the keg.

The court held that the sale of beer to a minor "gives rise to a cause of action against the vendor in favor of a purchaser or a third party injured as a proximate result of the unlawful sale" (p. 68). The court also held that the minor's claim could be reduced by comparative negligence. Finally, the court concluded that a jury could conclude that it was foreseeable for the keg of beer to be shared with other minors who could become intoxicated and injure themselves and others.

Social Host Liability In **Overbaugh v. McCutcheon,** 396 S.E.2d 153 (W. Va. 1990), the court held that there is no social host liability in West Virginia. Therefore, the social host was not liable for the injuries to third persons caused by a guest who had consumed alcohol at his party.

Wisconsin

1998 Cumulative Annual Pocket Part

Sale or Gift to a Minor In **Miller v. Thomack,** 563 N.W.2d 891 (Wis. 1997), the Wisconsin Supreme Court held that "a person who contributes money with the intent of bringing about the purchase of alcoholic beverages for consumption by an underage person whom the person knows, or should know, is under the legal drinking age," is in violation of the statute which makes if unlawful to procure alcohol for a minor.

Misrepresentation of Age Section 125.08, which authorized the Wisconsin government to issue I.D. cards to those of legal drinking age, was repealed, effective January 1, 1990.

Dramshop Liability In **Symes v. Milwaukee Mutual Ins. Co.**, 505 N.W.2d 143 (Wis. App. 1993), a bar patron who was beaten up by a minor ten blocks from the bar filed this action against the bar, alleging that they violated W.S.A. 127.07 by allowing the minor in the bar. The court refused to impose liability on the bar because the statute was not designed to prevent the harm that occurred to the plaintiff. The purpose of the statute is to protect minors from the harms associated with tavern activities. The court also stated that they would not hold the bar liable because it was not foreseeable for this altercation to occur ten blocks away from the tavern.

Kwiatkowski v. Capitol Indemnity Corp., 461 N.W.2d 150 (Wis. App. 1990), involved a thorough analysis of W.S.A. 125.035 and how it applies as a minor who suffers as a result of consuming alcohol that he purchased from an establishment. The court held that "[t]he legislature in sec. 125.035(4)(b), stats., has not sanctioned by clear , unambiguous and peremptory language a cause of action against a provider by a minor plaintiff whose injuries, at least in part, result from his own consumption of alcoholic beverages" (pp. 153-154). Therefore, the immunity from 125.035(4)(b) still applies when a plaintiff is injured as a result of his consumption of alcohol.

In **Paskiet By Fehring v. Quality State Oil**, 476 N.W.2d 871 (Wis. 1991), a minor who was injured from a fall after drinking alcohol provided to him by other minors, sued the store which sold the minors the alcohol. The court held that the traditional principles of tort law would apply and that the store could be liable for negligence if a jury found that the sale of alcohol was a substantial factor in causing the injuries. The court further held that if the store violated W.S.A. 127.07 by selling alcohol to a minor, this could constitute negligence per se. [Note: W.S.A. 125.035 was not in effect.]

Wyoming

Wyoming Statutes Annotated (1997 ed.)

In **Tietema v. State**, 926 P.2d 952 (Wyo. 1996), a minor who attended a keg party at a private residence appealed his conviction of illegal possession of alcohol based on the argument that the possession law did not apply to private property. The court disagreed and held that a minor can be charged with possession of alcohol under W.S. § 12-6-101(b) "regardless of location" (p. 955).

Possession or Consumption by a Minor

1999
Cumulative
Updated Tables:

DRAMSHOP LIABILITY

and

SOCIAL HOST LIABILITY

―――――――――

These tables include information for the fifty states and District of Columbia through January 1, 1999.

For the most current information, always refer to the latest updating state supplement.

Table I

Dramshop Liability in the Fifty States and The District of Columbia

Statutes, Common Law and Preconditions Necessary To Create Liability.

STATE	DRAM SHOP LIABILITY		STATUTE	CASE	PRECONDITION OF SALE WHICH CREATES LIABILITY				COMMENTS
✓ The presence or absence of Dramshop Liability is indicated by a check mark.	NO	YES			Minor	Intoxicated Adult	Intoxicated Minor	VIOLATION OF LAW	
Alabama		✓	6-5-71					✓	
Alaska		✓	04.21.020	**Nazareno** v. **Urie**, 638 P.2d 671 (Alaska 1981)	✓	✓			**Nazareno** held vendors have duty independent of statute. Amendment to statute in 1995 provides sale without a license would hold seller strictly liable for civil damages.
Arizona		✓		**Ontiveros** v. **Borak**, 667 P.2d 200 (Ariz. 1983)	✓	✓			4-311
Arkansas		✓		**Shannon** v. **Wilson**, 947 S.W.2d 349 (Ark. 1997)					Case overruled old common law rule of nonliability established in **Carr** v. **Turner**, 385 S.W.2d 656 (Ark. 1965).
California		✓	25602.1				✓		

State	DRAM SHOP LIABILITY		STATUTE	CASE	PRECONDITION OF SALE WHICH CREATES LIABILITY				COMMENTS
	NO	YES			Minor	Intoxicated Adult	Intoxicated Minor	VIOLATION OF LAW	
Colorado		✓	12-46-112.5 12-47-128.5	**Largo v. Crespin**, 727 P.2d 1098 (Colo. 1986)	✓	✓			Willful and knowing sale required.
Connecticut		✓	30-102			✓			
Delaware	✓			**Wright v. Moffitt**, 437 A.2d 554 (Del. 1981)					If common law is to be changed, legislature must do it.
District of Columbia		✓		**Rong Yao Zhou v. Jennifer Mall Rest.**, 534 A.2d 1268 (D.C. App. 1987)		✓			
Florida		✓	768.125	**Davis v. Shiappacossee**, 155 So. 2d 365 (Fla. 1963)	✓	*			Service must be willful and knowing. * Habitual drunk
Georgia		✓	OCGA §51-1-40	**Sutter v. Hutchings**, 327 S.E.2d 716 (Ga. 1985)	✓	✓			Willful, knowing and unlawful.
Hawaii		✓		**Ono v. Applegate**, 612 P.2d 533 (Hawaii 1980)				✓	

State			Statute / Case Citation					Comments
Idaho	✓		23-808				✓	Passed in 1986.
Illinois	✓		235 ILCS 5/6-16(a)		*	*	*	* Service that causes intoxication.
Indiana	✓		7.1-5-10-15.5			✓		Must knowingly serve.
Iowa	✓		123.92	✓		✓		1997 amendment to Dramshop Act extended the Act to those who serve minors.
Kansas		✓	Ling v. Jan's Liquors, 703 P.2d 731 (Ks. 1985)	✓		✓		In the absence of statute, there is no common-law liability.
Kentucky	✓		KRS 413.241			✓		Possible liability for sale to minor.
Louisiana	✓		Chausse v. Southland Corp. 400 So. 2d 1199 (La. App. 1981)	✓				
Maine	✓		28 § 1401	✓		✓		Sale must be negligent or reckless.
Maryland		✓	State v. Hatfield, 73 A.2d 754 (Md. 1951)					If common law is to be changed, legislature must do it.

STATE	DRAM SHOP LIABILITY NO	DRAM SHOP LIABILITY YES	STATUTE	CASE	Minor	Intoxicated Adult	Intoxicated Minor	VIOLATION OF LAW	COMMENTS
Massachusetts		✓		Adamian v. Three Sons, Inc., 233 A.2d 18 (Mass. 1968) Michmik-Ziberman v. Gordons 453 A.2d 430 (Mass. 1983)	✓	✓			
Michigan		✓	436.22	Weiss v. Hodge, 567 N.W.2d 468 (Mich. App. 1997)		✓		✓	Dramshop Act only applies to retailers. Tavern can be liable for intoxicated torts of patrons.
Minnesota		✓	340A. 801 subd. 1					✓	
Mississippi		✓	67-3-73	Munford v. Peterson, 368 So. 2d 213 (Miss. 1979)	✓	✓			Statute enacted 1987 makes consumption rather than furnishing the proximate cause of injuries **unless** there is unlawful sale, a sale to a visibly intoxicated person, there is forced consumption, or beverage is represented as non-alcoholic.
Missouri		✓	537.053		✓	✓			Applies only to those licensed to sell liquor by the drink on premises and must first be convicted of illegal sale.
Montana		✓	27-1-710	Nehring v. LaCounte, 712 P.2d 1329 (Mont. 1986)	✓*	✓*			Effective date of statute, 1986. * Also where consumption coerced or individual told drink contains NO alcohol.
Nebraska	✓			Holmes v. Circo, 244 N.W.2d 65 (Neb. 1976)					If common law is to be changed, legislature must do it.

The presence or absence of Dramshop Liability is indicated by a check mark.

State		Statute	Case				Comments
Nevada	✓		Hamm v. Carson City Nugget, Inc., 450 P.2d 358 (Nev. 1969)				Adheres to old common law.
New Hampshire	✓	507-F	Ramsey v. Anctil, 211 A.2d 900 (N.H. 1965)	✓	✓		
New Jersey	✓	2A:22A-1		✓	✓		
New Mexico	✓	41-11-1	Lopez v. Maez, 651 P.2d 1269 (N.M. 1982)	✓	✓		Statute effective 1986.
New York	✓		Berkley v. Park, 262 N.Y.S.2d 290 (Sup. Otsego Cty. 1965)			✓	
North Carolina	✓	18B-121	Hutchins v. Hankins, 303 S.E.2d 584 (N.C. App. 1983)	✓*	✓*		*Case provides liability where there is sale to intoxicated person. Statute provides liability for sale to minor.
North Dakota	✓	5-01-06.1		✓	✓		Requires knowingly sell.
Ohio	✓	4399.18	Mason v. Roberts, 294 N.E.2d 884 (Ohio 1973)	✓	✓		
Oklahoma	✓		Brigance v. Velvet Dove Rest. 725 P.2d 300 (Okl. 1986)	✓	✓		Minors are unable to deal responsibly with the effects of alcohol. See Busby v. Quail Creek Golf and Country Club, 885 P.2d 1326 (Okl. 1994).

STATE	DRAM SHOP LIABILITY NO	DRAM SHOP LIABILITY YES	STATUTE	CASE	Minor	Intoxicated Adult	Intoxicated Minor	VIOLATION OF LAW	COMMENTS
Oregon		✓	30.950	**Campbell v. Carpenter**, 566 P.2d 893 (Ore. 1977)	✓	✓			Liability for sale to minor attaches if no I.D. check.
Pennsylvania		✓	47 § 4-497	**Jardine v. Upper Darby Lodge**, 198 A.2d 550 (Pa. 1964).	✓	✓			
Rhode Island		✓	3-14-1		✓	✓			
South Carolina		✓		**Tobias v. Sports Club, Inc.**, 504 S.E.2d 318 (S.C. 1998)	prob.	✓			Intoxicated patron has no remedy.
South Dakota		✓	35-4-78	**Wildboer v. South Dakota Junior Chamber of Commerce**, 561 N.W.2d 666 (S.D. 1997)					There is no civil liability for serving alcohol to intoxicated persons.
Tennessee		✓	57-10-102	**Mitchell v. Ketner**, 393 S.W.2d 755 (Tenn. App. 1964)	✓	✓			
Texas		✓	2.01		✓	✓			Effective 1987.

✓ The presence or absence of *Dramshop Liability* is indicated by a check mark.

State	Statute	Case	Comments
Utah	32A-14-101		Effective 1985. The Act designed to provide a remedy only for third party injured by intoxicated tavern patron.
Vermont	7 § 501		After hours
Virginia		Williamson v. Old Brogue Inn, 350 S.E.2d 621 (Va. 1986)	If common law is to be changed, legislature must do it.
Washington		Halvorson v. Birchfield Boiler Inc., 458 P.2d 897 (Wash. 1969)	*Obviously intoxicated, those in a state of helplessness or those in "special relationship to furnisher." Only third party may recover.
West Virginia		Walker v. Griffith, 626 F. Supp. 350 (W.D. Va. 1986)	Comparative negligence doctrine would apply.
Wisconsin	125.035	Sorensen v. Jarvis, 350 N.W.2d 108 (Wisc. 1984)	Statute specifies liability can accrue if consumption coerced or individual told drink contains NO alcohol.
Wyoming	12-8-301(a)	McClellan v. Tottenhoff, 666 P.2d 408 (Wyo. 1983)	Statute only provides for liability if sale is at drive-up window.

Table II

Social Host Liability In the Fifty States and The District of Columbia

Statutes, Common Law and Preconditions Necessary To Create Liability.

✓ The presence or absence of Social Host Liability is indicated by a check mark.

STATE	SOCIAL HOST LIABILITY							STATUTE	CASE	COMMENTS
	NO		NOT DECIDED	POSSIBLY		YES				
	Minor	Intoxicated Adult		Minor	Intoxicated Adult	Minor	Intoxicated Adult			
Alabama						✓		6-5-71(a)	**Martin v. Watts,** 513 So. 2d 958 (Ala. 1987)	
Alaska	✓						*			**Chokwak v. Worley,** 912 P.2d 1248 (Alaska 1996). **Gordon v. Alaska Pacific Bancorporation,** 753 P.2d 721 (Alaska 1998). Liability only if injury takes place on premises.
Arizona		✓				✓		4-301	**Keckonen v. Robles,** 705 P.2d 945 (Ariz. App. 1985)	Case held no liability for serving adult guest. 1985 statute exempts host who serves those of legal age. **Estate of Hernandez v. Arizona Board of Regents,** 866 P.2d 1330 (Ariz. 1994).
Arkansas			✓							
California				✓	✓	*	*	Bus. & Prof. 25602.1	**Cantor v. Anderson,** 178 Cal. Rptr. 540 (Cal. App. 1982)	*Case held service must be to those with severe physical or mental conditions. No case law on new statute (1986).

STATE	SOCIAL HOST LIABILITY							STATUTE	CASE	COMMENTS
	NO		NOT DECIDED	POSSIBLY		YES				
	Minor	Intoxicated Adult		Minor	Intoxicated Adult	Minor	Intoxicated Adult			
Colorado						✓		12-47-801	**Charlton** v. **Kimeta**, 815 P.2d 946 (Colo. 1991)	Willfully and knowingly serve a minor (1986).
Connecticut						✓			**Ely** v. **Murphy**, 540 A.2d 54 (Conn. 1988)	Also see, **Bohan** v. **Last**, 674 A.2d 839 (Conn. 1996).
Delaware	✓								**Hooper** v. **Corridori Roofing Co**, 305 A.2d 309 (Del. 1973)	If liability is to be imposed, legislature must do so. However, see **DiOssi** v. **Maroney**, 548 A.2d 1361 (Del. 1988).
District of Columbia			✓							Probably not based on dicta in various cases.
Florida	✓				✓				**Bankston** v. **Brennan**, 507 So. 2d 1385 (Fla. 1987) **Bardy** v. **Walt Disney World Co**, 643 So. 2d 46 (Fla. App. 5 Dist. 1994). **Dowell** v. **Gracewood Fruit Co**, 559 So. 2d 217 (Fla. 1990)	
Georgia						✓	✓		**Sutter** v. **Hutchings**, 327 S.E.2d 716 (Ga. 1985)	Social hosts have a duty to prevent guests who are intoxicated from driving. See **Pirkle** v. **Hawley**, 405 S.E.2d 71 (Ga. App. 1991).
Hawaii	✓	✓								

✓ *The presence or absence of Social Host Liability is indicated by a check mark.*

346

State	Statute	Case citation	Comment
Idaho	23-808		1986 Statute.
Illinois		Cruse v. Aden, 20 N.E. 73 (Ill. 1889)	See **Cravens v. Inmann**, 586 N.E.2d 367 (Ill. 1991) for very limited social host liability.
Indiana	7.1-5-10-15.5	**Brattain v. Herron**, 309 N.E.2d 150 (Ind. App. 1974)	Statute requires service with knowledge guest is intoxicated (1986).
Iowa	123.49		1986 statute affirms old common law and abrogates **Clark v. Mincks** which imposed liability for providing to intoxicated person. Court has held in **Blesz v. Weisbrod**, 424 N.W.2d 451 (Iowa 1988) hosts can be liable if they serve to minors.
Kansas		**Thies v. Cooper**, 753 P.2d 1280 (Kans. 1988).	
Kentucky		**Grayson Fraternal Order of Eagles v. Claywell**, 736 S.W.2d 328 (Ky. 1987)	Dissenting judge said holding in this case effectively created social host liability. Service was to intoxicated adult.
Louisiana	9:2800.1	**Sanders v. Hercules Sheet Metal**, 385 So. 2d 772 (1980) **Gresham v. Davenport**, 524 So. 2d 48 (La. App. 1988)	Statute exempts host who serves those of legal age. Case held no liability for serving intoxicated adult. No exemption from liability where coerce consumption or falsely represents that the beverage contains NO alcohol.
Maine	28 § 1405(2)		Requires reckless or negligent furnishing (1985).
Maryland		**Kuykendall v. Top Notch**, 520 A.2d 1115 (Md. App. 1987) **Hebb v. Walker**, 536 A.2d 113 (Md. App. 1988)	

STATE	SOCIAL HOST LIABILITY							STATUTE	CASE	COMMENTS
	NO		NOT DECIDED	POSSIBLY		YES				
	Minor	Intoxicated Adult		Minor	Intoxicated Adult	Minor	Intoxicated Adult			
Massachusetts		✓				✓			**McGuiggan v. New England Tel. & Tel. Co.,** 496 N.E.2d 141 Mass. (1986)	Liability only if innocent third party is injured. No liability when intoxicated guest injured.
Michigan						✓			**Longstreth v. Gensel,** 377 N.W.2d 804 (Mich. 1985)	Unlawful furnishing to a minor. But see **Rogalski v. Tavernier,** 527 N.W.2d 73 (Mich. App. 1995) where court held violent acts *not* foreseeable result of serving alcohol to minors.
Minnesota	✓								**Cole v. City of Spring Lake,** 314 N.W.2d 836 (Minn. 1982)	Legislature removed words "or giving" from civil damages act.
Mississippi						✓		67-3-73	**Boutwell v. Sullivan,** 469 So. 2d 526 (Miss. 1985)	The 1987 statute makes consumption rather than furnishing the proximate cause of injuries **unless** alcohol is furnished to one who can not lawfully consume or there is forced consumption or beverage is represented as non-alcoholic.
Missouri	✓					*			**Andres v. Alpha Kappa Lambda Fraternity,** 730 S.W.2d 547 (Mo. 1987)	Could be liability where a minor is coerced to consume alcohol as a condition of membership. See **Nisbet v. Bucher,** 949 S.W.2d 111 (Mo. App. 1997).
Montana				✓	✓			27-1-710	**Nehring v. LaCounte,** 712 P.2d 1329 (Mont. 1986)	Civil damages act specifies "any person." Case holds statutes are the standard for due care (1986).
Nebraska	✓	✓							**Strong v. K&K Investment,** 343 N.W.2d 912 (Neb. 1984)	

348

State									Statute	Cases	Comments
Nevada						✓	✓				Based on court's adherence to old common law.
New Hampshire		✓		✓						State v. Small, 111 A.2d 201 (N.H. 1955) Hickingbotham v. Burke, 662 A.2d 297 (N.H. 1995)	Case held it was evidence of negligence for "any person" to provide to minor or intoxicated person. Service to a minor must be "reckless."
New Jersey	✓	✓							2A: 15-5.6		There are many conditions in the law which must be satisfied before a host can be held liable for serving an intoxicated adult.
New Mexico	✓	✓							41-11-1	Walker v. Key, 686 P.2d 973 (N.M. App. 1984)	Liability if alcohol supplied in reckless disregard of the rights of others (1983 & 1985).
New York		✓							ABC Laws 11-100	Montgomery v. Orr, 498 N.Y.S.2d 968 (Super. 1986)	(1983)
North Carolina		✓				✓				Chastain v. Litton Systems, 694 F.2d 957 (4th Cir. 1982) Hart v. Ivey, 420 S.E.2d 174 (N.C. 1992)	Social host has a duty to the driving public not to serve intoxicated persons known to be driving.
North Dakota			✓		✓				5-01-06.1	Born v. Mayers, 514 N.W.2d 687 (N.D. 1994)	Civil damages act specifies "any person" who knowingly serves alcohol to a minor or obviously intoxicated person is liable for 3rd party injury.
Ohio				✓						Settlemeyer v. Willmington Vet. Post 49, 464 N.E.2d 521 (1984); Mitseff v. Wheeler, 526 N.E.2d 798 (1988)	See Huston v. Konieczny, 556 N.E.2d 505 (Ohio 1990) for liability of parents who allow alcoholic beverages to be served in their home.
Oklahoma							✓	✓		Battles v. Cough, 947 P.2d 600 (Okl. Civ. App. 1997)	

STATE	SOCIAL HOST LIABILITY							STATUTE	CASE	COMMENTS
	YES		POSSIBLY		NOT DECIDED	NO				
	Intoxicated Adult	Minor	Intoxicated Adult	Minor		Intoxicated Adult	Minor			
Oregon	✓	✓				✓	✓	30.950 30.960	**Weiner v. Gamma Phi Chapter**, 485 P.2d 18 (Ore. 1971)	Liable if alcohol provided to visibly intoxicated adult or minor without I.D. check.
Pennsylvania		✓				✓			**Congini v. Portersville Valve**, 470 A.2d 515 (Pa. 1983); **Klein v. Raysinger**, 470 A.2d 507 (Pa. 1983)	Minor may not be liable as a social host. See **Kapres v. Heller**, 640 A.2d 888 (Pa. 1994).
Rhode Island						✓			**Vater v. HB Group**, 667 A.2d 283 (R.I. 1995) **Ferreira v. Strack**, 652 A.2d 965 (R.I. 1995)	If liability is to be imposed, the legislature must do it.
South Carolina						✓			**Garren v. Cummings & McCrady**, 345 S.E.2d 508 (S.C. App. 1986)	
South Dakota							✓	35-11-2		
Tennessee						✓			**Cecil v. Hardin**, 575 S.W.2d 268 (Tenn. 1978)	
Texas		*				✓			**Graff v. Beard**, 858 S.W.2d 918 (Tex. 1993); **Ryan v. Friesenhahn**, 911 S.W.2d 113 (Tex. App. San Antonio 1995)	Probably only applies when alcohol is served to minors under the age of eighteen [**Smith v. Merritt**, 940 S.W.2d 602 (Tex. 1997)].

✓ *The presence or absence of Social Host Liability is indicated by a check mark.*

State								Statute	Case	Comments
Utah	✓	✓						32A-14-101	Stephens v. Bonneville Travel, Inc., 935 P.2d 518 (Utah 1997)	Only applies when liquor is served; it does not apply when other forms of alcohol are served.
Vermont		✓	✓					7 § 501(g)	Langle v. Kurkul, 510 A.2d 1301 (Vt. 1986)	Statute specifies host not exempt from common law negligence. Case holds host liable for serving minor or intoxicated adult.
Virginia				✓	✓					Adheres to old common law.
Washington			✓	✓					Hanson v. Friend, 824 P.2d 483 (Wash. 1992)	Comparative negligence applies to bar recovery if minor is more than 50% at fault. Only injured minor can recover. Innocent third party does not have a remedy.
West Virginia				✓	✓				Walker v. Griffith, 626 F. Supp 350 (W.D. Va. 1986) Overbaugh v. McCutcheon, 396 S.E.2d 153 (W.Va. 1990).	Courts consistently hold the violation of a statute is negligence *per se.* But Overbaugh v. McCutcheon, 396 S.E.2d 153 (W. Va. 1990) says there is no social host liability.
Wisconsin		✓						125.035	Koback v. Crook, 366 N.W.2d 857 (Wis. 1985)	Statute holds liable "a person" who serves alcohol to minors or who forces consumption or states drink has NO alcohol. (1985)
Wyoming						✓	✓	12-8-301(a)		Statute specifies "no person" who "legally provided" alcohol is liable. (1985)

Cumulative
Alphabetical Table of Cases

Brett v. Great American Recreation, Inc., 652 A.2d 774
(N.J. Super. A.D. 1995) / 302
Brigance v. Velvet Dove Restaurant, Inc., 725 P.2d 300 (Okl. 1986) / 142, 312
Brinkerhoff v. Forsyth, 779 P.2d 685 (Utah 1989) / 325
Brockett v. Kitchen Boyd Motor Co., 70 Cal.Rptr. 136 (App. 5 Dist. 1968) / 178
Brookins v. The Round Table, Inc., 624 S.W.2d 547 (Tenn. 1981) / 161
Broussard v. Peltier, 499 So.2d 1026 (La. App. 3 Cir. 1986) / 86
Browder v. International Fidelity Insurance Company, 321 N.W.2d 668
(Mich. 1982) / 98
Brower v. Robert Chappell & Associates, Inc., 328 S.E.2d 45
(N.C. App. 1985) / 132
Brown v. Cathay Island, Inc., 480 A.2d 43 (N.H. 1984) / 118
Brown v. Hollywood Bar & Cafe, 942 P.2d 1363 (Colo. App. 1997) / 265
Brown v. Jones, 503 N.W.2d 735 (Mich. App. 1993) / 286, 291
Bruce v. Chas Roberts Air Conditioning, 801 P.2d 456 (Ariz. App. 1990) / 261
Brumbelow v. Shoney's Big Boy of Carrollton, 329 S.E.2d 319 (Ga. App. 1985) / 65
Bryant v. Alpha Entertainment Corp., 508 So.2d 1094 (Miss. 1987) / 105
Bryant v. Jax Liquors, 352 So.2d 542 (Fla. App. 1 Dist. 1978) / 61
Buchanan v. Merger Enterprises, Inc., 463 So.2d 121 (Ala. 1984) / 41
Buckley v. Estate of Pirolo, 500 A.2d 703 (N.J. 1985) / 120
Burkhart v. Brockway Glass Co., 507 A.2d 844 (Pa.Super. 1986) / 149
Burkhart v. Harrod, 755 P.2d 759 (Wash. 1988) / 243
Burkhard v. Sunset Cruises, Inc., 595 N.Y.S.2d 555 (A.D. 2 Dept. 1993) / 303
Burkis v. Contemporary Ind. Midwest, 435 N.W.2d 397 (Iowa App. 1988) / 226
Burns v. Bradley, 419 A.2d 1069 (N.H. 1980) / 118
Burrell v. Meads, 569 N.E.2d 637 (Ind. 1991) / 281
Burson v. Gate Petroleum Co., 401 So.2d 922 (Fla. App. 5 Dist. 1981) / 61
Busby v. Quail Creek Golf & Country Club, 885 P.2d 1326 (Okl. 1994) / 312
Byrd v. Gate Petroleum Co., 845 F.2d 86 (4th Cir. 1988) / 242

Cable v. Sahara Tahoe Corp., 155 Cal.Rptr. 770 (App. 2 Dist. 1979) / 51
Cady v. Coleman, 315 N.W.2d 593 (Minn. 1982) / 103
Callan v. O'Neil, 578 P.2d 890 (Wash. App. 1978) / 175, 178
Camalier v. Jeffries, 460 S.E.2d 133 (N.C. 1995) / 308
Camille v. Berry Fertilizers, Inc., 334 N.E.2d 205 (Ill. App. 4 Dist. 1975) / 72
Campbell v. Board of Trustees of Wabash College, 495 N.E.2d 227
(Ind. App. 1 Dist. 1986) / 75
Campbell v. Carpenter, 566 P.2d 893 (Ore. 1977) / 144, 145
Campbell v. Step/Lind Restaurant Corp., 531 N.Y.S.2d 567
(A.D. 2 Dept. 1988) / 235
Campos v. State, 623 S.W.2d 657 (Tex.Cr. App. 1981) / 163, 164
Canady v. McLeod, 446 S.E.2d 879 (N.C. App. 1994) / 308
Cantor v. Anderson, 178 Cal.Rptr. 540 (App. 3 Dist. 1981) / 51
Cantwell v. Peppermill, Inc., 31 Cal. Rptr. 2d 246
(Cal. App. 1 Dist. 1994) / 263
Cardinal v. Sante Pita, Inc., 286 Cal. Rptr. 275 (Cal. App. 4 Dist. 1991) / 263
Carey v. New Yorker of Worcester, Inc., 245 N.E.2d 420 (Mass. 1969) / 92
Carillo v. El Mirage Roadhouse, Inc., 793 P.2d 121 (Ariz. App. 1990) / 261
Carr v. Turner, 385 S.W.2d 656 (Ark. 1965) / 47, 48, 262
Carrick v. Franchise Associates, Inc., 671 A.2d 1243 (Vt. 1995) / 326
Cartwright v. Hyatt Corp., 460 F. Supp. 80 (D.C. 1978) / 182, 183
Carver v. Schafer, 647 S.W.2d 570 (Mo. App. 1983) / 107
Casebolt v. Cowan, 829 P.2d 352 (Colo. 1992) / 265
Casey's General Stores Inc. v. Downing, 757 S.W.2d 1 (Mo. App. 1988) / 230
Cassanello v. Luddy, 695 A.2d 325 (N.J Sup. Ct. 1997) / 301
Cecil v. Hardin, 575 S.W.2d 268 (Tenn. 1978) / 161
Chalup v. Aspen Mine Company, 221 Cal.Rptr. 97 (App. 4 Dist. 1985) / 50
Charles v. Seifried, 651 N.E.2d 154 (Ill. 1995) / 277
Charlton v. Kimata, 815 P.2d 946 (Colo. 1991) / 266
Chartrand v. Coos Bay Tavern, Inc., 696 P.2d 513 (Ore. 1985) / 144
Chastain v. Litton Systems, Inc., 694 F.2d 957 (4th Cir. 1982) / 133
Chausse v. Southland Corporation, 400 So.2d 1199 (La. App. 1 Cir. 1981) / 85, 286
Childress v. Sams, 736 S.W.2d 48 (Mo. en banc 1987) / 107, 108
Chokwak v. Worley, 912 P.2d 1248 (Alaska 1996) / 260
Christensen v. Parrish, 266 N.W.2d 826 (Mich. App. 1978) / 95, 99
Christiansen v. Campbell, 328 S.E.2d 351 (S.C. App. 1985) / 155, 318
Christoph v. Colorado Communications Corp., 946 P.2d 519
(Colo. 1997) / 265
Chung v. State, 751 S.W.2d 557 (Tex. App.-Texarkana 1988) / 240
Cimino v. Milford Keg, Inc., 431 N.E.2d 920 (Mass. 1982) / 92
City of Carbondale v. Nelson, 484 N.E.2d 392 (Ill. App. 5 Dist. 1985) / 70
Clark v. Inn West, 365 S.E.2d 682 (N.C. App. 1988) / 132
Clark v. Mincks, 364 N.W.2d 226 (Iowa 1985) / 178, 283
Clevenger v. District of Columbia, 106 Daily Wash .L. Rptr. 1561
(D.C.Super.Ct. July 11, 1978); 47 LW 2074 (Aug. 8, 1978) / 182, 183
Clymer v. Webster, 596 A.2d 905 (Vt. 1991) / 326
Coble v. Maloney, 643 A.2d 277 (Conn. App. 1994) / 266
Cole v. City of Spring Lake Park, 314 N.W.2d 836 (Minn. 1982) / 103
Cole v. O'Tooles of Utica, Inc., 643 N.Y.S.2d 283 (A.D. 4 Dept. 1996) / 306
Com. v. Penn Valley Resorts, Inc., 494 A.2d 1139 (Pa.Super. 1985) / 151

Com v. Tau Kappa Epsilon, 609 A.2d 791 (Pa. 1992) / 314
Commonwealth v. Demangone, 243 A.2d 187 (Pa.Super. 1968) / 147
Commonwealth, Pa. Liquor Control Board v. Abraham, 489 A.2d 306
(Pa.Cmwlth. 1985) / 148
Commonwealth, Pa. Liquor Control Bd. v. Tris-Dad, Inc., 448 A.2d 690
(Pa.Cmwlth. 1982) / 147
Commonwealth, Pa. Liquor Control Board v. Abraham, 489 A.2d 306
(Pa.Cmwlth. 1985) / 148
Commonwealth of Pennsylvania Liquors v. Grand Marcus One, 451 A.2d 810
(Pa.Cmwlth. 1982) / 148
Commonwealth of Pennsylvania Liquor Control Board v. Schiaffo, 456 A.2d
1120 (Pa.Cmwlth. 1983) / 147
Componile v. Maybee, 641 A.2d 1143 (N.J. Super. L. 1994) / 301
Congini by Congini v. Portersville Valve Co., 470 A.2d 515 (Pa. 1983) / 150
Conigliaro v. Franco, 504 N.Y.S.2d 186 (A.D.2 Dept. 1986) / 129
Connelly v. Ziegler, 380 A.2d 902 (Pa.Super. 1977) / 148
Conner v. Duffy, 652 A.2d 372 (Pa. Super. 1994) / 314
Connolly v. Conlan, 371 N.W.2d 832 (Iowa 1985) / 77
Cook v. Spinnaker's of Rivergate, Inc., 878 S.W.2d 934 (Tenn. 1994) / 320
Cooper v. Delta Chi Housing Corporation of Connecticut, 674 A.2d 858
(Ct. App. 1996) / 267
Corcoran v. McNeal, 161 A.2d 367 (Pa.Super. 1960) / 148
Cornack v. Sweeney, 339 N.W.2d 26 (Mich. App. 1983) / 97
Corrigan v. United States, 595 F. Supp. 1047 (D.C.Va. 1984) / 173
Corrigan v. United States, 609 F. Supp. 720 (D.C.Va. 1985);
reversed 815 F.2d 954 (4th Cir. 1987) / 173
Cory v. Shierloh, 174 Cal.Rptr. 500 (1981) / 50
Cotton v. State, 686 S.W.2d 140 (Tex.Cr. App. 1985) / 164
Coudriet v. Southland Corp., 244 Cal.Rptr. 69 (App. 4 Dist. 1988) / 50
Coulter v. Swearingen, 447 N.E.2d 561 (Ill. App. 3 Dist. 1983) / 72
Couts v. Ghion, 421 A.2d 1184 (Pa.Super. 1980) / 149
Cowin v. Huntington Hospital, 496 N.Y.S.2d 203
(Sup.Ct. Suffolk Cty. 1985) / 130
Cox v. Malcolm, 808 P.2d 758 (Wash. App. 1991) / 330
Cox v. Rolling Golf Course Corp., 532 N.W.2d 761 (Iowa 1995) / 282
Cravens v. Inman, 586 N.E.2d 367 (Ill. 1991) / 277
Creasy v. Coxon, 750 P.2d 903 (Ariz. App. 1987) / 46
Cremins v. Clancy, 612 N.E.2d 1183 (Mass. 1993) / 290
Crespin v. Largo Corp., 698 P.2d 826 (Colo. App. 1984) / 54
Crolley v. Hutchins, 387 S.E.2d 716 (S.C. App. 1989) / 318
Crowley v. State, 268 N.W.2d 616 (S.D. 1978) / 158
Crown Liquors of Broward, Inc. v. Evenrud, 436 So.2d 927 (Fla. App. 2 Dist.
1983) / 62
Cruse v. Aden, 20 N.E. 73 (Ill. 1889) / 71, 72
Cuevas v. Royal D'Iberville Hotel, 498 So.2d 346 (Miss. 1986) / 105
Cullivan v. Leston, 602 P.2d 1121 (Ore. App. 1979) / 146
Cummins v. Rubio, 622 N.E.2d 700 (Ohio App. 2 Dist. 1993) / 310
Cunningham v. Brown, 174 N.E.2d 153 (Ill. 1961) / 71
Custen v. Salty Dog, Inc. 566 N.Y.S.2d 348 (A.D. 2 Dept. 1991) / 305

D'Amico v. Christie, 524 N.Y.S.2d 1 (Ct. App. 1987) / 129
Daley v. Ward, 399 S.E.2d 13 (S.C. App. 1990) / 318
Dalrymple v. Southland Corp., 609 N.Y.S.2d 284 (A.D. 2 Dept. 1994) / 306
Darguzas v. Robinson, 515 N.E.2d 451 (Ill. App. 2 Dist. 1987) / 71
Davis v. Billy's Con-Teena, Inc., 587 P.2d 75 (Ore. 1978) / 144, 145
Davies v. Butler, 602 P.2d 605 (Nev. 1979) / 116
Davis v. Sam Goody, Inc., 480 A.2d 212 (N.J.Super. A.D. 1984) / 120
Davis v. Shiappacossee, 155 So.2d 365 (Fla. 1963) / 61
Davis v. Stinson, 508 N.E.2d 65 (Ind. App. 4 Dist. 1987) / 75
Deeds v. United States, 306 F. Supp. 348 (D.Mont. 1969) / 110
Del E. Webb v. Superior Court of Arizona, 726 P.2d 580 (Ariz. 1986) / 46
DeLoach v. Mayer Electric Supply Co., 378 So.2d 733 (Ala. 1979) / 41
Delozier v. Evans, 763 P.2d 986 (Az. App. 1988) / 219
DeMore by DeMore v. Dieters, 334 N.W.2d 734 (Iowa 1983) / 76, 283
Detwiler v. Brumbaugh, 656 A.2d 944 (Pa. Super. 1995) / 315
Dhuy v. Rude, 465 N.W.2d 32 (Mich. App. 1990) / 292
Dickinson v. Edwards, 716 P.2d 814 (Wash. 1986) / 177, 178, 179
Dickman v. Jackalope, Inc., 870 P.2d 1261 (Colo. App. 1994) / 265
Dimond v. Sacilotto, 233 N.E.2d 20 (Mass. 1968) / 93
Dines v. Henning, 459 N.W.2d 132 (Mich. App. 1990) / 291
Dinh v. State, 695 S.W.2d 797 (Tex. App. 1 Dist. 1985) / 162
DiOssi v. Maroney, 548 A.2d 1361 (Del. 1988) / 221
Dixon v. Saunders, 565 So. 2d 802 (Fla. App. 2 Dist. 1990) / 270
Dobozy v. Cochran Airport Systems, Inc., 330 S.E.2d 815 (Ga. App. 1985) / 65
Dobson v. Maki, 457 N.W.2d 132 (Mich. App. 1990) / 293
Dodge v. Victory Markets, Inc. 606 N.Y.S.2d 345 (A.D. 3 Dept. 1993) / 304
Donato v. McLaughlin, 599 N.Y.S.2d 754 (A.D. 3 Dept. 1993) / 303
Donnell v. Spring Sports, Inc. 920 S.W.2d 378
(Tex. App. Houston 1st Dist. 1996) / 322

Douglass v. Kenyon Oil Co., Inc., 618 A.2d 220 (Me. 1992) / 288
Dowell v. Gracewood Fruit Co., 559 So. 2d 217 (Fla. 1990) / 270
Dower v. Gamba, 647 A.2d 1364 (N.J. Super. A.D. 1994) / 302
Duckett v. Wilson Hotel Management Company, Inc., 669 So. 2d 977 (Ala. Civ. App. 1995) / 257
Dunagin v. City of Oxford, Mississippi, 718 F.2d 738 (5th Cir. 1983); cert.den. 467 US 1259 (1984) /104
Dynarski v. U-Crest Fire District, 447 N.Y.S.2d 86 (Sup.Ct. Erie Cty. 1981)/ 129
Dziewa v. Vossler , 438 N.W.2d 565 (Wisc. 1989) / 244

Eddy v. Casey's General Store, Inc., 485 N.W.2d 633 (Iowa 1992) / 282
Edgar v. Kajet, 375 N.Y.S.2d 548 (Sup.Ct. Nassau Cty. 1975); aff'd. 389 N.Y.S.2d 631 (A.D.2 Dept. 1976) / 130
Edison v. Walker, 573 So. 2d 545 (La. App. 1 Cir. 1991) / 286
El Chico Corp. v. Poole, 732 S.W.2d 306 (Tx. 1987) / 164, 165
Elder v. Fisher, 217 N.E.2d 847 (Ind. 1966) / 74
Eldridge v. Aronson, 472 S.E.2d 497 (Ga. App. 1996) / 271
Elliot v. Kessler, 799 S.W.2d 97 (Mo. App. W.D. 1990) / 297
Ellis v. N.G.N. of Tampa, Inc., 586 So. 2d 1042 (Fla. 1991) / 269
Elsperman v. Plump, 446 N.E.2d 1027 (Ind. App. 1 Dist. 1983) / 74
Ely v. Murphy, 540 A.2d 54 (Conn. 1988) / 56
Engel v. Lamplighter, Inc., 526 N.E.2d 641 (Ill. App. 3 Dist. 1988) / 224
Englund v. MN CA Partners / MN Joint Ventures, 555 N.W.2d 328 (Minn. App. 1997) / 295
Epsey v. Convenience Marketers, 578 So. 2d 1221 (Ala. 1991) / 257
Estate of Cummings v. PPG Industries, Inc., 651 N.E.2d 305 (Ind. App. 1995) / 279
Estate of Darby v. Monroe Oil Co., 488 S.E.2d 828 (N.C. App. 1997) / 307
Estate of Hernandez v. Arizona Board of Regents, 866 P.2d 1330 (Ariz. 1994) / 261
Estate of Hernandez v. Flavis, 930 P.2d 1309 (Ariz. en banc. 1997) / 261
Estate of Kelly by and through Kelly v. Falin, 896 P.2d 1245 (Wash. 1995) / 329
Estate of Mullis v. Monroe Oil Co., 488 S.E.2d 830 (N.C. App. 1997) / 308
Estate of Ritchie v. Farrell, 572 N.E.2d 367 (Ill. App. 3 Dist. 1991) / 278
Esther v. Wiemer, 859 P.2d 1140 (Okl. App. 1993) / 312
Etu v. Cumberland Farms, Inc., 538 N.Y.S.2d 657 (A.D. 3 Dept. 1989)/235, 236

Fabian v. Polish American Veterans, 466 N.E.2d 1239 (Ill. App. 1 Dist. 1984)/ 72
Fairbanks v. J.B. McLoughlin Company, Inc., 929 P.2d 433 (Wash. 1997)/330
Farrington v. Houston's Inc., 750 F.2d 492 (5th Cir. 1985) / 85
Fassett v. Delta Kappa Epsilon (New York), 807 F.2d 1150 (3rd Cir. 1986)/ 150
Fast Eddies v. Hall, 688 N.E.2d 1270 (Ind. App. 1997) / 279
Faulk v. Suzuki Motor Co. Ltd., 851 P.2d 332 (Hawaii App. 1993) / 274
Felder v. Butler, 438 A.2d 494 (Md. 1981) / 89
Feliciano v. Waikiki Deep Water, Inc., 752 P.2d 1076 (Hawaii 1988) / 67
Felix v. Milliken, 463 F. Supp. 1360 (E.D.Mich. 1978) / 95
Ferreira v. Strack, 652 A.2d 965 (R.I. 1995) / 317
Fifer v. Buffalo Cafe, 601 N.E.2d 601 (Ohio App. 6 Dist. 1991) / 310
Figuly v. Knoll, 449 A.2d 564 (N.J.Super.L. 1982) / 120
Findling v. T.P. Operating Company, 361 N.W.2d 376 (Mich. App. 1984) / 95
Finer v. Talbot, 552 A.2d 626 (N.J. Super. A.D. 1988) / 233
Finney v. Ren-bar Inc., 551 A.2d 535 (N.J. Super. A.D. 1988) / 233
First America Trust Co. v. McMurray, 620 N.E.2d 447 (Ill. App. 4 Dist. 1993)/ 277
Fisch v. Bellshot, 640 A.2d 801 (N.J. 1994) / 301
Fisher v. Cooper, 775 P.2d 1216 (Idaho 1989) / 223
Fisher v. O'Connor's, Inc., 452 A.2d 1313 (Md.Sp. App. 1982) / 90
Fishman v. Beach, 625 N.Y.S.2d 730 (A.D. 3 Dept. 1995) / 3044
Fitzer v. Bloom, 253 N.W.2d 395 (Minn. 1977) / 103
Fitzpatrick v. Carde Lounge, Ltd., 602 N.E.2d 19 (Ill. App. 1 Dist. 1992) / 278
Fladeland v. Mayer, 102 N.W.2d 121 (N.D. 1960) / 135
Flory v. Weaver, 553 N.E.2d 105 (Ill. App. 4 Dist. 1990) / 277
Floyd v. Bartley, 727 P.2d 1109 (Colo. 1986) / 53
Folda v. City of Bozeman, 582 P.2d 767 (Mont. 1978) / 110
Forrest v. Lorrigan, 833 P.2d 873 (Colo. App. 1992) / 266
Foster v. Purdue University, 567 N.E.2d 865 (Ind. App. 3 Dist. 1991) / 280
Freeland v. Pirozzi, 152 Cal.Rptr. 299 (App. 2 Dist. 1979) / 50
Freeman v. Finney, 309 S.E.2d 531 (N.C. App. 1983) / 132
Fudge v. City of Kansas City, 720 P.2d 1093 (Kansas 1986) / 79, 80
Fugate v. Safeway Stores, Inc., 897 P.2d 328 (Ore. App. 1995) / 314
Fuhrmam v. Total Petroleum, Inc., 398 N.W.2d 807 (Iowa 1987) / 77
Fullmar v. Tague, 500 N.W.2d 432 (Iowa 1993) / 283
Fulmer v. Timber Inn Restaurant and Lounge, 954 P.2d 201 (Ore. App. 1998) / 313
Futterleib v. Mr. Happy's Inc., 548 A.2d 728 (Conn. App. 1988) / 220

G & D Ramseur, Inc. v. Franklin, 652 S.W.2d 279 (Mo. App. 1983) / 106
Gabree v. King, 614 F.2d 1 (1st Cir. 1980) / 91
Gabrielle v. Craft, 428 N.Y.S.2d 84 (A.D.3 Dept. 1980) / 129
Gamble v. Neonatal Associates, P.A., 688 So. 2d 878 (Ala. Civ. App. 1997)/ 258

Garcia on Behalf of Garcia v. Jennings, 427 So.2d 1329 (La. App. 2 Cir. 1983)/ 85
Gardner v. Wood, 414 N.W.2d 706 (Mich. 1987) / 96
Gariup Construction Company, Inc. v. Foster, 519 N.E.2d 1224 (Ind. 1988)/ 75
Garren v. Cummings & McGrady, Inc., 345 S.E.2d 508 (S.C. App. 1986)/ 156
Giardina v. Solomon, 360 F. Supp. 262 (M.D.Pa. 1973) / 150
Gionfriddo v. Gartenhaus Cafe, 546 A.2d 284 (Conn. App. 1988) / 220
Glen's Grill No. 3, Inc. v. Board of Liquor Control, 166 N.E.2d 399 (Ohio App. 1959) / 138
Glinka v. Flame of Countryside, Inc., 524 N.E.2d 1102 (Ill. App. 1 Dist. 1988)/ 223
Goldberg v. Delta Tau Delta, 613 A.2d 1250 (Pa. Super. 1992) / 315
Gonzales v. Krueger, 799 P.2d 1318 (Alaska 1990) / 259
Gonzales v. Safeway Stores, Inc., 882 P.2d 389 (Alaska 1994) / 259
Goodnight v. Piraino, 554 N.E.2d 1 (Ill. App. 3 Dist. 1990) / 278
Gordon v. Alaska Pacific Bancorporation, 753 P.2d 721 (Alaska 1988) / 259
Gormon v. Albertson's Inc., 519 So. 2d 1119 (Fla. App. 2 Dist. 1988) / 221
Goss v. Richmond, 381 N.W.2d 776 (Mich. App. 1985) / 98
Goss v. Allen, 360 A.2d 388 (N.J. 1976) / 120
Gottlin v. Graves, 662 N.E.2d 711 (Mass. App. Ct. 1996) / 290
Graff v. Beard, 858 S.W.2d 918 (Tex. 1993) / 323
Graham v. General U.S. Grant Post No. 2665 V.F.W., 248 N.E.2d 657 (Ill. 1969) / 71
Graham v. Montana State University, 767 P.2d 301 (Mont. 1988) / 231
Grantham v. Tulsa Club, Inc., 918 P.2d 410 (Okl. App. 1996) / 312
Grasser v. Fleming, 253 N.W.2d 757 (Mich. App. 1977) / 97
Grayson Fraternal Order of Eagles v. Claywell, 736 S.W.2d 328 (Ky. 1987)/ 82, 83
Greer v. Ferrizz, 499 N.Y.S.2d 758 (A.D.2 Dept. 1986) / 130
Gregor v. Constitution State Insurance Co., 534 So. 2d 1340 (La. App. 4 Cir. 1988) / 287
Gregory v. Kurtis, 310 N.W.2d 415 (Mich. App. 1981) / 97, 98
Gresham v. Davenport, 524 So. 2d 48 (La. App. 1988) decided on appeal 537 So. 2d 1144 (La. 1989) / 227, 285
Gressman v. McClain, 533 N.E.2d 732 (Ohio 1988) / 237
Griesenbeck by Kuttner v. Walker, 488 A.2d 1038 (N.J.Super. A.D. 1985)/ 120
Griffin Motel Co. v. Strickland, 479 S.E.2d 401 (Ga. App. 1996) / 272
Gutwein v. Edwards, 419 N.W.2d 809 (Minn. App. 1988) / 229

Haafke v. Mitchell, 347 N.W.2d 381 (Iowa 1984) / 77
Haba v. Big Arm Bar & Grill, Inc., 468 S.W.2d 915 (W. Va. 1996) / 331
Haben v. Anderson, 597 N.E.2d 655 (Ill. App. 3 Dist. 1992) / 278
Hadaway v. State, 378 S.E.2d 127 (Ga. App. 1989) / 222
Hagen v. Dias, 185 Cal.Rptr. 530 (App. 2 Dist. 1982) / 51
Hale v. Commonwealth, 478 S.E.2d 710 (Va. App. 1996) / 327
Hall v. Budagher, 417 P.2d 71 (N.M. 1966) / 123
Halligan v. Pupo, 678 P.2d 1295 (Wash. App. 1984) / 179
Halvorson v. Birchfield Boiler, Inc., 458 P.2d 897 (Wash. 1969) / 177, 178, 179
Hamilton v. Ganias, 632 N.E.2d 407 (Mass. 1994) / 291
Hamm v. Carson City Nugget, Inc., 450 P.2d 358 (Nev. 1969) / 115
Hanewald v. Board of Liquor Control, 136 N.E.2d 77 (Ohio App. 1955) / 137
Hannah v. Chmielewski, Inc., 323 N.W.2d 781 (Minn. 1982) / 102
Hannah v. Jensen, 298 N.W.2d 52 (Minn. 1980) / 102
Hanson v. Friend, 824 P.2d 483 (Wash. 1992) / 329, 330
Harmann by Bertz v. Hadley, 382 N.W.2d 673 (Wis. 1986) / 189
Harriman v. Smith, 697 S.W.2d 219 (Mo. App. 1985) / 107, 108
Harris v. Gower, Inc., 506 N.E.2d 624 (Ill. App. 5 Dist. 1987) / 224
Harris v. Hurlburt, 373 N.Y.S.2d 480 (Sup.Ct. Seneca Cty. 1975) / 127
Harris v. Trojan Fireworks Co., 202 Cal.Rptr. 440 (App. 4 Dist. 1984) / 52
Hart v. Ivey, 420 S.E.2d 174 (N.C. 1992) / 308
Hasty v. Broughton, 348 N.W.2d 299 (Mich. App. 1984) / 97
Hatter v. Nations, 480 So.2d 1209 (Ala. 1985) / 41
Hawkins v. Conklin, 767 P.2d 66 (Ore. 1988) / 313
Hayward v. P.D.A., 573 N.W.2d 29 (Iowa 1997) / 282
Hebb v. Walker, 536 A.2d 113 (Md. App. 1988) / 90
Heldt v. Brei, 455 N.E.2d 842 (Ill. App. 1 Dist. 1983) / 72
Henry Grady Hotel Co. v. Sturgis, 28 S.E.2d 329 (Ga. App. 1943) / 64
Henry v. Vann, 508 N.Y.S.2d 502 (A.D.2 Dept. 1986) / 130
Hernandez v. Modesto Portuguese Pentecost Association, 48 Cal. Rptr. 2d 229 (App. 3 Dist. 1995) / 263
Herr v. Booten, 580 A.2d 1115 (Pa. Super. 1990) / 314
Heyler v. Dixon, 408 N.W.2d 121 (Mich. App. 1987) / 97, 291
Hickingbotham v. Burke, 662 A.2d 297 (N.H. 1995) / 300
Hickman v. Fraternal Order of Eagles, 758 P.2d 704 (Idaho 1988) / 275
Hiles v. Brandywine Club, 662 A.2d 16 (Pa. Super. 1995) / 315
Hinegardner v. Marcor Resorts, 844 P.2d 800 (Nev. 1992) / 299
Hobbiebrunken v. G&S Enterprises, Inc., 470 N.W.2d 19 (Iowa 1991) / 282
Hoffman v. Wiltscheck, 379 N.W.2d 145 (Minn. App. 1985) / 103
Hollerich v. City of Good Thunder, 340 N.W.2d 665 (Minn. 1983) / 102
Hollerud v. Malamis, 174 N.W.2d 626 (Mich. App. 1969) / 97
Hollis v. City of Baton Rouge, 593 So. 2d 388 (La. App. 1 Cir. 1991) / 287
Holmes v. Circo, 244 N.W.2d 65 (Neb. 1976) / 114
Holmquist v. Miller, 367 N.W.2d 468 (Minn. 1985) / 103, 296

Marusa v. District of Columbia, 484 F.2d 828 (D.C.Cir. 1973) /182, 183
Mason v. Roberts 294 N.E.2d 884 (Ohio 1973) / 138
Matter of Pirollo, 377 A.2d 1040 (Pa.Cmwlth. 1977) / 147
Matter of Tris-Dad, 439 A.2d 1286 (Pa.Cmwlth. 1981) / 147
Matthews v. Konieczny, 527 A.2d 508 (Pa. 1987) / 149
Matusak v. Chicago Transit Authority, 520 N.E2d 925
 (Ill. App. 1 Dist. 1988) / 224
McCall v. Villa Pizza, Inc., 636 A.2d 912 (Del. Supr. 1994) / 268
McCawley v. Carmel Lanes, Inc., 577 N.Y.S.2d 546 (A.D. 3 Dept. 1991) / 305
McClellan v. Tottenhoff, 666 P.2d 408 (Wyo. 1983) / 190, 191, 192
McDaniel v. Crapo, 40 N.W.2d 724 (Mich. 1950) / 97
McDonald v. Marriott Corp., 564 A.2d 1296 (Pa. Super. 1989) / 314
McGaha v. Matter, 528 A.2d 988 (Pa.Super. 1987) / 149
McGee by and through McGee v. Chalfant, 806 P.2d 980 (Kan. 1991) / 284
McGovern v. Koza's Bar & Grill, 604 A.2d 226 (N.J. Super. L. 1991) / 301
McGuiggan v. New England Telephone & Telegraph Company,
 496 N.E.2d 141 (Mass. 1986) / 92, 93
McIntyre v. Balentine, 833 S.W.2d 52 (Tenn. 1992) / 321
McIssaac v. Monte Carlo Club, Inc., 587 So. 2d 320 (Ala. 1991) / 256
McKeown v. Homoya, 568 N.E.2d 528 (Ill. App. 5 Dist. 1991) / 277
Mcleod v. Cannon Oil Corp., 603 So. 2d 889 (Ala. 1992) / 256
McNally v. Addis, 317 N.Y.S.2d 157 (Sup.Ct. Westchester Cty. 1970) / 126
Meany v. Newell, 367 N.W.2d 472 (Minn. 1985) / 103
Megge v. United States, 344 F.2d 31 (6th Cir. 1965) / 100
Menzie v. Kalmonowitz, 139 A. 698 (Conn. 1928) / 56
Merhi v. Becker, 325 A.2d 270 (Conn. 1973) / 57
Meshefski v. Shirnan Corp., 385 N.W.2d 474 (N.D. 1986) / 135
Mettling v. Mulligan, 225 N.W.2d 825 (Minn. 1975) / 102
Meyers v. Grubaugh, 750 P.2d 1031 (Kansas 1988) at 1037 / 227
Michnik-Zilberman v. Gordon's Liquor, Inc., 453 N.E.2d 430 (Mass. 1983) / 93
Migliore v. Crown Liquors of Broward, Inc., 448 So.2d 978 (Fla. 1984) / 61
Millard v. Osborne, 611 A.2d 715 (Pa. 1992) / 316
Miller v. City of Portland, 604 P.2d 1261 (Ore. 1980) / 144, 145
Miller v. Concordia Teachers College of Seward, Nebraska,
 296 F.2d 100 (8th Cir. 1961) / 114
Miller v. Moran, 421 N.E.2d 1046 (Ill. App. 4 Dist. 1981) / 72
Miller v. Ocampaugh, 477 N.W.2d 105 (Mich. App. 1991) / 291
Miller v. Owens-Illinois Glass Co., 199 N.E.2d 300 (Ill. App. 5 Dist. 1964) / 72
Miller v. Thomack, 563 N.W.2d 891 (Wis. 1997) / 332
Millross v. Plum Hollow Golf Club, 413 N.W.2d 17 (Mich. 1987) / 98, 99
Millross v. Tomakowski, 381 N.W.2d 786 (Mich. App. 1985) / 100
Mills v. City of Overland Park, 837 P.2d 370 (Kan. 1992) / 284
Mills v. Estate of Schwartz, 722 P.2d 1363 (Wash. App. 1986) / 175
Mills v. Harris, 615 So. 2d 533 (La. App. 3 Cir. 1993) / 282
Mitchell v. Ketner, 393 S.W.2d 755 (Tenn. App. 1964) / 160
Mitchell v. Shoals, Inc., 271 N.Y.S.2d 137 (A.D.1 Dept. 1966) / 127
Mitseff v. Wheeler, 526 N.E.2d 798 (Ohio 1988) / 237
Montgomery v. Orr, 498 N.Y.S.2d 968 (Sup.Ct. Oneida Cty. 1986) / 126, 129
Moore v. Bunk, 228 A.2d 510 (Conn. 1967) / 56
Moore v. Shoreline Ventures, Inc., 903 S.W.2d 900
 (Tex. App. Beaumont, 1995) / 322
Moran v. Foodmaker, Inc., 594 A.2d 587 (Md. App. 1991) / 289
Moreland v. Jitney Jungle, Inc., 621 So. 2d 285 (Ala. 1993) / 257
Morella v. Machu, 563 A.2d 881 (N.J. Super. A.D. 1989) / 302
Morgan v. Kirk Brothers, Inc., 444 N.E.2d 504 (Ill. App. 2 Dist. 1982) / 71
Morris v. Adolph Coors Co., 735 S.W.2d 578 (Tex. App. Fort Worth 1987) / 165
Morris v. Farley Enterprises, Inc., 661 P.2d 167 (Alaska 1983) / 44
Morris v. Markley, 371 N.W.2d 464 (Mich. App. 1985) / 97
Motz v. Johnson, 651 N.E.2d 1163 (Ind. App. 1995) / 280, 281
Moyer v. Lo Jim Cafe, Inc., 240 N.Y.S.2d 277 (A.D. 1963);
 aff'd. 251 N.Y.S.2d 30 (1964) / 127
MRC Properties, Inc. v. Gries, 652 P.2d 732 (N.M. 1982) / 123
Mueller v. JPA Foods, Inc., 767 S.W.2d 110 (Mo. App. 1989) / 230
Muex v. Hindel Bowling Lanes Inc., 596 N.E.2d 263 (Ind. App. 2 Dist. 1992) / 280
Mulvihill v. Union Oil Co., 859 P.2d 1310 (Alaska 1993) / 260
Munford, Inc. v. Peterson, 368 So.2d 213 (Miss. 1979) / 105
Murphy v. Tomada Enterprises, Inc., 819 P.2d (N.M. App. 1991) / 303
Myers v. South Seas Corporation, 871 P.2d 1235 (Hawaii App. 1992) / 274

Nally v. Blandford, 291 S.W.2d 832 (Ky. 1956) / 81
National Railroad Passenger Corp. v. Everton, 655 N.E.2d 360
 (Ind. App. 1995) / 280
Nazareno v. Urie, 638 P.2d 671 (Alaska 1981) / 43
Nehme v. Joseph, 554 N.Y.S.2d 642 (A.D. 2 Dept. 1990) / 303
Nehring v. LaCounte, 712 P.2d 1329 (Mont. 1986) / 110, 111
Nelson v. Araiza, 372 N.E.2d 637 (Ill. 1977) / 71
Nelson v. Dunaway, 536 So. 2d 955 (Ala. Civ. App. 1988) / 218
Nelson v. Steffens, 365 A.2d 1174 (Conn. 1976) / 56
Nesbitt v. Westport Square Ltd., 624 S.W.2d 519 (Mo. App. 1981) / 107
Nichols v. Hodges, 385 So.2d 298 (La. App. 1 Cir. 1980) / 86

Nieves v. Camacho Clothes, Inc., 645 So. 2d 507 (Fla. App. 5 Dist. 1994) / 268
Nisbet v. Bucher, 949 S.W.2d 111 (Mo. Ct. App. 1997) / 297
Nolan v. Morelli, 226 A.2d 383 (Conn. 1967) / 56
Northcutt v. Grilliot, 1997 WL 464785 (Ohio App. 2 Dist. 1997) / 310
Norton v. Opening Break of Aiken, Inc., 462 S.E.2d 861 (S.C. 1995) / 317
Norwood v. Marrocco, 586 F. Supp. 101 (D.C.Cir. 1984);
 aff'd. 780 F.2d 110 (D.C.Cir. 1986) / 183
Nunn v. Comidas Exquisitos, Inc., 305 S.E.2d 487 (Ga. App. 1983) / 64
Nutting v. Zieger, 482 N.W.2d 424 (Iowa 1992) / 282

O'Hanley v. Ninety-Nine, Inc., 421 N.E.2d 1217 (Mass. App. 1981) / 92
O'Neale v. Hershoff, 634 So. 2d 644 (Fla. App. 3 Dist. 1993) / 270
O'Sullivan v. Hemisphere Broadcasting, 520 N.E.2d 429 (Mass. 1996) / 290
Ocotillo West v. Superior Court, 844 P.2d 653 (Ariz. App. Div. 1 1992) / 262
Ohio Casualty Ins. Co. v. Todd / 312
Oja v. Grand Chapter of Theta Chi Fraternity, 667 N.Y.S.2d 650
 (Sup. Ct. Tompkins County, 1997) / 307
Oklahoma Broadcasters Association v. Crisp, 636 F. Supp. 978
 (W.D.Okl. 1985) / 142
146, Inc. v. Liquor Control Board, 527 A.2d 1083 (Pa.Cmwlth. 1987) / 148
Ono v. Applegate, 612 P.2d 533 (Hawaii 1980) / 66, 67
Ontiveros v. Borak, 667 P.2d 200 (Ariz. 1983) / 45, 46
Op. Att. Gen. 063-23 Feb. 22, 1963 / 61
Orner v. Mallick, 639 A.2d 491 (Pa. Super. 1994) / 150, 315
Otis Engineering Corp. v. Clark, 668 S.W.2d 307 (Tex. 1983) / 165
Overbaugh v. McCutcheon, 396 S.E.2d 153 (W. Va. 1990) / 332

Pa. Liquor Central Board v. Mignogna, 548 A.2d 689 (Pa. Cmwlth. 1988) / 238
Pakes v. Megaw, 565 A.2d 914 (Del. Supr. 1989) / 268
Pardey v. Boulevard Billiard Club, 518 A.2d 1349 (R.I. 1986) / 153
Parker v. Miller Brewing Co., 560 So. 2d 1030 (Ala. 1990) / 257
Parrett v. Lebamoff, 408 N.E.2d 1344 (Ind. App. 3 Dist. 1980) / 74
Parsons v. Jow, 480 P.2d 396 (Wyo. 1971) / 192
Paskiet By Fehring v. Quality State Oil, 476 N.W.2d 871 (Wis. 1991) / 332
Passini v. Decker, 467 A.2d 442 (Conn.Super. 1983) / 56
Pastor v. Champs Restaurant, Inc., 750 S.W.2d 335
 (Tex. App.-Houston 1988) / 241
Paul v. Hogan, 392 N.Y.S.2d 766 (A.D. 1977) / 128
Paul v. Ron Moore Oil Co., 487 N.W.2d 337 (Iowa 1997) / 282
Peal by Peal v. Smith, 444 S.E.2d 673 (N.C. App. 1994),
 aff'd. 457 S.E.2d 599 (N.C. 1995) / 308
Pelzek v. American Legion, 463 N.W.2d 321 (Neb. 1990) / 298
Pena v. Neal, Inc., 901 S.W.2d 663 (Tex. App. San Antonio, 1995) / 322
Pence v. Ketchum, 326 So.2d 831 (La. 1976) / 85
People v. Armstrong, 203 N.Y.S.2d 552 (Cty. Ct. 1960) / 125
People v. Binder, 536 N.E.2d 218 (Ill. App. 4 Dist. 1989) / 223
People v. Byrne, 494 N.Y.S.2d 257 (Sup. 1985) / 125
People v. Danchak, 261 N.Y.S.2d 722 (A.D. 1965) / 125
People v. Helt, 526 N.E. 842 (Ill. App. 3 Dist. 1987) / 223
People v. Jackson, 487 N.Y.S.2d 270 (Co.Cty. 1985) / 126
People v. Johnson, 185 P.2d 105 (Cal. App. Sup.Ct. LA Cty 1947) / 49
People v. Kaufman, 504 N.Y.S.2d 361 (City Ct. 1986) / 126
People v. Monroe, 333 N.E.2d 239 (Ill. App. 2 Dist. 1975) / 70
People v. Rhoes, 612 N.E.2d 536 (Ill. App. Dist. 4 1993) / 275
People v. Williams, 215 N.Y.S.2d 841 (City Ct. 1961) / 126
People's Restaurant v. Sabo, 591 So. 2d 907 (Fla. 1991) / 269
Perryman v. Lufran, Inc., 434 S.E.2d 112 (Ga. App. 1993) / 272
Persilver v. Louisiana Department of Transportation,
 592 So. 2d 1344 (La. App. 1 Cir. 1991) / 286
Person v. Southland Corporation, 656 So. 2d 453 (Fla. 1995) / 269
Peschke v. Carroll College, 929 P.2d 874 (Mont. 1996) / 298
Peters v. Saft, 597 A.2d 50 (Me. 1991) / 288
Petolicchio v. Santa Cruz County Fair and Rodeo Association, Inc.,
 866 P.2d 1342 (Ariz. 1994) / 261
Pfeifer v. Copperstone Restaurant & Lounge, Inc., 693 P.2d 644
 (Ore. App. 1985) / 145
Picadilly, Inc. v. Colvin, 519 N.E.2d 1217 (Ind. 1988) / 74
Pierce v. Albanese, 129 A.2d. 606 (Conn. 1957) / 56
Pike v. George, 434 S.W.2d 626 (Ky. 1968) / 82
Pinkham v. Apple Computer, Inc., 699 S.W.2d 387 (Tex. App. 2 Dist. 1985) / 165
Pirkle v. Hawley, 405 S.E.2d 71 (Ga. App. 1991) / 273
Plattner v. VIP's Industries, Inc., 768 P.2d 440 (Ore. App. 1989) / 313
Point Cafe, Inc. v. Board of Liquor Control, 168 N.E.2d 157 (Ohio App. 1960) / 137
Pollard v. Village of Ovid, 446 N.W.2d 574 (Mich. App. 1989) / 292
Porter v. Ortiz, 665 P.2d 1149 (N.M. App. 1983) / 123
Powers v. Niagara Mohawk Power Corp., 516 N.Y.S.2d 811 (A.D. 1987) / 127, 128
Prelvitz v. Milsop, 831 F.2d 806, 810 (8th Cir. 1987) / 260
Prest v. Delta Delta Delta Sorority, 686 N.E.2d 293 (Ohio App. 1996) / 311
Prevatt v. McClennan, 201 So.2d 780 (Fla. App. 2 Dist. 1967) / 61, 62

Pritchard v. Jax Liquors, Inc., 499 So.2d 926 (Fla. App. 1 Dist. 1986) / 61
Provigo Corporation v. ABC Appeals Board, 28 Cal. Rptr. 2d 638,
869 P.2d 1163 (Cal. 1994) / 262
Publix Supermarkets, Inc. v. Austin, 658 So. 2d 1064
(Fla. App. 5 Dist. 1995) / 270
Puckett v. Mr. Luckey's Ltd., 529 N.E.2d 1169 (Ill. App. 4 Dist. 1989) / 224, 277
Purchase v. Meyer, 737 P.2d 661 (Wash. 1987) / 175, 177, 178
Putman v. Cromwell, 475 So.2d 524 (Ala. 1985) / 41

Quinn v. Sigma Rho Chapter of Beta Theta Pi Fraternity,
507 N.E.2d 1193 (Ill. App. 4 Dist. 1987) / 72, 278
Quinn v. Winkel's, Inc., 279 N.W.2d 65 (Minn. 1979) / 102

R. Hughes, Inc. v. Mitchell, 617 So. 2d 767 (Fla. App. 1 Dist. 1993) / 269
Rainey v. Pickera, 651 N.E.2d 747 (Ill. App. 5th Div. 1995) / 277
Raithel v. Dustcutter, Inc., 634 N.E.2d 1163 (Ill. App. 4 Dist. 1994) / 276
Ramsey v. Anctil, 211 A.2d 900 (N.H. 1965) / 118
Ramsay v. Kenyon College, 85-CA-01 (5th Dist., Ct. App., Knox 10-31-85) / 139
Rancher Bar & Lounge v. State, 514 P.2d 634 (Wyo. 1973) / 190, 191
Randall v. Village of Excelsior, 103 N.W.2d 131 (Minn. 1960) / 102
Rann by Rann v. Hamilton, 599 N.Y.S.2d 51 (A.D. 2 Dept. 1993) / 305
Rappaport v. Nichols, 156 A.2d 1 (N.J. 1959) / 119, 120
Rauck v. Hawn, 564 N.E.2d 334 (Ind. App. Dist. 1 1996) / 279
Reber v. Commonwealth of Pennsylvania Liquor Control Board,
516 A.2d 440 (Pa.Cmwlth. 1986) / 149
Reed for Use and Ben. of Reed v. Fleming, 477 N.E.2d 733
(Ill. App. 3 Dist. 1985) / 71
Rees v. Albertson's, Inc., 587 P.2d 130 (Utah 1978) / 166
Reeves v. Bridges, 284 S.E.2d 416 (Ga. 1981) / 63
Reeves v. Gentile, 813 P.2d 111 (Utah 1991) / 324
Reickert v. Misciagna, 590 N.Y.S.2d 100 (A.D. 2 Dept. 1992) / 306
Reilly v. Tiergarten Inc., 633 A.2d 208 (Pa. Super. 1993) / 314
Reinert v. Dolezel, 383 N.W.2d 148 (Mich. App. 1985) / 99
Reyes v. Kuboyama, 870 P.2d 1281 (Hawaii 1994) / 274
Reynolds v. Hicks, 951 P.2d 761 (Wash 1998) / 329
Reynolds v. Nichols, 556h P.2d 102 (Ore. 1976) / 146
Rhea v. Grandview School District No. JT 116-200, 694 P.2d 666
(Wash. App. 1985) / 180
Richardson v. Carnegie Library Restaurant Inc., 763 P.2d 1153 (N.M. 1988) / 234
Richardson v. Matador Steak House, Inc., 948 P.2d 347 Utah 1997) / 325
Riddle v. Arizona Oncology Services, Inc., 924 P.2d 468 (Ariz. App. 1996) / 261
Riley v. H&H Operations, Inc. 436 S.E.2d 659 (Ga. 1993) / 272
Rinks v. Bearss, 921 P.2d 558 (Wash. App. Div. 1 1996) / 329
Riverside Enterprises, Inc. v. Rahn, 320 S.E.2d 595 (Ga. App. 1984) / 64
Roberts v. Roman, 457 So.2d 578 (Fla. App. 2 Dist. 1984) / 60
Robertson v. Okraj, 620 N.E.2d 612 (Ill. App. 4 Dist. 1993) / 277
Robinson v. Lamott, 289 N.W.2d 60 (Minn. 1979) / 102, 103
Rogalski v. Tavernier, 527 N.W.2d 73 (Mich. App. 1995) / 292, 293
Rogers v. Alvas, 207 Cal.Rptr. 60 (App. 1 Dist. 1984) / 50
Rollins v. Winn Dixie, 780 S.W.2d 765 (Tenn. App. 1989) / 320
Romano v. Stanley, 643 N.Y.S.2d 238 (A.D. 3 Dept. 1996) / 303
Romeo v. Van Otterloo, 323 N.W.2d 693 (Mich. App. 1982) / 100
Rong Yao Zhou v. Jennifer Mall Restaurant 534 A.2d 1268 (D.C. App. 1987) / 183
Rosas v. Damore, 430 N.W.2d 783 (Mich. App. 1988) / 229
Ross v. Ross, 200 N.W.2d 149 (Minn. 1972) / 103
Ross by Kanta v. Scott, 386 N.W.2d 18 (N.D. 1986) / 135
Ross's Dairies, Ltd. v. Rohan, 202 N.Y.S.2d 807 (Sup. 1960) / 125
Roster v. Moulton, 602 So. 2d 975 (Fla. App. 4 Dist. 1992) / 269
Roy v. Race Tavern, Inc., 423 N.W.2d 54 (Mich. App. 1988) / 229
Runge v. Watts, 589 P.2d 145 (Mont. 1979) / 110
Russell v. Olkowski, 535 N.Y.S.2d 187 (A.D. 3 Dept. 1988) / 235
Russo v. Plant City Moose Lodge No. 1668, 656 So. 2d 957
(Fla. App. 2 Dist. 1995) / 270
Rust v. Reyer, 670 N.Y.S.2d 822 (N.Y. 1998) / 305
Ruth v. Benvenutti, 449 N.E.2d 209 (Ill. App. 3 Dist. 1983) / 71
Ryan v. Friesenhahn, 911 S.W.2d 113 (Tex. App. San Antonio, 1995) / 323

S. & A. Beverage Co. of Beaumont No. 2 v. De Roven, 753 S.W.2d 507
(Tex. App.-Beaumont 1988) / 241
S.W. v. State, 431 So.2d 342 (Fla. App. 2 Dist. 1983) / 60
Saatzer v. Smith, 176 Cal.Rptr. 68 (App. 2 Dist. 1981) / 51
Sabatelli v. Omni International Hotels, Inc., 379 So.2d 444
(Fla. App. 3 Dist. 1980) / 62
Sagadin v. Ripper, 221 Cal.Rptr. 675 (App. 3 Dist. 1985) / 50
Sage v. Johnson, 437 N.W.2d 582 (Iowa 1989) / 283
Sager v. McClenden, 672 P.2d 697 (Ore. 1983) / 145
Sampson v. W. F. Enterprises, Inc., 611 S.W.2d 333 (Mo. App. 1980) / 107
Samson v. Smith, 560 A.2d 1024 (Del. 1989) / 221
Sanders v. Crosstown Market, Inc., 850 P.2d 1061 (Okl. 1993) / 313
Sanders v. Hercules Sheet Metal, Inc., 385 So.2d 772 (La. 1980) / 86
Sanders v. Officers Club of Connecticut, Inc., 493 A.2d 184 (Conn. 1985) / 55

Scatorchia v. Caputo, 32 N.Y.S.2d 534 (A.D. 1942) / 127
Schaffield v. Abboud, 19 Cal. Rptr. 205 (15 C.A. 4th 1133) / 263
Schelin v. Goldberg, 146 A.2d 648 (Pa.Super. 1958) / 148
Schirmer v. Yost, 400 N.Y.S.2d 655 (A.D. 1977) / 128, 130
Schooley v. Pinch's Deli Market, Inc., 912 P.2d 1044
(Wash. App. Div. 2 1996) / 328
Schooley v. Pinch's Deli Market, Inc., 951 P.2d 749 (Wash 1998) / 328
Schrader v. Carney, 586 N.Y.S.2d 687 (A.D. 4 Dept. 1992) / 306
Schreier v. Sonderleiter, 420 N.W.2d 821 (Iowa 1988) / 77
Schroer v. Synowiecki, 435 N.W.2d 875 (Neb. 1989) / 298
Schulker v. Roberson, 676 So. 2d 684 (La. App. 3 Cir. 1996) / 287
Seeley v. Sobczak, 281 N.W.2d 368 (Minn. 1979) / 102
Selchert v. Lien, 371 N.W.2d 791 (S.D. 1985) / 158
Senn v. Scudieri, 567 N.Y.S.2d 665
(Sup. Ct. App. Div. 1 Dept. 1991) / 303, 305
Settlemeyer v. Wilmington Veterans Post No. 49, 464 N.E.2d 251
(Ohio 1984) / 139, 237
Shannon v. Wilson, 947 S.W.2d 349 (Ark. 1997) / 262
Sheeky v. Big Flats Community, 543 N.Y.S.2d 18 (1989) / 235
Shelter Mut. Ins. Co. v. White, 930 S.W.2d 1 (Mo. App. W.D. 1996) / 297
Sherman v. Robinson, 591 N.Y.S.2d 974 (Ct. App. 1992) / 304, 306
Sigman v. Seafood Ltd. Partnership I, 817 P.2d 527 (Colo. 1991) / 265
Siltman v. Tulenchik, 1995 WL 6426 (Minn. App.) / 295
Silverhorn v. State, 358 P.2d 226 (Okl.Cr. App. 1960) / 141
Simpson v. Kilcher, 749 S.W.2d 386 (Mo. 1988) / 230
Sissle v. Stefenoni, 152 Cal.Rptr. 56 (App. 1 Dist. 1979) / 51
Sites v. Cloonan, 477 A.2d 547 (Pa.Super. 1984) / 149
Skruck v. State, 740 S.W.2d 819 (Tex. App. Houston [1 Dist.] 1987) / 164
Slade v. Smith's Management Corp., 808 P.2d 401 (Idaho 1991) / 275
Slager v. HWA Corp., 435 N.W.2d 349 (Iowa 1989) / 225
Slawson v. State, 276 S.W.2d 811 (Tex.Cr. App. 1955) / 163
Slicer v. Quigley, 429 A.2d 855 (Conn. 1980) / 56
Slocum v. D's & Jayes Valley Restaurant, 582 N.Y.S.2d 544
(A.D. 3 Dept. 1992) / 305
Smith v. Clark, 190 A.2d 441 (Pa. 1963) / 148
Smith v. Gregg, 946 S.W.2d 807 (Mo. App. 1997) / 297
Smith v. Harms, 865 P.2d 486 (Ore. App. 1993) / 314
Smith v. Kappel, 433 N.W.2d 588 (Wisc. App. 1988)
[rev. den. 439 N.W.2d 141 (Wisc. 1989)] / 244
Smith v. Merritt, 940 S.W.2d 602 (Tex 1997) / 323
Smith v. Sewell, 858 S.W.2d 350 (Tex. 1993) / 321
Smith v. Shaffer, 395 N.W.2d 853 (Iowa 1986) / 78
Smith v. The 10th Inning, Inc., 551 N.E.2d 1296 (Ohio 1990) / 302
Smith v. Tully, 665 A.2d 1333 (R.I. 1994) / 316
Smith v. West Rochelle Travel Agency, Inc., 656 N.Y.S.2d 340
(N.Y. App. 1997) / 306
Snyder v. Davenport, 323 N.W.2d 225 (Iowa 1982) / 77
Snyder v. Fish, 539 N.W.2d 197 (Iowa App. 1995) / 283
Snyder v. Viani, 885 P.2d 610 (Nev. 1994) / 299
Snyder v. West Rawlins Properties, Inc., 531 F. Supp. 701 (D.Wyo. 1982) / 192
Solberg v. Johnson, 760 P.2d 867 (Or. 1988) / 238
Soronen v. Olde Milford Inn, Inc., 218 A.2d 630 (N.J. 1966) / 120
Sorensen by Kerscher v. Jarvis, 350 N.W.2d 108 (Wis. 1984) / 188, 189
Sorrells v. M.Y.B. Hospitality Ventures, 435 S.E.2d 320(N.C. 1993) / 307
South Dakota v. Dole, 107 S.Ct. 2793 (1987) / 157
Southern Bell Telephone & Telegraph Co. v. Altman, 359 S.E.2d 385
(Ga. App. 1987) / 64
Southland Corp. v. Lewis, 940 S.W.2d 83 (Tex. 1997) / 322
Sparks v. Ober, 192 So.2d 81 (Fla. App. 3 Dist. 1966) / 62
Sparks v. Warren, 856 P.2d 337 (Ore. 1993) / 314
Spears v. Bradford, 652 So. 2d 628 (La. App. 1 Cir. 1995) / 287
Sports, Inc. v. Gilbert, 431 N.E.2d 534 (Ind. App. 1 Dist. 1982) / 74
Stachniewicz v. Mar-Cam Corporation, 488 P.2d 436 (Ore. 1971) / 144
Starr v. State, 734 S.W.2d 52 (Tex. App. Houston [1 Dist.] 1987) / 163
State v. Bohl, 317 N.W.2d 790 (N.D. 1982) / 134
State v. Buglione, 558 A.2d 51 (N.J. Super. A.D. 1989) / 232
State v. Chrisman, 676 P.2d419 (1984) / 232
State v. Comerford, 484 N.E.2d 993 (Ind. App. 3 Dist. 1985) / 73
State v. Connor, 202 N.W.2d 172 (Neb. 1972) / 113
State v. Dalton, 865 P.2d 575 (Wash. App. Div. 3 1994) / 328
State v. Denhardt, 760 P.2d 988 (Wyo. 1988) / 245
State v. DeVilliers, 633 P.2d 756 (Okl.Cr. App. 1981) / 141
State v. Eberhardt, 125 N.W.2d 1 (Neb. 1963) / 112
State v. Embrey, 198 N.W.2d 322 (Neb. 1972) / 112
State v. Gear, 143 P. 890 (Ore. 1914) / 143
State v. Graves, 42 N.W.2d 153 (Wis. 1950) / 187
State v. Gulley, 70 P. 385 (Ore. 1902) / 143
State v. Haarde, 554 A.2d 872 (N.J. Super. A.D. 1989) / 232

Cumulative
Table of Cases by State

Williams v. Saga Enterprises, 274 Cal. Rptr. 901 (Cal. App. 2 Dist. 1992) / 264
Zavala v. Regents of the University of California, 178 Cal.Rptr. 185 (App. 2 Dist. 1981) / 51

Colorado

Brown v. Hollywood Bar & Cafe, 942 P.2d 1363 (Colo. App. 1997) / 265
Casebolt v. Cowan, 829 P.2d 352 (Colo. 1992) / 265
Charlton v. Kimata, 815 P.2d 946 (Colo. 1991) / 266
Christoph v. Colorado Communications Corp., 946 P.2d 519 (Colo. App. 1997) / 265
Crespin v. Largo Corp., 698 P.2d 826 (Colo. App. 1984) / 54
Dickman v. Jackalope, Inc., 870 P.2d 1261 (Colo. App. 1994) / 265
Floyd v. Bartley, 727 P.2d 1109 (Colo. 1986) / 53
Forrest v. Lorrigan, 833 P.2d 873 (Colo. App. 1992) / 266
Hull v. Rund, 374 P.2d 351 (Colo. 1962) / 54
Kerby v. Flamingo Club, Inc., 532 P.2d 975 (Colo. App. 1974) / 54
Largo Corp. v. Crespin, 727 P.2d 1098 (Colo. 1986) / 54, 220
Leake v. Cain, 720 P.2d 152 (Colo. 1986) / 54
Lyons v. Nasby, 770 P.2d. 1250 (Colo. 1989) / 220
Sigman v. Seafood Ltd. Partnership I, 817 P.2d 527 (Colo. 1991) / 265
Thomas v. Pete's Satire, Inc., 717 P.2d 509 (Colo. App. 1985) / 54

Connecticut

Belanger v. Village Pub I, Inc., 603 A.2d 1173 (Conn. App. 1992) / 267
Boehm v. Kish, 517 A.2d 624 (Conn. 1986) / 55, 56
Bohan v. Last, 674 A.2d 839 (Conn. 1996) / 267
Coble v. Maloney, 643 A.2d 277 (Conn. App. 1994) / 266
Cooper v. Delta Chi Housing Corporation of Connecticut, 674 A.2d 858 (Ct. App. 1996) / 267
Ely v. Murphy, 540 A.2d 54 (Conn. 1988) / 56
Futterleib v. Mr. Happy's Inc., 548 A.2d 728 (Conn. App. 1988) / 220
Gionfriddo v. Gartenhaus Cafe, 546 A.2d 284 (Conn. App. 1988) / 220
Kelehear v. Larcon, Inc. 577 A.2d 746 (Conn. App. 1990) / 266
Kowal v. Hofhe, 436 A.2d 1 (Conn. 1980) /·56
London and Lancashire Indemnity Co. v. Duryea, 119 A.2d 325 (Conn. 1955) / 56
Menzie v. Kalmonowitz, 139 A. 698 (Conn. 1928) / 56
Merhi v. Becker, 325 A.2d 270 (Conn. 1973) / 57
Moore v. Bunk, 228 A.2d 510 (Conn. 1967) / 56
Nelson v. Steffens, 365 A.2d 1174 (Conn. 1976) / 56
Nolan v. Morelli, 226 A.2d 383 (Conn. 1967) / 56
Passini v. Decker, 467 A.2d 442 (Conn.Super. 1983) / 56
Pierce v. Albanese, 129 A.2d. 606 (Conn. 1957) / 56
Sanders v. Officers Club of Connecticut, Inc., 493 A.2d 184 (Conn. 1985) / 55
Slicer v. Quigley, 429 A.2d 855 (Conn. 1980) / 56

Delaware

Acker v. S.W. Cantinas, Inc., 586 A.2d 1178 (Del. Supr. 1991) / 268
DiOssi v. Maroney, 548 A.2d 1361 (Del. 1988) / 221
Hopper v. F.W. Corridori Roofing Co., 305 A.2d 309 (Del. 1973) / 59
McCall v. Villa Pizza, Inc., 636 A.2d 912 (Del. Supr. 1994) / 268
Pakes v. Megaw, 565 A.2d 914 (Del. Supr. 1989) / 268
Samson v. Smith, 560 A.2d 1024 (Del. 1989) / 221
State v. Peo, 42 A. 623 (Del.Ct.Gen.Sess. 1899) / 58
State v. Salkowski, 69 A. 839 (Del.Ct.Gen.Sess. 1907) / 58
Taylor v. Ruiz, 394 A.2d 765 (Del.Super. 1978) / 58
Wright v. Moffitt, 437 A.2d 554 (Del. 1981) / 58, 221

Florida

Allen v. Babrab, Inc., 438 So.2d 356 (Fla. 1983) / 62
Armstrong v. Munford, Inc., 451 So.2d 480 (Fla. 1984) / 61
Bankston v. Brennan, 480 So.2d 246 (Fla. App. 4 Dist 1985) / 61
Bankston v. Brennan, 507 So.2d 1385 (Fla. 1987) / 61
Bardy v. Walt Disney World Co., 643 So. 2d 46 (Fla. App. 5 Dist. 1994) / 270
Barnes v. B.K. Credit Service, Inc., 461 So.2d 217 (Fla. App. 1 Dist. 1984) / 61
Bennett v. Godfather's Pizza, Inc., 570 So.2d 1351 (Fla. App. 3 Dist. 1990)/269
Booth v. Abbey Road Beef and Booze, Inc., 532 So. 2d 1288 (Fla. App. 4 Dist. 1988) / 221
Bryant v. Jax Liquors, 352 So.2d 542 (Fla. App. 1 Dist. 1978) / 61
Burson v. Gate Petroleum Co., 401 So.2d 922 (Fla. App. 5 Dist. 1981) / 61
Crown Liquors of Broward, Inc. v. Evenrud, 436 So.2d 927 (Fla. App. 2 Dist. 1983) / 62
Davis v. Shiappacossee, 155 So.2d 365 (Fla. 1963) / 61
Dixon v. Saunders, 565 So. 2d 802 (Fla. App. 2 Dist. 1990) / 270
Dowell v. Gracewood Fruit Co., 559 So. 2d 217 (Fla. 1990) / 270
Ellis v. N.G.N. of Tampa, Inc., 586 So. 2d 1042 (Fla. 1991) / 269
Gormon v. Albertson's Inc., 519 So. 2d 1119 (Fla. App. 2 Dist. 1988) / 221
Kirkland v. Johnson, 499 So.2d 899 (Fla. App. 1 Dist. 1986) / 61
Lonestar Florida, Inc. v. Cooper, 408 So.2d 758 (Fla. App. 4 Dist. 1982) / 60
Migliore v. Crown Liquors of Broward, Inc., 448 So.2d 978 (Fla. 1984) / 61

Nieves v. Camacho Clothes, Inc., 645 So. 2d 507 (Fla. App. 5 Dist. 1994) / 268
O'Neale v. Hershoff, 634 So. 2d 644 (Fla. App. 3 Dist. 1993) / 270
Op. Att. Gen. 063-23 Feb. 22, 1963 / 61
People's Restaurant v. Sabo, 591 So. 2d 907 (Fla. 1991) / 269
Person v. Southland Corporation, 656 So. 2d 453 (Fla. 1995) / 269
Prevatt v. McClennan, 201 So.2d 780 (Fla. App. 2 Dist. 1967) / 61, 62
Pritchard v. Jax Liquors, Inc., 499 So.2d 926 (Fla. App. 1 Dist. 1986) / 61
Publix Supermarkets, Inc. v. Austin, 658 So. 2d 1064 (Fla. App. 5 Dist. 1995)/270
R. Hughes, Inc. v. Mitchell, 617 So. 2d 767·(Fla. App. 1 Dist. 1993) / 269
Roberts v. Roman, 457 So.2d 578 (Fla. App. 2 Dist. 1984) / 60
Roster v. Moulton, 602 So. 2d 975 (Fla. App. 4 Dist. 1992) / 269
Russo v. Plant City Moose Lodge No. 1668, 656 So. 2d 957 (Fla. App. 2 Dist. 1995) / 270
S.W. v. State, 431 So.2d 342 (Fla. App. 2 Dist. 1983) / 60
Sabatelli v. Omni International Hotels, Inc., 379 So.2d 444 (Fla. App. 3 Dist. 1980) / 62
Sparks v. Ober, 192 So.2d 81 (Fla. App. 3 Dist. 1966) / 62
Stevens v. Jefferson, 436 So.2d 33 (Fla. 1983) / 62
United Services Automobile Association v. Butler, 359 So.2d 498 (Fla. App. 4 Dist. 1978) / 60, 61
Williams v. Anheuser-Busch, Inc., 957 F. Supp. 1246 (M.D. Fla. 1997) 270

Georgia

Belding v. Johnson, 12 S.E. 304 (Ga. 1890) / 64
Bishop v. Fair Lanes Bowling, Inc., 623 F. Supp. 1195 (D.C.Ga. 1985) / 64
Bishop v. Fair Lanes Georgia Bowling, Inc., 803 F.2d 1548 (11th Cir. 1986)/222
Borders v. Board of Trustees, VFW Club, 500 S.E.2d 362 (Ga. App. 1998) / 273
Brumbelow v. Shoney's Big Boy of Carrollton, 329 S.E.2d 319 (Ga. App. 1985)/65
Dobozy v. Cochran Airport Systems, Inc., 330 S.E.2d 815 (Ga. App. 1985)/ 65
Eldridge v. Aronson, 472 S.E.2d 497 (Ga. App. 1996) / 271
Griffin Motel Co. v. Strickland, 479 S.E.2d 401 (Ga. App. 1996) / 272
Hadaway v. State, 378 S.E.2d 127 (Ga. App. 1989) / 222
Henry Grady Hotel Co. v. Sturgis, 28 S.E.2d 329 (Ga. App. 1943) / 64
Ihesiaba v. Pelletier, 448 S.E.2d 920 (Ga. App. 1994) / 272
Jaques v. Kendrick, 43 F.3d 628 (11th Cir. 1995) / 272
Kalpa v. Perczak, 658 F. Supp. 235 (N.D. Ga. 1987) / 222
Kappa Sigma International Fraternity v. Tootle, 473 S.E.2d 213 (Ga. App. 1996) / 272
Keaton v. Kroger Co., 237 S.E.2d 443 (Ga. App. 1977) / 64
Lee v. State, 412 S.E.2d 563 (Ga. App. 1991) / 271
Manuel v. Koonce, 425 S.E.2d 921 (Ga. App. 1992) / 273
Nunn v. Comidas Exquisitos, Inc., 305 S.E.2d 487 (Ga. App. 1983) / 64
Perryman v. Lufran, Inc., 434 S.E.2d 112 (Ga. App. 1993) / 272
Pirkle v. Hawley, 405 S.E.2d 71 (Ga. App. 1991) / 273
Reeves v. Bridges, 284 S.E.2d 416 (Ga. 1981) / 63
Riley v. H&H Operations, Inc. 436 S.E.2d 659 (Ga. 1993) / 272
Riverside Enterprises, Inc. v. Rahn, 320 S.E.2d 595 (Ga. App. 1984) / 64
Southern Bell Telephone & Telegraph Co. v. Altman, 359 S.E.2d 385 (Ga. App. 1987) / 64
Steedley v. Huntley's Jiffy Stores, Inc., 432 S.E.2d 625 (Ga. App. 1993) / 272
Stepperson, Inc. v. Long, 353 S.E.2d 461 (Ga. 1987) / 63, 222
Sutter v. Hutchings, 327 S.E.2d 716 (Ga. 1985) / 64, 65, 272
Taylor v. N.I.L., Inc., 470 S.E.2d 491 (Ga. App. 1996) / 272
Tibbs v. Studebaker's of Savannah, 362 S.E.2d 377 (Ga. App. 1987) / 65
Viau v. Fred Dean, Inc., 418 S.E.2d 604 (Ga. App. 1992) / 271
Whelchel v. Laing Properties, Inc., 378 S.E.2d 478 (Ga. App. 1989) / 273
White v. Hubbard, 416 S.E.2d 568 (Ga. App. 1996) / 272

Hawaii

Bertelmann v. TAAS Associates, 735 P.2d 930 (Hawaii 1987) / 67
Faulk v. Suzuki Motor Co. Ltd., 851 P.2d 332 (Hawaii App. 1993) / 274
Feliciano v. Waikiki Deep Water, Inc., 752 P.2d 1076 (Hawaii 1988) / 67
Johnston v. KFC National Management Co., 788 P.2d 159 (Hawaii 1990)/ 274
Myers v. South Seas Corporation, 871 P.2d 1235 (Hawaii App. 1992) / 274
Ono v. Applegate, 612 P.2d 533 (Hawaii 1980) / 66, 67
Reyes v. Kuboyama, 870 P.2d 1281 (Hawaii 1994) / 274
Winters v. Silver Fox Bar, 797 P.2d 51 (Hawaii 1990) / 274
Wong-Leong v. Hawaiian Indep. Refinery, Inc., 879 P.2d 538 (Hawaii 1994)/274

Idaho

Alegria v. Payonk, 619 P.2d 135 (Idaho 1980) / 69, 275
Bergman v. Henry, 766 P.2d 729 (Idaho 1988) / 223
Fisher v. Cooper, 775 P.2d 1216 (Idaho 1989) / 223
Hickman v. Fraternal Order of Eagles, 758 P.2d 704 (Idaho 1988) / 275
Slade v. Smith's Management Corp., 808 P.2d 401 (Idaho 1991) / 275

Illinois

Bachman v. Sharon & Lo's Place, Inc., 541 N.E.2d 153 (Ill. App. 3 Dist. 1989)/224
Bass v. Rothschild Liquor Stores, Inc., 232 N.E.2d 19 (Ill. App. 1 Dist. 1967)/71
Beukema v. Yomac, Inc., 672 N.E.2d 755 (Ill. App. 1 Dist. 1996) / 276

Camille v. Berry Fertilizers, Inc., 334 N.E.2d 205 (Ill. App. 4 Dist. 1975) / 72
Charles v. Seifried, 651 N.E.2d 154 (Ill. 1995) / 277
City of Carbondale v. Nelson, 484 N.E.2d 392 (Ill. App. 5 Dist. 1985) / 70
Coulter v. Swearingen, 447 N.E.2d 561 (Ill. App. 3 Dist. 1983) / 72
Cravens v. Inman, 586 N.E.2d 367 (Ill. 1991) / 277
Cruse v. Aden, 20 N.E. 73 (Ill. 1889) / 71, 72
Cunningham v. Brown, 174 N.E.2d 153 (Ill. 1961) / 71
Darguzas v. Robinson, 515 N.E.2d 451 (Ill. App. 2 Dist. 1987) / 71
Engel v. Lamplighter, Inc., 526 N.E.2d 641 (Ill. App. 3 Dist. 1988) / 224
Estate of Ritchie v. Farrell, 572 N.E.2d 367 (Ill. App. 3 Dist. 1991) / 279
Fabian v. Polish American Veterans, 466 N.E.2d 1239 (Ill. App. 1 Dist. 1984) / 72
First America Trust Co. v. McMurray, 620 N.E.2d 447 (Ill. App. 4 Dist. 1993) / 277
Fitzpatrick v. Carde Lounge, Ltd., 602 N.E.2d 19 (Ill. App. 1 Dist. 1992) / 278
Flory v. Weaver, 553 N.E.2d 105 (Ill. App. 4 Dist. 1990) / 277
Glinka v. Flame of Countryside, Inc., 524 N.E.2d 1102 (Ill. App. 1 Dist. 1988) / 223
Goodnight v. Piraino, 554 N.E.2d 1 (Ill. App. 3 Dist. 1990) / 278
Graham v. General U.S. Grant Post No. 2665 V.F.W., 248 N.E.2d 657
   (Ill. 1969) / 71
Haben v. Anderson, 597 N.E.2d 655 (Ill. App. 3 Dist. 1992) / 278
Harris v. Gower, Inc., 506 N.E.2d 624 (Ill. App. 5 Dist. 1987) / 224
Heldt v. Brei, 455 N.E.2d 842 (Ill. App. 1 Dist. 1983) / 72
Hopkins v. Powers, 497 N.E.2d 757 (Ill. 1986) / 71
Jackson v. Moreno, 663 N.E.2d 27 (Ill. App. 1 Dist. 1996) / 276
Jodelis v. Harris, 517 N.E.2d 1055 (Ill. 1987) / 224
Krawczyk v. Polinski, 642 N.E.2d 185 (Ill. App. 2 Dist. 1994) / 277
Linnabery v. De Pauw, 695 F. Supp. 411 (C.D. Ill. 1988) / 223
Lowe v. Rubin, 424 N.E.2d 710 (Ill. App. 1 Dist. 1981) / 72
Martin v. Palazzolo Produce Co., Inc., 497 N.E.2d 881 (Ill. App. 5 Dist. 1986) / 224
Matusak v. Chicago Transit Authority, 520 N.E.2d 925
   (Ill. App. 1 Dist. 1988) / 224
McKeown v. Homoya, 568 N.E.2d 528 (Ill. App. 5 Dist. 1991) / 277
Miller v. Moran, 421 N.E.2d 1046 (Ill. App. 4 Dist. 1981) / 72
Miller v. Owens-Illinois Glass Co., 199 N.E.2d 300 (Ill. App. 5 Dist. 1964) / 72
Morgan v. Kirk Brothers, Inc., 444 N.E.2d 504 (Ill. App. 2 Dist. 1982) / 71
Nelson v. Araiza, 372 N.E.2d 637 (Ill. 1977) / 71
People v. Binder, 536 N.E.2d 218 (Ill. App. 4 Dist. 1989) / 223
People v. Helt, 526 N.E. 842 (Ill. App. 3 Dist. 1987) / 223
People v. Monroe, 333 N.E.2d 239 (Ill. App. 2 Dist. 1975) / 70
People v. Rhoes, 612 N.E.2d 536 (Ill. App. Dist. 4 1993) / 275
Puckett v. Mr. Luckey's Ltd., 529 N.E.2d 1169 (Ill. App. 4 Dist. 1989) / 224, 277
Quinn v. Sigma Rho Chapter of Beta Theta Pi Fraternity,
   507 N.E.2d 1193 (Ill. App. 4 Dist. 1987) / 72, 278
Raithel v. Dustcutter, Inc., 634 N.E.2d 1163 (Ill. App. 4 Dist. 1994) / 276
Rainey v. Pickera, 651 N.E.2d 747 (Ill. App. 5th Div. 1995) / 277
Reed for Use and Ben. of Reed v. Fleming, 477 N.E.2d 733
   (Ill. App. 3 Dist. 1985) / 71
Robertson v. Okraj, 620 N.E.2d 612 (Ill. App. 4 Dist. 1993) / 277
Ruth v. Benvenutti, 449 N.E.2d 209 (Ill. App. 3 Dist. 1983) / 71
Sterenberg v. Sir Lion, Inc. 546 N.E.2d 294 (Ill. App. 1 Dist. 1989) / 224
Tate v. Coonce, 421 N.E.2d 1385 (Ill. App. 3 Dist. 1981) / 71
Thompson v. Trickle, 449 N.E.2d 910 (Ill. App. 1 Dist. 1983) / 72
Walter v. Carriage House Hotels, Ltd., 646 N.E.2d 599 (Ill. 1995) / 276
Weiner v. Trasatti, 311 N.E.2d 313 (Ill. App. 1 Dist. 1974) . 71
Wienke v. ChaCmpaign Cty. Grain Ass'n., 447 N.E.2d 1388
   (Ill. App. 4 Dist. 1983) / 72
Woodward v. Mainer, 521 N.E.2d 303 (Ill. App. 5 Dist. 1988) / 224
Zamiar v. Linderman, 478 N.E.2d 534 (Ill. App. 1 Dist. 1985) / 72

Indiana

Ashlock v. Norris, 475 N.E.2d 1167 (Ind. App. 3 Dist. 1985) / 74, 75
Baxter v. Galligher, 604 N.E.2d 1245 (Ind. App. 3 Dist. 1992) / 281
Bearman v. University of Notre Dame, 453 N.E.2d 1196
   (Ind. App. 3 Dist. 1983) / 75, 280
Booker, Inc. v. Morrill, 639 N.E.2d 358 (Ind. 1994) / 280
Bowling v. Popp, 536 N.E.2d 511 (Ind. App. 1 Dist. 1989) / 225
Brattain v. Herron, 309 N.E.2d 150 (Ind. App. 1 Dist. 1974) / 74
Burrell v. Meads, 569 N.E.2d 637 (Ind. 1991) / 281
Campbell v. Board of Trustees of Wabash College, 495 N.E.2d 227
   (Ind. App. 1 Dist. 1986) / 75
Davis v. Stinson, 508 N.E.2d 65 (Ind. App. 4 Dist. 1987) / 75
Elder v. Fisher, 217 N.E.2d 847 (Ind. 1966) / 74
Elsperman v. Plump, 446 N.E.2d 1027 (Ind. App. 1 Dist. 1983) / 74
Estate of Cummings v. PPG Industries, Inc., 651 N.E.2d 305
   (Ind. App. 1995) / 279
Fast Eddies v. Hall, 688 N.E.2d 1270 (Ind. App. 1997) / 279
Foster v. Purdue University, 567 N.E.2d 865 (Ind. App. 3 Dist. 1991) / 280
Gariup Construction Company, Inc. v. Foster, 519 N.E.2d 1224 (Ind. 1988) / 75
Jackson v. Gore, 634 N.E.2d 503 (Ind. App. 1 Dist. 1994) / 280

Kolkman v. Falstaff Brewing Corporation, 511 N.E.2d 478
   (Ind. App. 4 Dist. 1987) / 75
Lather v. Berg, 519 N.E.2d 755 (Ind. App. 2 Dist. 1988) / 73
Motz v. Johnson, 651 N.E.2d 1163 (Ind. App. 1995) / 280, 281
Muex v. Hindel Bowling Lanes Inc., 596 N.E.2d 263 (Ind. App. 2 Dist. 1992) / 280
National Railroad Passenger Corp. v. Everton, 655 N.E.2d 360
   (Ind. App. 1995) / 280
Parrett v. Lebamoff, 408 N.E.2d 1344 (Ind. App. 3 Dist. 1980) / 74
Picadilly, Inc. v. Colvin, 519 N.E.2d 1217 (Ind. 1988) / 74
Rauck v. Hawn, 564 N.E.2d 334 (Ind. App. Dist. 1 1996) / 279
Sports, Inc. v. Gilbert, 431 N.E.2d 534 (Ind. App. 1 Dist. 1982) / 74
State v. Comerford, 484 N.E.2d 993 (Ind. App. 3 Dist. 1985) / 73
Thompson v. Ferdinand Sesquicentennial Committee, Inc., 637 N.E.2d 178
   (Ind. App. 1 Dist. 1985) / 279
Whisman v. Fawcett, 470 N.E.2d 73 (Ind. 1984) / 74
Williams v. Crist, 484 N.E.2d 576 (Ind. 1985) / 75

Iowa

Atkins v. Baxter, 423 N.W.2d 6 (Iowa 1988) / 225
Bauer v. Cole, 467 N.W.2d 221 (Iowa 1991) / 283
Bauer v. Dann, 428 N.W.2d 658 (Iowa 1988) / 225
Blesz v. Weisbrod, 424 N.W.2d 451 (Iowa 1988) / 226
Burkis v. Contemporary Ind. Midwest, 435 N.W.2d 397 (Iowa App. 1988) / 226
Clark v. Mincks, 364 N.W.2d 226 (Iowa 1985) / 178, 283
Connolly v. Conlan, 371 N.W.2d 832 (Iowa 1985) / 77
Cox v. Rolling Golf Course Corp., 532 N.W.2d 761 (Iowa 1995) / 282
DeMore by DeMore v. Dieters, 334 N.W.2d 734 (Iowa 1983) / 76, 283
Eddy v. Casey's General Store, Inc., 485 N.W.2d 633 (Iowa 1992) / 282
Fuhrmam v. Total Petroleum, Inc., 398 N.W.2d 807 (Iowa 1987) / 77
Fullmar v. Tague, 500 N.W.2d 432 (Iowa 1993) / 283
Haafke v. Mitchell, 347 N.W.2d 381 (Iowa 1984) / 77
Hayward v. P.D.A., 573 N.W.2d 29 (Iowa 1997) / 282
Hobbiebrunken v. G&S Enterprises, Inc., 470 N.W.2d 19 (Iowa 1991) / 282
Hoth v. Meisner, 548 N.W.2d 152 (Iowa 1996) / 282
Kelly v. Sinclair Oil Corp., 476 N.W.2d 341 (Iowa 1991) / 282
Kone v. Joe Lang Tap, Inc., 418 N.W.2d 377 (Iowa App. 1987) / 77
Lewis v. State, 256 N.W.2d 181 (Iowa 1977) / 77
Nutting v. Zieger, 482 N.W.2d 424 (Iowa 1992) / 282
Paul v. Ron Moore Oil Co., 487 N.W.2d 337 (Iowa 1997) / 282
Sage v. Johnson, 437 N.W.2d 582 (Iowa 1989) / 283
Schreier v. Sonderleiter, 420 N.W.2d 821 (Iowa 1988) / 77
Slager v. HWA Corp., 435 N.W.2d 349 (Iowa 1989) / 225
Smith v. Shaffer, 395 N.W.2d 853 (Iowa 1986) / 78
Snyder v. Davenport, 323 N.W.2d 225 (Iowa 1982) / 77
Snyder v. Fish, 539 N.W.2d 197 (Iowa App. 1995) / 283
State v. Rosenstiel, 473 N.W.2d 59 (Iowa 1991) / 281
Summerhays v. Clark, 509 N.W.2d 748 (Iowa 1993) / 282
Thorp v. Casey's General Stores, Inc., 446 N.W.2d 457 (Iowa 1989) / 282

Kansas

Fudge v. City of Kansas City, 720 P.2d 1093 (Kansas 1986) / 79, 80
Ling v. Jan's Liquors, 703 P.2d 731 (Kansas 1985) / 79
McGee by and through McGee v. Chalfant, 806 P.2d 980 (Kan. 1991) / 284
Meyers v. Grubaugh, 750 P.2d 1031 (Kansas 1988) at 1037 / 227
Mills v. City of Overland Park, 837 P.2d 370 (Kan. 1992) / 284
State v. Robinson, 718 P.2d 1313 (Kansas 1986) / 79
State v. Sleeth, 664 P.2d 883 (Kan. App. 1983) / 79
Thies v. Cooper, 753 P.2d 1280 (Kan. 1988) / 284

Kentucky

Grayson Fraternal Order of Eagles v. Claywell, 736 S.W.2d 328 (Ky. 1987) / 82, 83
Nally v. Blandford, 291 S.W.2d 832 (Ky. 1956) / 81
Pike v. George, 434 S.W.2d 626 (Ky. 1968) / 82

Louisiana

Bertrand v. Kratzer's Country Market, 563 So. 2d 1302
   (La. App. 3 Cir. 1990) / 287
Bourgeois v. Puglisi, 615 So. 2d 1047 (La. App. 1 Cir. 1993) / 287
Broussard v. Peltier, 499 So.2d 1026 (La. App. 3 Cir. 1986) / 86
Chausse v. Southland Corporation, 400 So.2d 1199 (La. App. 1 Cir. 1981) / 85, 286
Farrington v. Houston's Inc., 750 F.2d 492 (5th Cir. 1985) / 85
Edison v. Walker, 573 So. 2d 545 (La. App. 1 Cir. 1991) / 286
Garcia on Behalf of Garcia v. Jennings, 427 So.2d 1329 (La. App. 2 Cir. 1983) / 85
Gregor v. Constitution State Insurance Co., 534 So. 2d 1340
   (La. App. 4 Cir. 1988) / 287
Gresham v. Davenport, 524 So. 2d 48 (La. App. 1988) decided on appeal
   537 So. 2d 1144 (La. 1989) / 227, 285
Hollis v. City of Baton Rouge, 593 So. 2d 388 (La. App. 1 Cir. 1991) / 287
Hopkins v. Sovereign Fire & Casualty Ins. Co., 626 So. 2d 880
   (La. App. 3 Cir. 1993 / 286

Lee v. Peerless Insurance Company, 183 So.2d 328 (La. 1966) / 85
Lowe v. Patterson, 492 So.2d 110 (La. App. 1 Cir. 1986) / 86
Mills v. Harris, 615 So. 2d 533 (La. App. 3 Cir. 1993) / 282
Nichols v. Hodges, 385 So.2d 298 (La. App. 1 Cir. 1980) / 86
Pence v. Ketchum, 326 So.2d 831 (La. 1976) / 85
Persilver v. Louisiana Department of Transportation, 592 So. 2d 1344
  (La. App. 1 Cir. 1991) / 286
Sanders v. Hercules Sheet Metal, Inc., 385 So.2d 772 (La. 1980) /86
Schulker v. Roberson, 676 So. 2d 684 (La. App. 3 Cir. 1996) / 287
Spears v. Bradford, 652 So. 2d 628 (La. App. 1 Cir. 1995) / 287
State v. Peterson, 343 So.2d 1038 (La. 1977) / 85
Thrasher v. Leggett, 373 So.2d 494 (La. 1979) / 86
Vaughan v. Hair, 645 So. 2d 1177 (La. App. 3 Cir. 1994) / 286

Maine

Albano v. Colby College, 822 F. Supp 840 (D. Maine 1993) / 288
Douglass v. Kenyon Oil Co., Inc., 618 A.2d 220 (Me. 1992) / 288
Peters v. Saft, 597 A.2d 50 (Me. 1991) / 288
Swan v. Sohio Oil Co., 618 A.2d 214 (Me. 1992) / 288

Maryland

Boyd v. Board of Liquor License Commission for Baltimore City,
  692 A.2d 1 (Md. App. 1997) / 289
Felder v. Butler, 438 A.2d 494 (Md. 1981) / 89
Fisher v. O'Connor's, Inc., 452 A.2d 1313 (Md.Sp. App. 1982) / 90
Hebb v. Walker, 536 A.2d 113 (Md. App. 1988) / 90
Kuykendall v. Top Notch Laminates, Inc., 520 A.2d 1115 (Md. App. 1987) / 90
Moran v. Foodmaker, Inc., 594 A.2d 587 (Md. App. 1991) / 289
State v. Hatfield, 78 A.2d 754 (Md. 1951) / 89
Valentine v. On Target, 686 A.2d 636 (Md. App. 1996) / 289

Massachusetts

Adamian v. Three Sons, Inc., 233 N.E.2d 18 (Mass. 1968) / 92
Alioto v. Marnell, 520 N.E.2d 1284 (Mass. 1988) / 93
Allenby v. M. & C. Enterprises, Inc., 322 N.E.2d 422 (Mass. App. 1975) / 92
Bennett v. Eagle Brook Country Store, 557 N.E.2d 1166 (Mass. 1990) / 289
Brown v. Jones, 503 N.W.2d 735 (Mich. App. 1993) / 286
Carey v. New Yorker of Worcester, Inc., 245 N.E.2d 420 (Mass. 1969) / 92
Cimino v. Milford Keg, Inc., 431 N.E.2d 920 (Mass. 1982) / 92
Cremins v. Clancy, 612 N.E.2d 1183 (Mass. 1993) / 290
Dimond v. Sacilotto, 233 N.E.2d 20 (Mass. 1968) / 93
Gabree v. King, 614 F.2d 1 (1st Cir. 1980) / 91
Gottlin v. Graves, 662 N.E.2d 711 (Mass. App. Ct. 1996) / 290
Hamilton v. Ganias, 632 N.E.2d 407 (Mass. 1994) / 291
Howard Johnson Co. v. Alcoholic Beverage Control, 510 N.E.2d 293
  (Mass. App. Ct. 1987) / 228
Irwin v. Town of Ware, 467 N.E.2d 1292 (Mass. 1984) / 93
Kane v. Fields Corner Grille, Inc., 171 N.E.2d 287 (Mass. 1961) / 92
Kirby v. LeDisco, 614 N.E.2d 1016 (Mass. App. Ct. 1993) / 290
Langemann v. Davis, 495 N.E.2d 847 (Mass. 1986) / 93
Makynen v. Mustakangas, 655 N.E.2d 1284 (Mass. App. Ct. 1995) / 291
Manning v. Nobile, 582 N.E.2d 942 (Mass. 1991) / 291
McGuiggan v. New England Telephone & Telegraph Company, 496 N.E.2d 141
  (Mass. 1986) / 92, 93
Michnik-Zilberman v. Gordon's Liquor, Inc., 453 N.E.2d 430 (Mass. 1983) / 93
O'Hanley v. Ninety-Nine, Inc., 421 N.E.2d 1217 (Mass. App. 1981) / 92
O'Sullivan v. Hemisphere Broadcasting, 520 N.E.2d 429 (Mass. 1996) / 290
Stock v. Fife, 430 N.E.2d 845 (Mass. App. 1982) / 93
Tobin v. Norwood Country Club, Inc., 661 N.E.2d 627 (Mass. 1996) / 290
Vickowski v. Polish American Cit. Club, 664 N.E.2d 429 (Mass. 1996) / 290
Wallace v. Wilson, 575 N.E.2d 1134 (Mass. 1991) / 2291
Wiska v. St. Stanislaus Social Club, Inc., 390 N.E.2d 1133 (Mass. 1979) / 93
Wood v. Ray-Al Cafe, Inc., 208 N.E.2d 225 (Mass. 1965) / 92

Michigan

Arbelius v. Poletti, 469 N.W.2d 436 (Mich. App. 1991) / 293
Barrett v. Campbell, 345 N.W.2d 614 (Mich. App. 1983) / 98
Behnke v. Pierson, 175 N.W.2d 303 (Mich. 1970) / 99
Browder v. International Fidelity Insurance Company, 321 N.W.2d 668
  (Mich. 1982) / 98
Brown v. Jones, 503 N.W.2d 735 (Mich. App. 1993) / 291
Christensen v. Parrish, 266 N.W.2d 826 (Mich. App. 1978) / 95, 99
Cornack v. Sweeney, 339 N.W.2d 26 (Mich. App. 1983) / 97
Dhuy v. Rude, 465 N.W.2d 32 (Mich. App. 1990) / 292
Dines v. Henning, 459 N.W.2d 132 (Mich. App. 1990) / 291
Dobson v. Maki, 457 N.W.2d 132 (Mich. App. 1990) / 293
Felix v. Milliken, 463 F. Supp. 1360 (E.D.Mich. 1978) / 95
Findling v. T.P. Operating Company, 361 N.W.2d 376 (Mich. App. 1984) / 95
Gardner v. Wood, 414 N.W.2d 706 (Mich. 1987) / 96
Goss v. Richmond, 381 N.W.2d 776 (Mich. App. 1985) / 98

Grasser v. Fleming, 253 N.W.2d 757 (Mich. App. 1977) / 97
Gregory v. Kurtis, 310 N.W.2d 415 (Mich. App. 1981) / 97, 98
Hasty v. Broughton, 348 N.W.2d 299 (Mich. App. 1984) / 97
Heyler v. Dixon, 408 N.W.2d 121 (Mich. App. 1987) / 97, 291
Hollerud v. Malamis, 174 N.W.2d 626 (Mich. App. 1969) / 97
Jackson v. PKM Corporation, 403 N.W.2d 106 (Mich. App. 1987) / 228
Jackson v. PKM Corp. 422 N.W.2d 657 (Mich. 1988) / 229
Kerry v. Turnage, 397 N.W.2d 543 (Mich. App. 1986) / 98
Klotz v. Persenaire, 360 N.W.2d 255 (Mich. App. 1984) / 99
Lamson v. Martin, after remand, 549 N.W.2d 878 (Mich. App. 1996) / 291
Larrow v. Miller, 548 N.W.2d 704 (Mich. App. 1996) / 293
Longstreth v. Gensel, 377 N.W.2d 804 (Mich. 1985) / 95, 99, 293
Lover v. Sampson, 205 N.W.2d 69 (Mich. App. 1972) / 95, 97
Lucido v. Apollo Lanes & Bar, Inc., 333 N.W.2d 246 (Mich. App. 1983) / 97, 98
Manuel v. Weitzman, 191 N.W.2d 474 (Mich. 1971) / 98
McDaniel v. Crapo, 40 N.W.2d 724 (Mich. 1950) / 97
Megge v. United States, 344 F.2d 31 (6th Cir. 1965) / 100
Miller v. Ocampaugh, 477 N.W.2d 105 (Mich. App. 1991) / 291
Millross v. Plum Hollow Golf Club, 413 N.W.2d 17 (Mich. 1987) / 98, 99
Millross v. Tomakowski, 381 N.W.2d 786 (Mich. App. 1985) / 100
Morris v. Markley, 371 N.W.2d 464 (Mich. App. 1985) / 97
Pollard v. Village of Ovid, 446 N.W.2d 574 (Mich. App. 1989) / 292
Reinert v. Dolezel, 383 N.W.2d 148 (Mich. App. 1985) / 99
Rogalski v. Tavernier, 527 N.W.2d 73 (Mich. App. 1995) / 292, 293
Romeo v. Van Otterloo, 323 N.W.2d 693 (Mich. App. 1982) / 100
Rosas v. Damore, 430 N.W.2d 783 (Mich. App. 1988) / 229
Roy v. Race Tavern, Inc., 423 N.W.2d 54 (Mich. App. 1988) / 229
Tennile v. Action Distribution Co. 570 N.W.2d 130 (Mich. App. 1997) / 292
Thaut v. Finley, 213 N.W.2d 820 (Mich. App. 1973) / 95
Todd v. Biglow, 214 N.W.2d 733 (Mich. 1974) / 98
Town & Country Lanes, Inc. v. Liquor Control Commission,
  446 N.W.2d 335 (Mich. App. 1990) / 291
Traxler v. Koposky, 384 N.W.2d 819 (Mich. App. 1986) / 99
Verdusco v. Miller, 360 N.W.2d 281 (Mich. App. 1984) / 98
Waynick v. Chicago's Last Department Store, 269 F.2d 322 (7th Cir. 1959) / 97
Weiss v. Hodge, 567 N.W.2d 468 (Mich. App. 1997) / 292
Westcoat v. Mielke, 310 N.W.2d 293 (Mich. App. 1981) / 99
Whittaker v. Jet-Way, Inc., 394 N.W.2d 111 (Mich. App. 1986) / 9

Minnesota

Alholm v. Wilt, 348 N.W.2d 106 (Minn. App. 1984) / 103
Beseke v. Garden Center, Inc., 401 N.W.2d 428 (Minn. App. 1987) / 103
Cady v. Coleman, 315 N.W.2d 593 (Minn. 1982) / 103
Cole v. City of Spring Lake Park, 314 N.W.2d 836 (Minn. 1982) / 103
Englund v. MN CA Partners / MN Joint Ventures, 555 N.W.2d 328
  (Minn. App. 1997) / 295
Fitzer v. Bloom, 253 N.W.2d 395 (Minn. 1977) / 103
Gutwein v. Edwards, 419 N.W.2d 809 (Minn. App. 1988) / 229
Hannah v. Chmielewski, Inc., 323 N.W.2d 781 (Minn. 1982) / 102
Hannah v. Jensen, 298 N.W.2d 52 (Minn. 1980) / 102
Hoffman v. Wiltscheck, 379 N.W.2d 145 (Minn. App. 1985) / 103
Hollerich v. City of Good Thunder, 340 N.W.2d 665 (Minn. 1983) / 102
Holmquist v. Miller, 367 N.W.2d 468 (Minn. 1985) / 103, 296
Jewett v. Deutsch, 437 N.W.2d 717 (Minn. App. 1989) / 294
Knudsen v. Peickert, 221 N.W.2d 785 (Minn. 1974) / 102
Kryzer v. Champlin Am. Leg. No. 600, 494 N.W.2d 35, 37 (Minn. 1992) / 294, 295
Larson v. Carchedi, 419 N.W.2d 132 (Minn. App. 1988) / 102, 229
Larson v. Moorhead Country Club, 395 N.W.2d 448 (Minn. App. 1986) / 102
Lefto v. Hoggsbreath Enterprises, 567 N.W.2d 746 (Minn. App. 1997) / 294
Martinson v. Monticello Municipal Liquors, 209 N.W.2d 902 (Minn. 1973) / 102
Meany v. Newell, 367 N.W.2d 472 (Minn. 1985) / 103
Mettling v. Mulligan, 225 N.W.2d 825 (Minn. 1975) / 102
Quinn v. Winkel's, Inc., 279 N.W.2d 65 (Minn. 1979) / 102
Randall v. Village of Excelsior, 103 N.W.2d 131 (Minn. 1960) / 102
Robinson v. Lamott, 289 N.W.2d 60 (Minn. 1979) / 102, 103
Ross v. Ross, 200 N.W.2d 149 (Minn. 1972) / 103
Seeley v. Sobczak, 281 N.W.2d 368 (Minn. 1979) / 102
Siltman v. Tulenchik, 1995 WL 6426 (Minn. App.) / 295
Stevens v. Thielen, 394 N.W.2d 834 (Minn. App. 1986) / 103
Strand v. Village of Watson, 72 N.W.2d 609 (Minn. 1955) / 101
Trail v. Village of Elk River, 175 N.W.2d 916 (Minn. 1970) / 102
Vanwagner v. Mattison, 533 N.W.2d 75 (Minn. App. 1995) / 295
Wagner v. Schwegmann's South Town Liquor, Inc., 485 N.W.2d 730
  (Minn. Ct. App. 1992) / 294
Weber v. Au, 512 N.W.2d 348 (Minn. Ct. App. 1994) / 294

Mississippi

Boutwell v. Sullivan, 469 So.2d 526 (Miss. 1985) / 105
Bryant v. Alpha Entertainment Corp., 508 So.2d 1094 (Miss. 1987) / 105
Cuevas v. Royal D'Iberville Hotel, 498 So.2d 346 (Miss. 1986) / 105

Dunagin v. City of Oxford, Mississippi, 718 F.2d 738 (5th Cir. 1983); cert.den. 467 US 1259 (1984) / 104
Maine v. Office Depot, Inc., 914 F. Supp. 1413 (S.D. Miss. 1996) / 296
Munford, Inc. v. Peterson, 368 So.2d 213 (Miss. 1979) / 105

Missouri

Andres v. Alpha Kappa Lambda Fraternity, 730 S.W.2d 547 (Mo.banc 1987) / 107, 108
Bernickus v. Bomar, 768 S.W.2d 210 (Mo. App. 1989) / 230
Carver v. Schafer, 647 S.W.2d 570 (Mo. App. 1983) / 107
Casey's General Stores Inc. v. Downing, 757 S.W.2d 1 (Mo. App. 1988) / 230
Childress v. Sams, 736 S.W.2d 48 (Mo. en banc 1987) / 107, 108
Elliot v. Kessler, 799 S.W.2d 97 (Mo. App. W.D. 1990) / 297
G & D Ramseur, Inc. v. Franklin, 652 S.W.2d 279 (Mo. App. 1983) / 106
Harriman v. Smith, 697 S.W.2d 219 (Mo. App. 1985) / 107, 108
Kelley v. Supervisor of Liquor Control, State of Missouri, 823 S.W.2d 147 (Mo. App. 1992) / 296
Lambing v. Southland Corp., 739 S.W.2d 717 (Mo.banc 1987) / 107
Mueller v. JPA Foods, Inc., 767 S.W.2d 110 (Mo. App. 1989) / 230
Nesbitt v. Westport Square Ltd., 624 S.W.2d 519 (Mo. App. 1981) / 107
Nisbet v. Bucher, 949 S.W.2d 111 (Mo. Ct. App. 1997) / 297
Sampson v. W. F. Enterprises, Inc., 611 S.W.2d 333 (Mo. App. 1980) / 107
Shelter Mut. Ins. Co. v. White, 930 S.W.2d 1 (Mo. App. W.D. 1996) / 297
Simpson v. Kilcher, 749 S.W.2d 386 (Mo. 1988) / 230
Smith v. Gregg, 946 S.W.2d 807 (Mo. App. 1997) / 297
State v. Henry, 254 S.W.2d 307 (Mo. App. 1953) / 106
State v. Larson, 623 S.W.2d 69 (Mo. App. 1981) / 106
State v. Patton, 336 S.W.2d 726 (Mo. App. 1960) / 106
State v. Perkins, 773 S.W.3d 237 (Mo. App. 1989) / 230
Trammell v. Mathis, 744 St.W.2d 474 (Mo. App. 1987) / 107
Withers v. Supervisor of Liquor Control, 655 S.W.2d 857 (Mo. App. 1983) / 106

Montana

Ballou v. Sigma Nu General Fraternity, 352 S.E.2d 488 (S.C. App. 1986) / 110
Bissett v. DMI, Inc., 717 P.2d 545 (Mont. 1986) / 110
Deeds v. United States, 306 F. Supp. 348 (D.Mont. 1969) / 110
Folda v. City of Bozeman, 582 P.2d 767 (Mont. 1978) / 110
Graham v. Montana State University, 767 P.2d 301 (Mont. 1988) / 231
Jevning v. Skyline Bar, 726 P.2d 326 (Mont. 1986) / 111
Nehring v. LaCounte, 712 P.2d 1329 (Mont. 1986) / 110, 111
Peschke v. Carroll College, 929 P.2d 874 (Mont. 1996) / 298
Runge v. Watts, 589 P.2d 145 (Mont. 1979) / 110
Swartzenberger v. Billings Labor Temple Ass'n., 586 P.2d 712 (Mont. 1978) / 110
Thoring v. LaCounte, 733 P.2d 340 (Mont. 1987) / 111

Nebraska

Holmes v. Circo, 244 N.W.2d 65 (Neb. 1976) / 114
Miller v. Concordia Teachers College of Seward, Nebraska, 296 F.2d 100 (8th Cir. 1961) / 114
Pelzek v. American Legion, 463 N.W.2d 321 (Neb. 1990) / 298
Schroer v. Synowiecki, 435 N.W.2d 875 (Neb. 1989) / 298
State v. Connor, 202 N.W.2d 172 (Neb. 1972) / 113
State v. Eberhardt, 125 N.W.2d 1 (Neb. 1963) / 112
State v. Embrey, 198 N.W.2d 322 (Neb. 1972) / 112
State v. Harris, 352 N.W.2d 581 (Neb. 1984) / 112
State v. Laue, 402 N.W.2d 313 (Neb. 1987) / 113
State v. Lesiak, 449 N.W.2d 550 (Neb. 1989) / 298
State v. Masur, 432 N.W.2d 815 (Neb. 1988) / 231
State v. Reeder, 160 N.W.2d 753 (Neb. 1968) / 113
State v. Rys, 183 N.W.2d 253 (Neb. 1971) / 113
State v. Smith, 377 N.W.2d 527 (Neb. 1985) / 113
Strong v. K & K Investments, Inc. 343 N.W.2d 912 (Neb. 1984) / 114

Nevada

Bell v. Alpha Tau Omega Fraternity, 642 P.2d 161 (Nev. 1982) / 116
Davies v. Butler, 602 P.2d 605 (Nev. 1979) / 116
Hamm v. Carson City Nugget, Inc., 450 P.2d 358 (Nev. 1969) / 115
Hinegardner v. Marcor Resorts, 844 P.2d 800 (Nev. 1992) / 299
Snyder v. Viani, 885 P.2d 610 (Nev. 1994) / 299
Van Cleave v. Kietz-Mill Minit Mart, 633 P.2d 1220 (Nev. 1981) / 116
Yoscovitch v. Wasson, 645 P.2d 975 (Nev. 1982) / 116

New Hampshire

Brown v. Cathay Island, Inc., 480 A.2d 43 (N.H. 1984) / 118
Burns v. Bradley, 419 A.2d 1069 (N.H. 1980) / 118
Hickingbotham v. Burke, 662 A.2d 297 (N.H. 1995) / 300
MacLeod v. Ball, 663 A.2d 632 (N.H. 1995) / 300
Ramsey v. Anctil, 211 A.2d 900 (N.H. 1965) / 118
State v. Small, 111 A.2d 201 (N.H. 1955) / 117, 118

State v. Zeta Chi Fraternity, 696 A.2d 536 (N.H. 1997) /. 299
Weldy v. Town of Kingston, 514 A.2d 1257 (N.H. 1986) / 117, 118

New Jersey

Aliulis v. Tunnel Hill Corporation, 284 A.2d 180 (N.J. 1971) / 120
Allen v. Rutgers State University, 523 A.2d 262 (N.J.Super. A.D. 1987) / 121
Batten by Batten v. Bobo, 528 A.2d 572 (N.J.Super.L. 1986) / 120
Blair v. Anik Liquors, 510 A.2d 314 (N.J.Super.L. 1986) / 119
Brett v. Great American Recreation, Inc., 652 A.2d 774 (N.J. Super. A.D. 1995) / 302
Buckley v. Estate of Pirolo, 500 A.2d 703 (N.J. 1985) / 120
Cassanello v. Luddy, 695 A.2d 325 (N.J Sup. Ct. 1997) / 301
Componile v. Maybee, 641 A.2d 1143 (N.J. Super. L. 1994) / 301
Davis v. Sam Goody, Inc., 480 A.2d 212 (N.J.Super. A.D. 1984) / 120
Dower v. Gamba, 647 A.2d 1364 (N.J. Super. A.D. 1994) / 302
Figuly v. Knoll, 449 A.2d 564 (N.J.Super.L. 1982) / 120
Finer v. Talbot, 552 A.2d 626 (N.J. Super. A.D. 1988) / 233
Finney v. Ren-bar Inc., 551 A.2d 535 (N.J. Super. A.D. 1988) / 233
Fisch v. Bellshot, 640 A.2d 801 (N.J. 1994) / 301
Goss v. Allen, 360 A.2d 388 (N.J. 1976) / 120
Griesenbeck by Kuttner v. Walker, 488 A.2d 1038 (N.J.Super. A.D. 1985) / 120
Kelly v. Gwinnell, 476 A.2d 1219 (N.J. 1984) / 120, 301
Kollar v. Lozier, 669 A.2d 845 (N.J. Super. A.D. 1996) / 302
Lee v. Kiku Restaurant, 603 A.2d 503 (N.J. 1992) / 301
Linn v. Rand, 356 A.2d 15 (N.J.Super. A.D. 1976) / 120
McGovern v. Koza's Bar & Grill, 604 A.2d 226 (N.J. Super. L. 1991) / 301
Morella v. Machu, 563 A.2d 881 (N.J. Super. A.D. 1989) / 302
Rappaport v. Nichols, 156 A.2d 1 (N.J. 1959) / 119, 120
Soronen v. Olde Milford Inn, Inc., 218 A.2d 630 (N.J. 1966) / 120
State v. Buglione, 558 A.2d 51 (N.J. Super. A.D. 1989) / 232
State v. Haarde, 554 A.2d 872 (N.J. Super. A.D. 1989) / 232
State v. Zarrilli, 523 A.2d 284 (N.J.Super.L. 1987) / 119
Thomas v. Romeis, 560 A.2d 1267 (N.J. Super. A.D. 1989) / 232
Tilton v. Brombacher, 556 A.2d 1337 (N.J. Super. L. 1989) / 233
Wagner v. Schlue, 605 A.2d 294 (N.J. Super. 1992) / 301
Witter by Witter v. Leo, 635 A.2d 580 (N.J. Super. A.D. 1994) / 302

New Mexico

Baxter v. Noce, 752 P.2d 245 (N.M. App. 1987) / 123
Hall v. Budagher, 417 P.2d 71 (N.M. 1966) / 123
Karbel v. Francis, 709 P.2d 190 (N.M. App. 1985) / 124
Lopez v. Maez, 651 P.2d 1269 (N.M. 1982) / 123
Marchiondo v. Roper, 563 P.2d 1160 (N.M. 1977) / 123
MRC Properties, Inc. v. Gries, 652 P.2d 732 (N.M. 1982) / 123
Murphy v. Tomada Enterprises, Inc., 819 P.2d (N.M. App. 1991) / 303
Porter v. Ortiz, 665 P.2d 1149 (N.M. App. 1983) / 123
Richardson v. Carnegie Library Restaurant Inc., 763 P.2d 1153 (N.M. 1988) / 234
Trujillo v. Trujillo, 721 P.2d 1310 (N.M. App. 1986) / 123
Walker v. Key, 686 P.2d 973 (N.M. App. 1984) / 124

New York

Aleski v. Freilich, 164 N.Y.S.2d 151 (Sup.Ct. Richmond Cty. 1957) / 128
Allen v. County of Westchester, 492 N.Y.S.2d 772 (A.D.2 Dept. 1985) / 128
Allen v. County of Westchester, 567 N.Y.S.2d 826 (A.D. 2 Dept. 1991) / 305
Barnett v. O'Connell, 111 N.Y.S.2d 166 (A.D.3 Dept. 1952) / 125
Berkeley v. Park, 262 N.Y.S.2d 290 (Sup.Ct. Otsego Cty. 1965) / 128
Besner v. Bucci, 523 N.Y.S.2d 300 (A.D.4 Dept. 1987) / 128
Beyrle v. Finneron, 606 N.Y.S.2d 467 (A.D. 4 Dept. 1993) / 304
Bongiorno v. D.I.G.I. Inc., 529 N.Y.S.2d 804 (A.D. 2 Dept. 1988) / 236
Burkhard v. Sunset Cruises, Inc., 595 N.Y.S.2d 555 (A.D. 2 Dept. 1993) / 303
Campbell v. Step/Lind Restaurant Corp., 531 N.Y.S.2d 567 (A.D. 2 Dept. 1988) / 235
Cole v. O'Tooles of Utica, Inc., 643 N.Y.S.2d 283 (A.D. 4 Dept. 1996) / 306
Conigliaro v. Franco, 504 N.Y.S.2d 186 (A.D.2 Dept. 1986) / 129
Cowin v. Huntington Hospital, 496 N.Y.S.2d 203 (Sup.Ct. Suffolk Cty. 1985) / 130
Custen v. Salty Dog, Inc. 566 N.Y.S.2d 348 (A.D. 2 Dept. 1991) / 305
D'Amico v. Christie, 524 N.Y.S.2d 1 (Ct. App. 1987) / 129
Dalrymple v. Southland Corp., 609 N.Y.S.2d 284 (A.D. 2 Dept. 1994) / 306
Dodge v. Victory Markets, Inc. 606 N.Y.S.2d 345 (A.D. 3 Dept. 1993) / 304
Donato v. McLaughlin, 599 N.Y.S.2d 754 (A.D. 3 Dept. 1993) / 303
Dynarski v. U-Crest Fire District, 447 N.Y.S.2d 86 (Sup.Ct. Erie Cty. 1981) / 129
Edgar v. Kajet, 375 N.Y.S.2d 548 (Sup.Ct. Nassau Cty. 1975); aff'd. 389 N.Y.S.2d 631 (A.D.2 Dept. 1976) / 130
Etu v. Cumberland Farms, Inc., 538 N.Y.S.2d 657 (A.D. 3 Dept. 1989) / 235, 236
Fishman v. Beach, 625 N.Y.S.2d 730 (A.D. 3 Dept. 1995) / 3044
Gabrielle v. Craft, 428 N.Y.S.2d 84 (A.D.3 Dept. 1980) / 129
Greer v. Ferrizz, 499 N.Y.S.2d 758 (A.D.2 Dept. 1986) / 130
Harris v. Hurlburt, 373 N.Y.S.2d 480 (Sup.Ct. Seneca Cty. 1975) / 127
Henry v. Vann, 508 N.Y.S.2d 502 (A.D.2 Dept. 1986) / 130

Huyler v. Rose, 451 N.Y.S.2d 478 (A.D.4 Dept. 1982) / 129
Jacobs v. Amodeo, 618 N.Y.S.2d 120 (A.D. 3 Dept. 1994) / 306
James G. Karas, Inc. v. Hostetter, 289 N.Y.S.2d 40 (A.D.2 Dept. 1968) / 125
Kinney v. 1809 Forest Ave., Inc., 165 N.Y.S.2d 149
   (Sup.Ct. Richmond Cty. 1957) / 128
Kohler v. Wray, 452 N.Y.S.2d 831 (Sup.Ct. Steuben Cty. 1982) / 129
Lane v. Barker, 660 N.Y.S.2d 194 (A.D. Sup. Ct. 1997 / 305
Lyons v. Tiedemann, 522 N.Y.S.2d 159 (A.D.2 Dept. 1987) / 127
MacGilvray v. Denino, 540 N.Y.S.2d 449 (A.D. 2 Dept. 1989) / 306
Maniccia v. State Liquor Authority, 172 N.Y.S.2d 333 (A.D.2 Dept. 1958) / 125
Marsico v. Southland Corp., 539 N.Y.S.2d 378 (A.D. 2 Dept. 1989) / 236
Martinez v. Camardella, 558 N.Y.S.2d 211 (A.D. 3 Dept. 1990) / 304
McCawley v. Carmel Lanes, Inc., 577 N.Y.S.2d 546 (A.D. 3 Dept. 1991) / 305
McNally v. Addis, 317 N.Y.S.2d 157 (Sup.Ct. Westchester Cty. 1970) / 126
Mitchell v. Shoals, Inc., 271 N.Y.S.2d 137 (A.D.1 Dept. 1966) / 127
Montgomery v. Orr, 498 N.Y.S.2d 968 (Sup.Ct. Oneida Cty. 1986) / 126, 129
Moyer v. Lo Jim Cafe, Inc., 240 N.Y.S.2d 277 (A.D. 1963);
   aff'd. 251 N.Y.S.2d 30 (1964) / 127
Nehme v. Joseph, 554 N.Y.S.2d 642 (A.D. 2 Dept. 1990) / 303
Oja v. Grand Chapter of Theta Chi Fraternity, 667 N.Y.S.2d 650
   (Sup. Ct. Tompkins County, 1997) / 307
Paul v. Hogan, 392 N.Y.S.2d 766 (A.D. 1977) / 128
People v. Armstrong, 203 N.Y.S.2d 552 (Cty. Ct. 1960) / 125
People v. Byrne, 494 N.Y.S.2d 257 (Sup. 1985) / 125
People v. Danchak, 261 N.Y.S.2d 722 (A.D. 1965) / 125
People v. Jackson, 487 N.Y.S.2d 270 (Co.Cty. 1985) / 126
People v. Kaufman, 504 N.Y.S.2d 361 (City Ct. 1986) / 126
People v. Williams, 215 N.Y.S.2d 841 (City Ct. 1961) / 126
Powers v. Niagara Mohawk Power Corp., 516 N.Y.S.2d 811 (A.D. 1987) / 127, 128
Rann by Rann v. Hamilton, 599 N.Y.S.2d 51 (A.D. 2 Dept. 1993) / 305
Reickert v. Misciagna, 590 N.Y.S.2d 100 (A.D. 2 Dept. 1992) / 306
Romano v. Stanley, 643 N.Y.S.2d 238 (A.D. 3 Dept. 1996) / 303
Ross's Dairies, Ltd. v. Rohan, 202 N.Y.S.2d 807 (Sup. 1960) / 125
Russell v. Olkowski, 535 N.Y.S.2d 187 (A.D. 3 Dept. 1988) / 235
Rust v. Reyer, 670 N.Y.S.2d 822 (N.Y. 1998) / 305
Scatorchia v. Caputo, 32 N.Y.S.2d 534 (A.D. 1942) / 127
Schirmer v. Yost, 400 N.Y.S.2d 655 (A.D. 1977) / 128, 130
Schrader v. Carney, 586 N.Y.S.2d 687 (A.D. 4 Dept. 1992) / 306
Senn v. Scudieri, 567 N.Y.S.2d 665 (Sup. Ct. App. Div. 1 Dept. 1991) / 303, 305
Sheeky v. Big Flats Community, 543 N.Y.S.2d 18 (1989) / 235
Sherman v. Robinson, 591 N.Y.S.2d 974 (Ct. App. 1992) / 304, 306
Slocum v. D's & Jayes Valley Restaurant, 582 N.Y.S.2d 544
   (A.D. 3 Dept. 1992) / 305
Smith v. West Rochelle Travel Agency, Inc., 656 N.Y.S.2d 340
   (N.Y. App. 1997) / 306
Stevens v. Spec Inc., 637 N.Y.S.2d 979 (A.D. 3 Dept. 1996) / 304
Strassner v. Saleem, 594 N.Y.S.2d 559 (Sup. 1993) / 305
Tyrrell v. Quigley, 60 N.Y.S.2d 821 (Sup. Kings Cty. 1946) / 128
Vadasy v. Bill Feigel's Tavern, Inc., 391 N.Y.S.2d 32
   (Sup.Ct. Onondaga Cty. 1973); aff'd. 391 N.Y.S.2d 999 (A.D. 1977) / 127, 128
Vandenberg v. Brosnan, 514 N.Y.S.2d 784 (A.D. 2 Dept. 1987) / 235
Wellcome v. Student Co-op of Stony-Brook, 509 N.Y.S.2d 816 (A.D. 1986) / 127
Wilkins v. Weresiuk, 316 N.Y.S.2d 360 (Sup.Ct. Saratoga Cty. 1970) / 127, 128
Winje v. Cavalry Veterans of Syracuse, Inc., 508 N.Y.S.2d 768 (A.D. 1986) / 128
Wright v. Sunset Recreation, Inc., 457 N.Y.S.2d 606 (A.D. 1982) / 128
Yashar v. Yakovac, 48 N.Y.S.2d 128 (City Ct. NY 1944) / 128

North Carolina
Brower v. Robert Chappell & Associates, Inc., 328 S.E.2d 45
   (N.C. App. 1985) / 132
Camalier v. Jeffries, 460 S.E.2d 133 (N.C. 1995) / 308
Canady v. McLeod, 446 S.E.2d 879 (N.C. App. 1994) / 308
Chastain v. Litton Systems, Inc., 694 F.2d 957 (4th Cir. 1982) / 133
Clark v. Inn West, 365 S.E.2d 682 (N.C. App. 1988) / 132
Estate of Darby v. Monroe Oil Co., 488 S.E.2d 828 (N.C. App. 1997) / 307
Estate of Mullis v. Monroe Oil Co., 488 S.E.2d 830 (N.C. App. 1997) / 308
Freeman v. Finney, 309 S.E.2d 531 (N.C. App. 1983) / 132
Hart v. Ivey, 420 S.E.2d 174 (N.C. 1992) / 308
Hutchens v. Hankins, 303 S.E.2d 584 (N.C. App. 1983);
   rev.den. 305 S.E.2d 734 (N.C. 1983) / 131, 132
Peal by Peal v. Smith, 444 S.E.2d 673 (N.C. App. 1994),
   aff'd. 457 S.E.2d 599 (N.C. 1995) / 308
Sorrells v. M.Y.B. Hospitality Ventures, 435 S.E.2d 320(N.C. 1993) / 307
Wilson by Wilson v. Bellamy, 414 S.E.2d 347 (N.C. App. 1992) / 308

North Dakota
Aanenson v. Bastien, 438 N.W.2d 151 (N.D. 1989) / 309
Anderson v. K.S., 500 N.W.2d 603 (N.D. 1993) / 309
Born v. Mayers, 514 N.W.2d 687 (N.D. 1994) / 309
Fladeland v. Mayer, 102 N.W.2d 121 (N.D. 1960) / 135

Meshefski v. Shirnan Corp., 385 N.W.2d 474 (N.D. 1986) / 135
Ross by Kanta v. Scott, 386 N.W.2d 18 (N.D. 1986) / 135
State v. Bohl, 317 N.W.2d 790 (N.D. 1982) / 134
Thoring v. Bottonsek, 350 N.W.2d 586 (N.D. 1984) / 135
Wanna v. Miller, 136 N.W.2d 563 (N.D. 1965) / 135
Zueger v. Carlson, 542 N.W.2d 92 (N.D. 1996) / 309

Ohio
Cummins v. Rubio, 622 N.E.2d 700 (Ohio App. 2 Dist. 1993) / 310
Fifer v. Buffalo Cafe, 601 N.E.2d 601 (Ohio App. 6 Dist. 1991) / 310
Glen's Grill No. 3, Inc. v. Board of Liquor Control, 166 N.E.2d 399
   (Ohio App. 1959) / 138
Gressman v. McClain, 533 N.E.2d 732 (Ohio 1988) / 237
Hanewald v. Board of Liquor Control, 136 N.E.2d 77 (Ohio App. 1955) / 137
Horwath v. Smith, 683 N.E.2d 846 (Ohio App. 1996) / 311
Hosom v. Eastland Lanes, Inc., 595 N.E.2d 534 (Ohio App. 10 Dist. 1991) / 310
Huston v. Konieczny, 556 N.E.2d 505 (Ohio 1990) / 311
In Re Sons Bars & Grills Co., 117 N.E.2d 526 (Ohio Comm. Pleas 1954) / 137
Kemock v. The Mark II, 404 N.E.2d 766 (Ohio App. 1978) / 138
Lape v. Rose, 621 N.E.2d 173 (Ohio App. 12 Dist. 1993) / 310
Love v. Fountas, 200 N.E.2d 715 (Ohio App. 1963) / 138
Malone v. Miami University, 625 N.E.2d 640 (Ohio App. 1993) / 311
Mason v. Roberts 294 N.E.2d 884 (Ohio 1973) / 138
Mitseff v. Wheeler, 526 N.E.2d 798 (Ohio 1988) / 237
Northcutt v. Grilliot, 1997 WL 464785 (Ohio App. 2 Dist. 1997) / 310
Point Cafe, Inc. v. Board of Liquor Control, 168 N.E.2d 157 (Ohio App. 1960) / 137
Prest v. Delta Delta Delta Sorority, 686 N.E.2d 293 (Ohio App. 1996) / 311
Ramsay v. Kenyon College, 85-CA-01 (5th Dist., Ct. App., Knox 10-31-85) / 139
Settlemeyer v. Wilmington Veterans Post No. 49, 464 N.E.2d 251
   (Ohio 1984) / 139, 237
Smith v. The 10th Inning, Inc., 551 N.E.2d 1296 (Ohio 1990) / 302
State v. McGhee, 468 N.E.2d 400 (Ohio Mun. 1984) / 137
State v. Morello, 158 N.E.2d 525 (Ohio 1959) / 137
State v. Pi Kappa Alpha Fraternity, 491 N.E.2d 1129 (Ohio 1986);
   cert.den. 107 S.Ct. 104 (1986) / 139
State v. Scullen, 372 N.E.2d 1349 (Ohio Mun. 1977) / 138
Steed v. Chances Entertainment, Inc., 1996 WL 488850
   (Ohio App. 5 Dist. 1996) / 310
Stevens v. United Auto Workers, Local 1112, 673 N.E.2d 930
   (Ohio App. 1996) / 311
Stillweel v. Johnson, 602 N.E.2d 1254 (Ohio App. 1 Dist. 1991) / 310
Taggart v. Bitzenhofer 299 N.E.2d 901 (Ohio App. 1972);
   aff'd. 294 N.E.2d 226 (Ohio 1973) / 138
Terry v. Markoff, 497 N.E.2d 1133 (Ohio App. 1986) / 139
Tillett v. Tropicana Lounge & Restaurant, 610 N.E.2d 453
   (Ohio App. 9 Dist. 1991) / 310
Tome v. Berea Pewter Mug, Inc., 446 N.E.2d 848 (Ohio App. 1982) / 138
Tomlinson v. McCutcheon, 554 F. Supp. 186 (N.D.Ohio 1982) / 138, 139
VanHaverbeke v. Bernhard, 654 F. Supp. 255 (S.D.Ohio 1986) / 139
Williams v. Veterans of Foreign Wars, 650 N.E.2d 175
   (Ohio App. 2 Dist. 1994) / 311

Oklahoma
Battles v. Cough, 947 P.2d 600 (Okl. Civ. App. 1997) / 313
Brigance v. Velvet Dove Restaurant, Inc., 725 P.2d 300 (Okl. 1986) / 142, 312
Busby v. Quail Creek Golf & Country Club, 885 P.2d 1326 (Okl. 1994) / 312
Esther v. Wiemer, 859 P.2d 1140 (Okl. App. 1993) / 312
Grantham v. Tulsa Club, Inc., 918 P.2d 410 (Okl. App. 1996) / 312
Kellogg v. Ohler, 825 P.2d 1346 (Okl. 1992) / 313
Kyle v. State, 366 P.2d 961 (Okl.Cr. App. 1961) / 142
Mansfield v. Circle K Corp., 877 P.2d 1130 (Okl. 1994) / 312
Ohio Casualty Ins. Co. v. Todd / 312
Oklahoma Broadcasters Association v. Crisp, 636 F. Supp. 978
   (W.D.Okl. 1985) / 142
Sanders v. Crosstown Market, Inc., 850 P.2d 1061 (Okl. 1993) / 313
Silverhorn v. State, 358 P.2d 226 (Okl.Cr. App. 1960) / 141
State v. DeVilliers, 633 P.2d 756 (Okl.Cr. App. 1981) / 141
Tomlinson v. Love's County Stores, Inc., 854 P.2d 910 (Okl. 1993) / 312
Troxell v. Bingham, 774 P.2d 1073 (Okl. App. 1989) / 237

Oregon
Blunt v. Bocci, 704 P.2d 534 (Ore. App. 1985) / 144, 145
Campbell v. Carpenter, 566 P.2d 893 (Ore. 1977) / 144, 145
Chartrand v. Coos Bay Tavern, Inc., 696 P.2d 513 (Ore. 1985) / 144
Cullivan v. Leston, 602 P.2d 1121 (Ore. App. 1979) / 146
Davis v. Billy's Con-Teena, Inc., 587 P.2d 75 (Ore. 1978) / 144, 145
Fugate v. Safeway Stores, Inc., 897 P.2d 328 (Ore. App. 1995) / 314
Fulmer v. Timber Inn Restaurant and Lounge, 954 P.2d 201
   (Ore. App. 1998) / 313
Hawkins v. Conklin, 767 P.2d 66 (Ore. 1988) / 313

Hunt v. Evenhoff, 829 P.2d 1051 (Ore. App. 1992) / 313
Johnson v. Paige, 615 P.2d 1185 (Ore. App. 1980) / 144, 146
Miller v. City of Portland, 604 P.2d 1261 (Ore. 1980) / 144, 145
Pfeifer v. Copperstone Restaurant & Lounge, Inc., 693 P.2d 644
 (Ore. App. 1985) / 145
Plattner v. VIP's Industries, Inc., 768 P.2d 440 (Ore. App. 1989) / 313
Reynolds v. Nichols, 556h P.2d 102 (Ore. 1976) / 146
Sager v. McClenden, 672 P.2d 697 (Ore. 1983) / 145
Smith v. Harms, 865 P.2d 486 (Ore. App. 1993) / 314
Solberg v. Johnson, 760 P.2d 867 (Or. 1988) / 238
Sparks v. Warren, 856 P.2d 337 (Ore. 1993) / 314
Stachniewicz v. Mar-Cam Corporation, 488 P.2d 436 (Ore. 1971) / 144
State v. Gear, 143 P. 890 (Ore. 1914) / 143
State v. Gulley, 70 P. 385 (Ore. 1902) / 143
State v. Raper, 149 P.2d 165 (Ore. 1944) / 143
State v. Ritner, 675 P.2d 1085 (Ore. App. 1984) / 143
Stein v. Beta Rho Alumni Association, Inc., 621 P.2d 632
 (Ore. App. 1980) / 146
Wiener v. Gamma Phi Chapter of Alpha Tau Omega Fraternity 485 P.2d 18
 (Ore. 1971) / 145, 146

Pennsylvania

146, Inc. v. Liquor Control Board, 527 A.2d 1083 (Pa.Cmwlth. 1987) / 148
Alumni Association v. Sullivan, 535 A.2d 1095 (Pa. Super. 1987) / 239
Appeal of Skowronek, 379 A.2d 906 (Pa.Cmwlth. 1977) / 148
Booker v. Lehigh University, 800 F. Supp. 234 (E.D. Pa. 1992) / 315
Bradshaw v. Rawlings, 612 F.2d 135 (3rd Cir. 1979) / 151
Burkhart v. Brockway Glass Co., 507 A.2d 844 (Pa.Super. 1986) / 149
Com. v. Penn Valley Resorts, Inc., 494 A.2d 1139 (Pa.Super. 1985) / 151
Com v. Tau Kappa Epsilon, 609 A.2d 791 (Pa. 1992) / 314
Commonwealth, Pa. Liquor Control Board v. Abraham, 489 A.2d 306
 (Pa.Cmwlth. 1985) / 148
Commonwealth v. Demangone, 243 A.2d 187 (Pa.Super. 1968) / 147
Commonwealth of Pennsylvania Liquor Control Board v. Schiaffo, 456 A.2d
 1120 (Pa.Cmwlth. 1983) / 147
Commonwealth, Pa. Liquor Control Bd. v. Tris-Dad, Inc., 448 A.2d 690
 (Pa.Cmwlth. 1982) / 147
Commonwealth of Pennsylvania Liquors v. Grand Marcus One, 451 A.2d 810
 (Pa.Cmwlth. 1982) / 148
Congini by Congini v. Portersville Valve Co., 470 A.2d 515 (Pa. 1983) / 150
Connelly v. Ziegler, 380 A.2d 902 (Pa.Super. 1977) / 148
Conner v. Duffy, 652 A.2d 372 (Pa. Super. 1994) / 314
Corcoran v. McNeal, 161 A.2d 367 (Pa.Super. 1960) / 148
Couts v. Ghion, 421 A.2d 1184 (Pa.Super. 1980) / 149
Detwiler v. Brumbaugh, 656 A.2d 944 (Pa. Super. 1995) / 315
Fassett v. Delta Kappa Epsilon (New York), 807 F.2d 1150 (3rd Cir. 1986) / 150
Giardina v. Solomon, 360 F. Supp. 262 (M.D.Pa. 1973) / 150
Goldberg v. Delta Tau Delta, 613 A.2d 1250 (Pa. Super. 1992) / 315
Herr v. Booten, 580 A.2d 1115 (Pa. Super. 1990) / 314
Hiles v. Brandywine Club, 662 A.2d 16 (Pa. Super. 1995) / 315
Holpp v. Fez, Inc., 656 A.2d 147 (Pa. Super. 1995) / 315
In Re Peter's Pub, Inc., 503 A.2d 499 (Pa. Cmwlth. 1986) / 147
Jardine v. Upper Darby Lodge No. 1973, Inc., 198 A.2d 550
 (Pa. 1964) / 132, 148
Jeffries v. Commonwealth, 537 A.2d 355 (Pa. Super. 1988) / 315
Johnson v. Harris, 615 A.2d 771 (Pa. Super. 1992) / 315
Kapres v. Heller, 640 A.2d 888 (Pa. 1994) / 315
Klein v. Raysinger, 470 A.2d 507 (Pa. 1983) / 149, 150
Liquor Central Board v. K.V.M. Inc., 547 A.2d 517 (Pa. Cmwlth. 1988) / 238
Macleary v. Hines, 817 F.2d 1081 (3rd Cir. 1987) / 150
Majors v. Brodhead Hotel, 205 A.2d 873 (Pa. 1965) / 148
Manning v. Andy, 310 A.2d 75 (Pa. 1973) / 149
Matter of Pirollo, 377 A.2d 1040 (Pa.Cmwlth. 1977) / 147
Matter of Tris-Dad, 439 A.2d 1286 (Pa.Cmwlth. 1981) / 147
Matthews v. Konieczny, 527 A.2d 508 (Pa. 1987) / 149
McDonald v. Marriott Corp., 564 A.2d 1296 (Pa. Super. 1989) / 314
McGaha v. Matter, 528 A.2d 988 (Pa.Super. 1987) / 149
Millard v. Osborne, 611 A.2d 715 (Pa. 1992) / 316
146, Inc. v. Liquor Control Board, 527 A.2d 1083 (Pa.Cmwlth. 1987) / 148
Orner v. Mallick, 527 A.2d 521 (Pa. 1987) / 150
Orner v. Mallick, 639 A.2d 491 (Pa. Super. 1994) / 315
Pa. Liquor Central Board v. Mignogna, 548 A.2d 689 (Pa. Cmwlth. 1988) / 238
Reber v. Commonwealth of Pennsylvania Liquor Control Board,
 516 A.2d 440 (Pa.Cmwlth. 1986) / 149
Reilly v. Tiergarten Inc., 633 A.2d 208 (Pa. Super. 1993) / 314
Schelin v. Goldberg, 146 A.2d 648 (Pa.Super. 1958) / 148
Sites v. Cloonan, 477 A.2d 547 (Pa.Super. 1984) / 149
Smith v. Clark, 190 A.2d 441 (Pa. 1963) / 148
Turgiss v. Fassett, 107 S.Ct. 2463 (1987) / 150

Rhode Island

Beauchesne v. David London & Co., 375 A.2d 920 (R.I. 1977) / 154
Beaupre v. Boulevard Billiard Club, 510 A.2d 415 (R.I. 1986) / 153
Ferreira v. Strack, 652 A.2d 965 (R.I. 1995) / 317
Lawrence v. Anheuser-Busch, Inc., 523 A.2d 864 (R.I. 1987) / 153
Pardey v. Boulevard Billiard Club, 518 A.2d 1349 (R.I. 1986) / 153
Smith v. Tully, 665 A.2d 1333 (R.I. 1994) / 316
Vater v. HB Group, 667 A.2d 283 (R.I. 1995) / 317

South Carolina

Ballou v. Sigma Nu General Fraternity, 352 S.E.2d 488 (S.C. App. 1986) / 156
Christiansen v. Campbell, 328 S.E.2d 351 (S.C. App. 1985) / 155, 318
Crolley v. Hutchins, 387 S.E.2d 716 (S.C. App. 1989) / 318
Daley v. Ward, 399 S.E.2d 13 (S.C. App. 1990) / 318
Garren v. Cummings & McGrady, Inc., 345 S.E.2d 508 (S.C. App. 1986) / 156
Jamison v. The Pantry, Inc., 392 S.E.2d 474 (S.C. App. 1990) / 318
Norton v. Opening Break of Aiken, Inc., 462 S.E.2d 861 (S.C. 1995) / 317
Steele v. Rogers, 413 S.E.2d 329 (S.C. App. 1992) / 318
Tobias v. Sports Club, Inc., 504 S.E.2d 318 (S.C. 1998) / 318
Whitlaw v. Kroger Co., 410 S.E.2d 251 (S.C. 1991) / 317

South Dakota

Baatz v. Arrow Bar, 426 N.W.2d 298 (S.D. 1988) at 302 / 240
 on remand 452 N.W.2d 138 (S.D. 1990) / 319
Crowley v. State, 268 N.W.2d 616 (S.D. 1978) / 158
Selchert v. Lien, 371 N.W.2d 791 (S.D. 1985) / 158
South Dakota v. Dole, 107 S.Ct. 2793 (1987) / 157
Walz v. City of Hudson, 327 N.W.2d 120 (S.D. 1982) / 158, 240
Wildboer v. South Dakota Junior Chamber of Commerce, 561 N.W.2d 666
 (S.D. 1997) / 319
Walz v. City of Hudson, 327 N.W.2d 120 (S.D. 1982) / 158, 240

Tennessee

Brookins v. The Round Table, Inc., 624 S.W.2d 547 (Tenn. 1981) / 161
Cecil v. Hardin, 575 S.W.2d 268 (Tenn. 1978) / 161
Cook v. Spinnaker's of Rivergate, Inc., 878 S.W.2d 934 (Tenn. 1994) / 320
Kirksey v. Overton Pub, Inc., 804 S.W.2d 68 (Tenn. App. 1990) / 320
Larue v. Lake Incorporated, 966 S.W.2d 423 (Tenn. App. 1997) / 320
McIntyre v. Balentine, 833 S.W.2d 52 (Tenn. 1992) / 321
Mitchell v. Ketner, 393 S.W.2d 755 (Tenn. App. 1964) / 160
Rollins v. Winn Dixie, 780 S.W.2d 765 (Tenn. App. 1989) / 320
Worley v. Weigels, 919 S.W.2d 589 (Tenn. 1996) / 320

Texas

Barfield v. City of Houston, 846 S.W.2d 399 (Tex. App. Houston,
 14th Dist. 1992) / 323
Campos v. State, 623 S.W.2d 657 (Tex.Cr. App. 1981) / 163, 164
Chung v. State, 751 S.W.2d 557 (Tex. App.-Texarkana 1988) / 240
Cotton v. State, 686 S.W.2d 140 (Tex.Cr. App. 1985) / 164
Dinh v. State, 695 S.W.2d 797 (Tex. App. 1 Dist. 1985) / 162
Donnell v. Spring Sports, Inc. 920 S.W.2d 378
 (Tex. App. Houston 1st Dist. 1996) / 322
El Chico Corp. v. Poole, 732 S.W.2d 306 (Tx. 1987) / 164, 165
Graff v. Beard, 858 S.W.2d 918 (Tex. 1993) / 323
I-Gotcha, Inc. v. McInnis, 903 S.W.2d 829 (Tex. App. Fort Worth, 1995) / 322
Martin v. State, 734 S.W.2d 32 (Tex. App. Houston [1 Dist.] 1987) / 164
Moore v. Shoreline Ventures, Inc., 903 S.W.2d 900
 (Tex. App. Beaumont, 1995) / 322
Morris v. Adolph Coors Co., 735 S.W.2d 578 (Tex. App. Fort Worth 1987) / 165
Otis Engineering Corp. v. Clark, 668 S.W.2d 307 (Tex. 1983) / 165
Pastor v. Champs Restaurant, Inc., 750 S.W.2d 335
 (Tex. App.-Houston 1988) / 241
Pena v. Neal, Inc., 901 S.W.2d 663 (Tex. App. San Antonio, 1995) / 322
Pinkham v. Apple Computer, Inc., 699 S.W.2d 387
 (Tex. App. 2 Dist. 1985) / 165
Ryan v. Friesenhahn, 911 S.W.2d 113 (Tex. App. San Antonio, 1995) / 323
S. & A. Beverage Co. of Beaumont No. 2 v. De Roven, 753 S.W.2d 507
 (Tex. App.-Beaumont 1988) / 241
Skruck v. State, 740 S.W.2d 819 (Tex. App. Houston [1 Dist.] 1987) / 164
Slawson v. State, 276 S.W.2d 811 (Tex.Cr. App. 1955) / 163
Smith v. Merritt, 940 S.W.2d 602 (Tex 1997) / 323
Smith v. Sewell, 858 S.W.2d 350 (Tex. 1993) / 321
Southland Corp. v. Lewis, 940 S.W.2d 83 (Tex. 1997) / 322
Starr v. State, 734 S.W.2d 52 (Tex. App. Houston [1 Dist.] 1987) / 163
Sturgeon v. State, 176 S.W.2d 331 (Tex.Cr. App. 1943) / 162
Texas Alcoholic Beverage Commission v. J. Square Enterprises,
 650 S.W.2d 531 (Tex. App. Dallas [5 Dist.] 1983) / 163
Texas Liquor Control Board v. Coggins, 402 S.W.2d 935
 (Civ. App. El Paso 1966) / 162